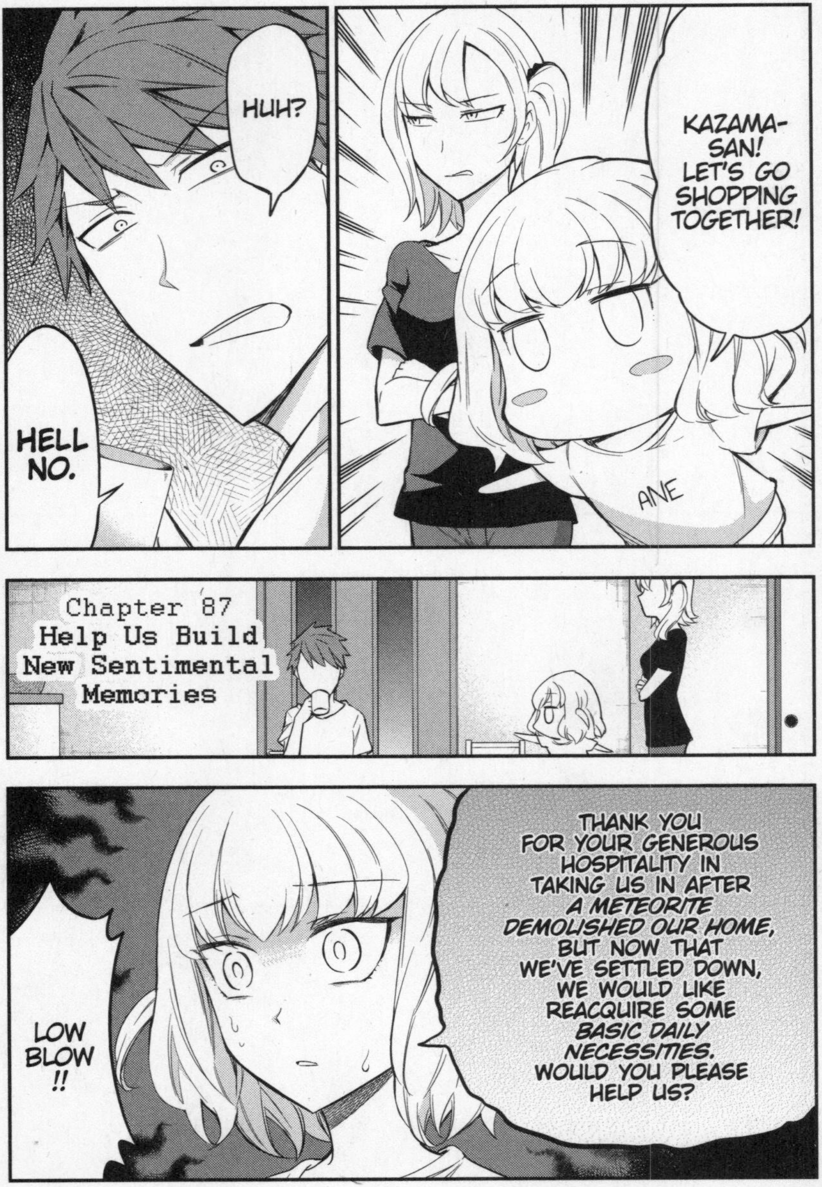
KAZAMA-SAN! LET'S GO SHOPPING TOGETHER!
ANE
HUH?
HELL NO.
Chapter 87
Help Us Build New Sentimental Memories
THANK YOU FOR YOUR GENEROUS HOSPITALITY IN TAKING US IN AFTER *A METEORITE DEMOLISHED OUR HOME*, BUT NOW THAT WE'VE SETTLED DOWN, WE WOULD LIKE REACQUIRE SOME *BASIC DAILY NECESSITIES*. WOULD YOU PLEASE HELP US?
LOW BLOW !!

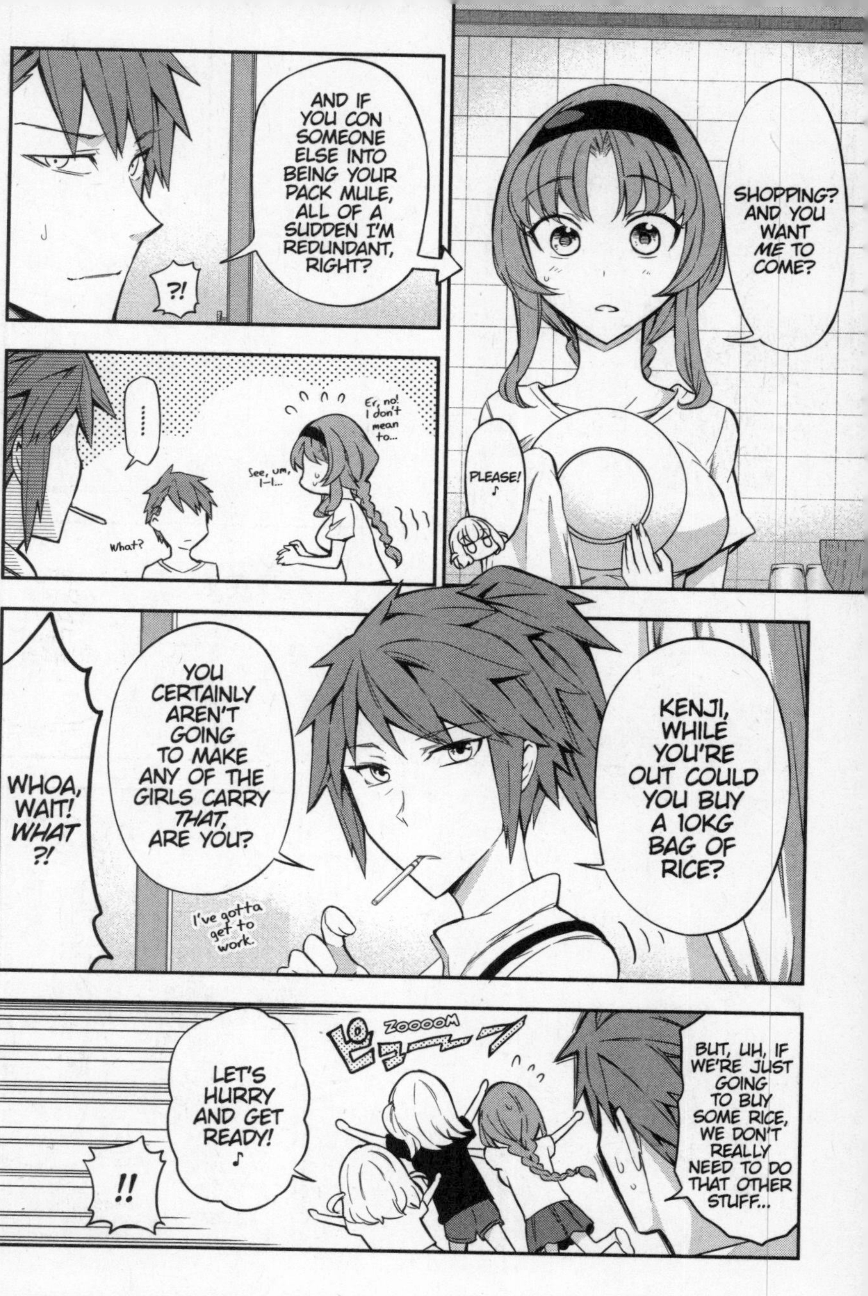
SHOPPING? AND YOU WANT ME TO COME?
PLEASE! ♪
AND IF YOU CON SOMEONE ELSE INTO BEING YOUR PACK MULE, ALL OF A SUDDEN I'M REDUNDANT, RIGHT?
?!
......
Er, no! I don't mean to...
See, um, I-I...
What?
KENJI, WHILE YOU'RE OUT COULD YOU BUY A 10KG BAG OF RICE?
YOU CERTAINLY AREN'T GOING TO MAKE ANY OF THE GIRLS CARRY THAT, ARE YOU?
WHOA, WAIT! WHAT?!
I've gotta get to work.
BUT, UH, IF WE'RE JUST GOING TO BUY SOME RICE, WE DON'T REALLY NEED TO DO THAT OTHER STUFF...
ZOOOOM
LET'S HURRY AND GET READY! ♪
!!

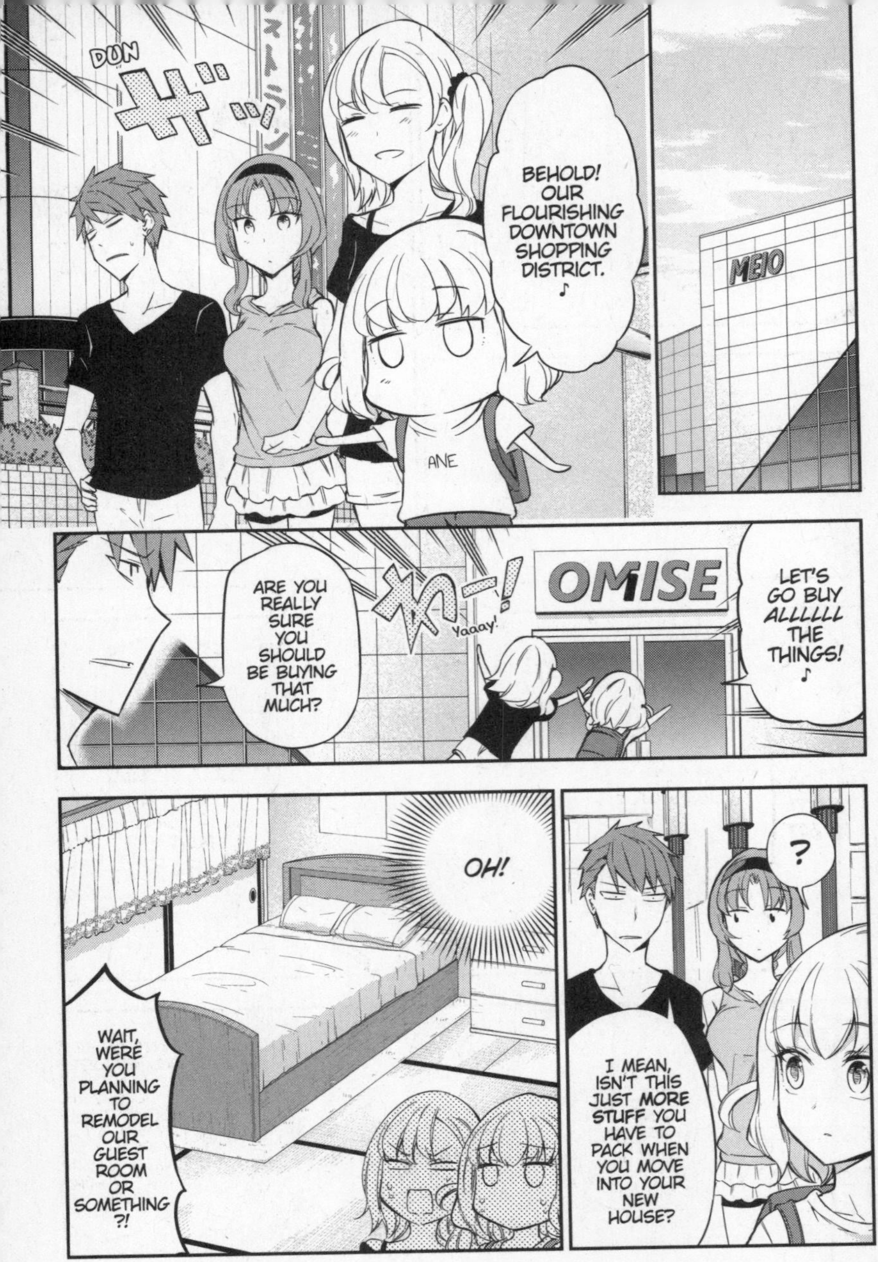
MEIO
BEHOLD! OUR FLOURISHING DOWNTOWN SHOPPING DISTRICT. ♪
DUN
ザッ
ANE
LET'S GO BUY ALLLLLL THE THINGS! ♪
OMISE
ワー!
Yaaay!
ARE YOU REALLY SURE YOU SHOULD BE BUYING THAT MUCH?
?
I MEAN, ISN'T THIS JUST MORE STUFF YOU HAVE TO PACK WHEN YOU MOVE INTO YOUR NEW HOUSE?
OH!
WAIT, WERE YOU PLANNING TO REMODEL OUR GUEST ROOM OR SOMETHING?!

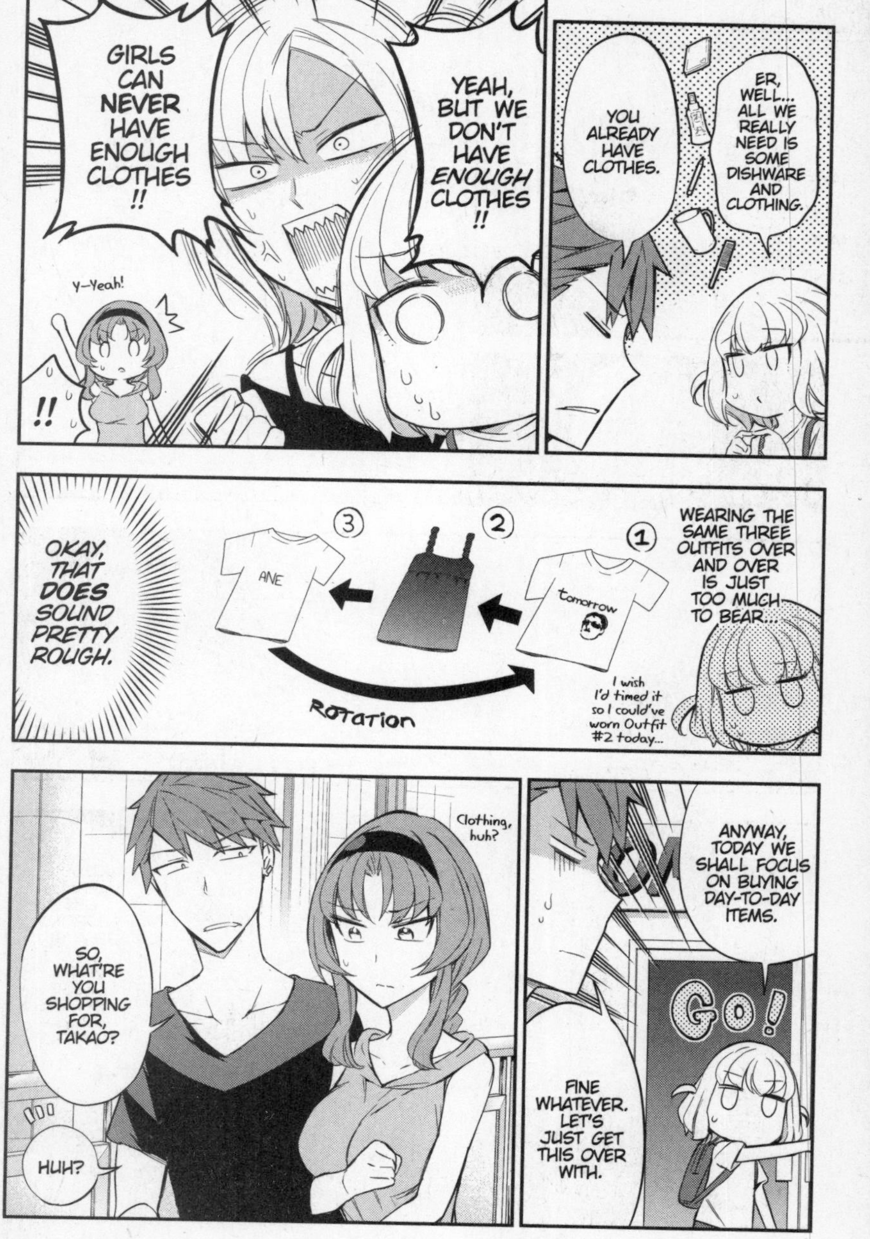
ER, WELL... ALL WE REALLY NEED IS SOME DISHWARE AND CLOTHING.
YOU ALREADY HAVE CLOTHES.
YEAH, BUT WE DON'T HAVE *ENOUGH* CLOTHES !!
GIRLS CAN NEVER HAVE ENOUGH CLOTHES !!
Y-Yeah!
!!
WEARING THE SAME THREE OUTFITS OVER AND OVER IS JUST TOO MUCH TO BEAR...
I wish I'd timed it so I could've worn Outfit #2 today...
1
tomorrow
2
3
ANE
ROTATION
OKAY, THAT **DOES** SOUND PRETTY ROUGH.
ANYWAY, TODAY WE SHALL FOCUS ON BUYING DAY-TO-DAY ITEMS.
GO!
FINE WHATEVER. LET'S JUST GET THIS OVER WITH.
Clothing, huh?
SO, WHAT'RE YOU SHOPPING FOR, TAKAO?
HUH?

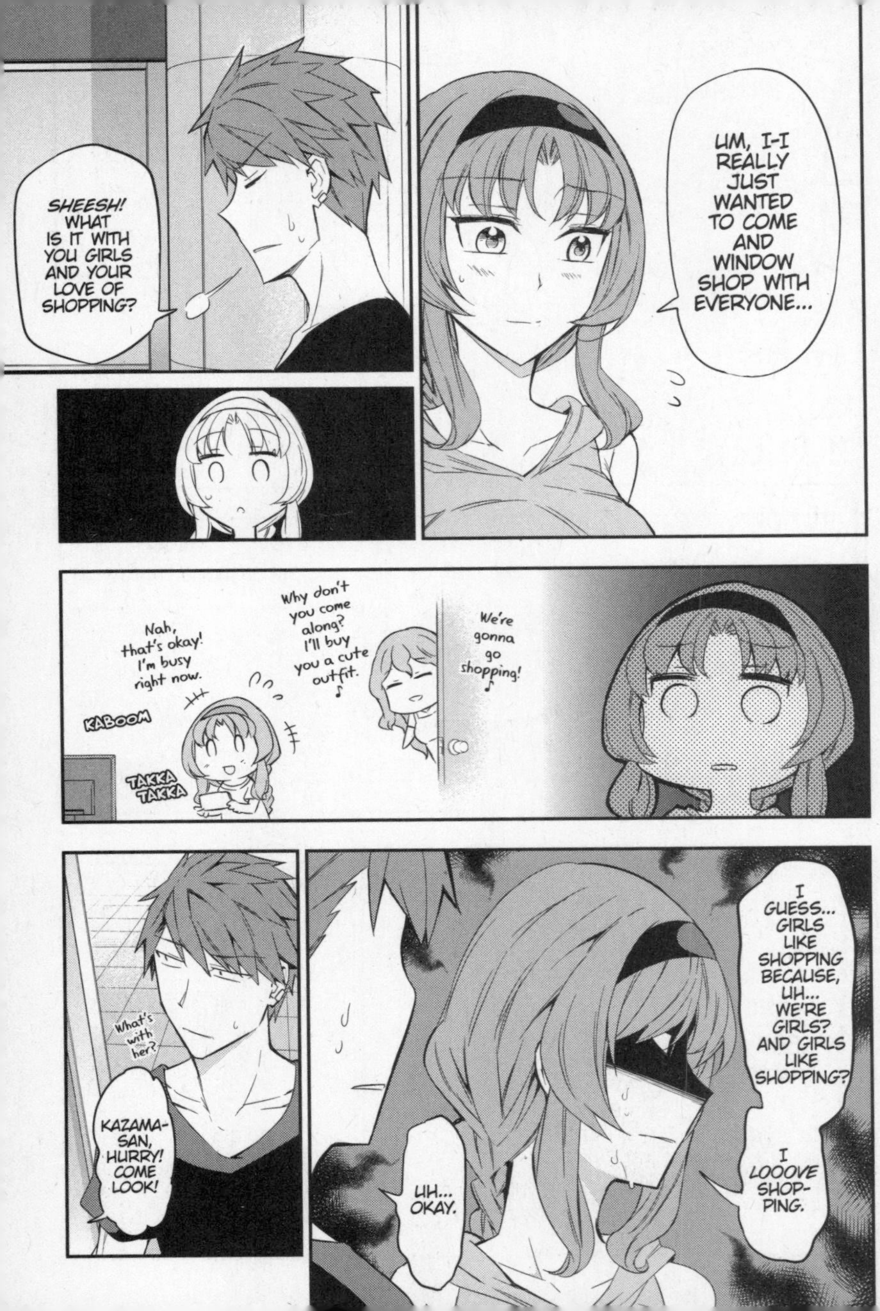
UM, I-I REALLY JUST WANTED TO COME AND WINDOW SHOP WITH EVERYONE...
SHEESH! WHAT IS IT WITH YOU GIRLS AND YOUR LOVE OF SHOPPING?
We're gonna go shopping! ♪
Why don't you come along? I'll buy you a cute outfit. ♪
Nah, that's okay! I'm busy right now.
KABOOM
TAKKA TAKKA
I GUESS... GIRLS LIKE SHOPPING BECAUSE, UH... WE'RE GIRLS? AND GIRLS LIKE SHOPPING?
I LOOOVE SHOP-PING.
UH... OKAY.
What's with her?
KAZAMA-SAN, HURRY! COME LOOK!

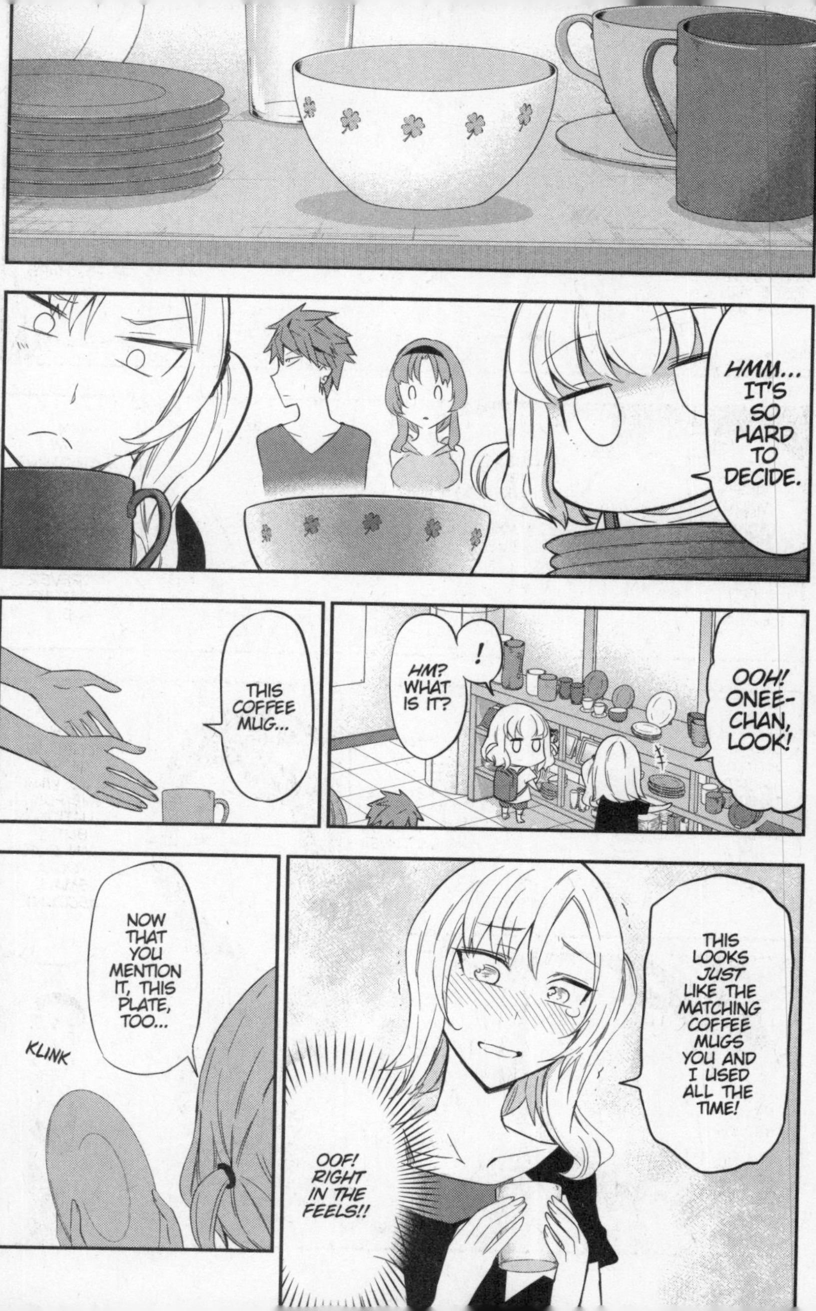
HMM... IT'S SO HARD TO DECIDE.
OOH! ONEE-CHAN, LOOK!
!
HM? WHAT IS IT?
THIS COFFEE MUG...
THIS LOOKS JUST LIKE THE MATCHING COFFEE MUGS YOU AND I USED ALL THE TIME!
OOF! RIGHT IN THE FEELS!!
NOW THAT YOU MENTION IT, THIS PLATE, TOO...
KLINK

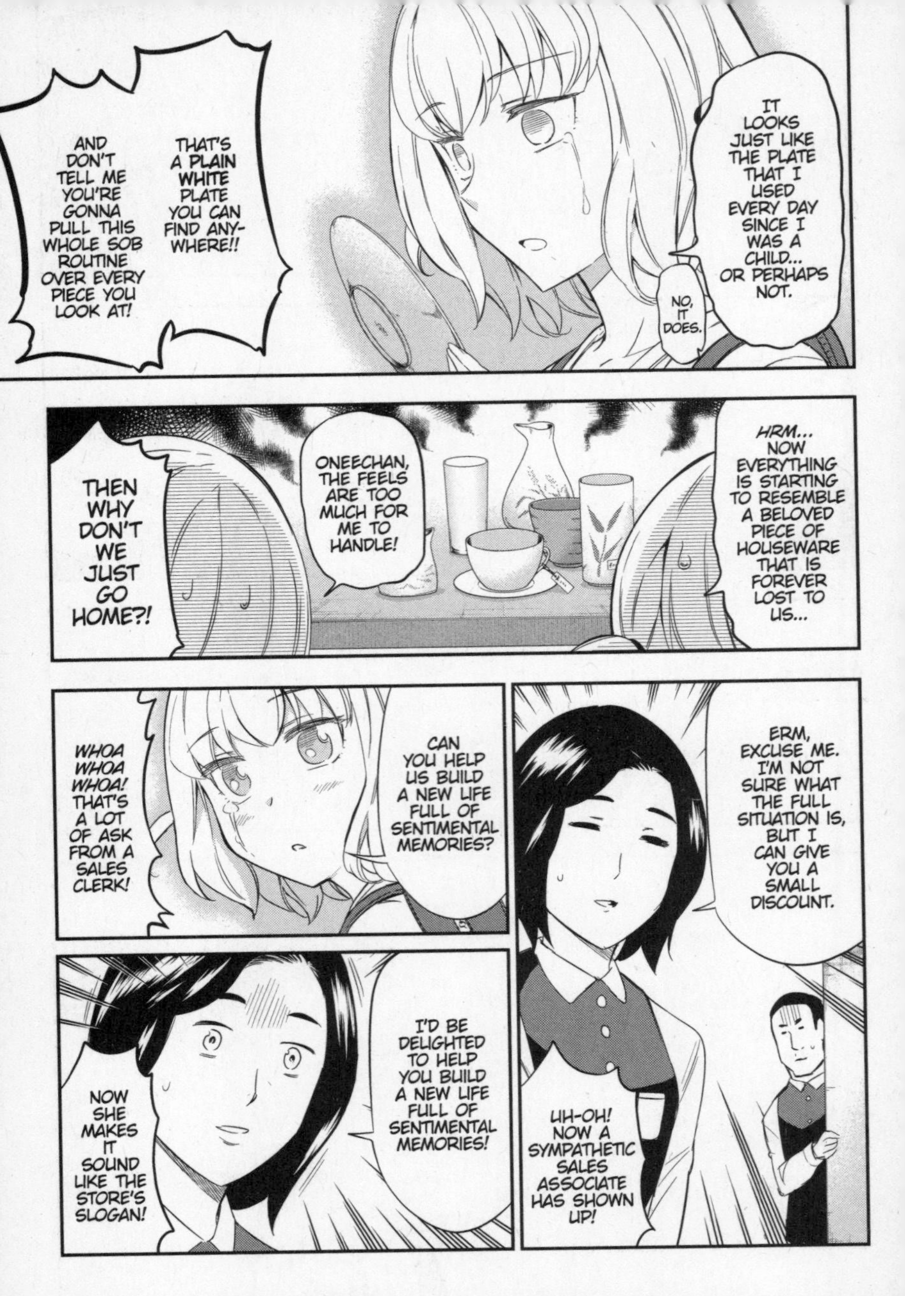
IT LOOKS JUST LIKE THE PLATE THAT I USED EVERY DAY SINCE I WAS A CHILD... OR PERHAPS NOT.
NO, IT DOES.
THAT'S A PLAIN WHITE PLATE YOU CAN FIND ANY-WHERE!!
AND DON'T TELL ME YOU'RE GONNA PULL THIS WHOLE SOB ROUTINE OVER EVERY PIECE YOU LOOK AT!
HRM... NOW EVERYTHING IS STARTING TO RESEMBLE A BELOVED PIECE OF HOUSEWARE THAT IS FOREVER LOST TO US...
ONEECHAN, THE FEELS ARE TOO MUCH FOR ME TO HANDLE!
THEN WHY DON'T WE JUST GO HOME?!
ERM, EXCUSE ME. I'M NOT SURE WHAT THE FULL SITUATION IS, BUT I CAN GIVE YOU A SMALL DISCOUNT.
UH-OH! NOW A SYMPATHETIC SALES ASSOCIATE HAS SHOWN UP!
CAN YOU HELP US BUILD A NEW LIFE FULL OF SENTIMENTAL MEMORIES?
WHOA WHOA WHOA! THAT'S A LOT OF ASK FROM A SALES CLERK!
I'D BE DELIGHTED TO HELP YOU BUILD A NEW LIFE FULL OF SENTIMENTAL MEMORIES!
NOW SHE MAKES IT SOUND LIKE THE STORE'S SLOGAN!

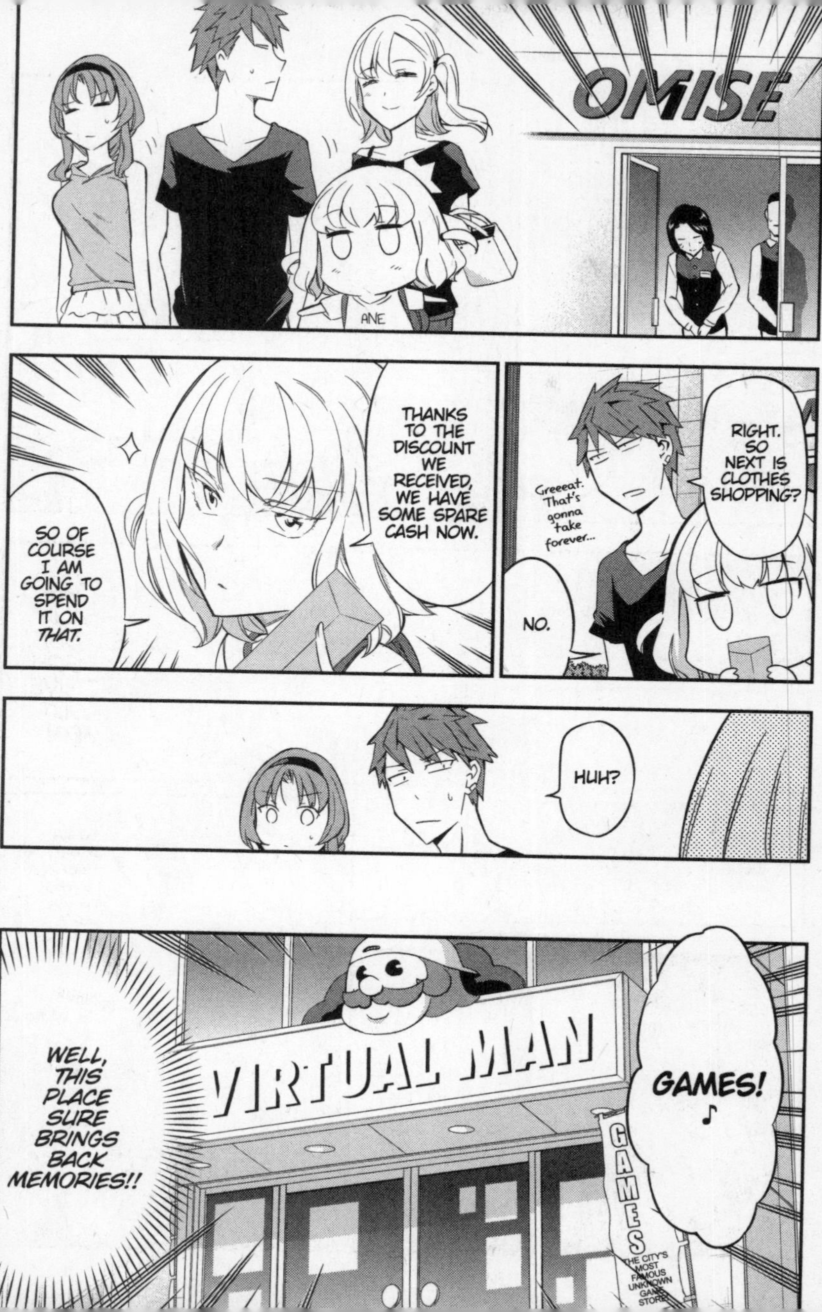
OMISE
ANE
RIGHT. SO NEXT IS CLOTHES SHOPPING?
Greeeat. That's gonna take forever...
NO.
THANKS TO THE DISCOUNT WE RECEIVED, WE HAVE SOME SPARE CASH NOW.
SO OF COURSE I AM GOING TO SPEND IT ON *THAT.*
HUH?
GAMES! ♪
VIRTUAL MAN
WELL, THIS PLACE SURE BRINGS BACK MEMORIES!!
GAMES
THE CITY'S MOST FAMOUS UNKNOWN GAME STORE!

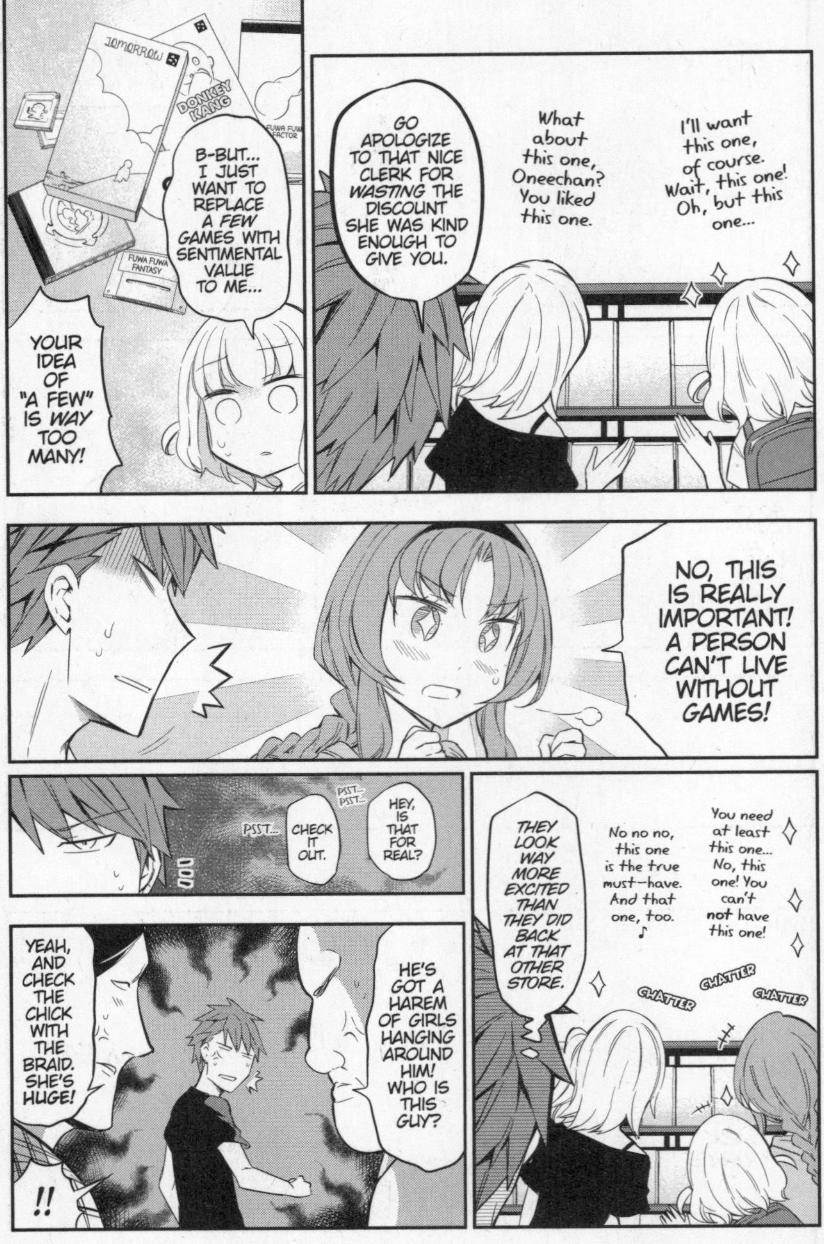
I'll want this one, of course. Wait, this one! Oh, but this one...
What about this one, Oneechan? You liked this one.
GO APOLOGIZE TO THAT NICE CLERK FOR *WASTING* THE DISCOUNT SHE WAS KIND ENOUGH TO GIVE YOU.
TOMORROW
DONKEY KANG
FUWA FUWA FACTOR
FUWA FUWA FANTASY
B-BUT... I JUST WANT TO REPLACE A *FEW* GAMES WITH SENTIMENTAL VALUE TO ME...
YOUR IDEA OF "A FEW" IS *WAY* TOO MANY!
NO, THIS IS REALLY IMPORTANT! A PERSON CAN'T LIVE WITHOUT GAMES!
You need at least this one... No, this one! You can't *not* have this one!
No no no, this one is the true must-have. And that one, too. ♪
THEY LOOK WAY MORE EXCITED THAN THEY DID BACK AT THAT OTHER STORE.
CHATTER
CHATTER
CHATTER
PSST... PSST...
HEY, IS THAT FOR REAL?
CHECK IT OUT.
PSST...
HE'S GOT A HAREM OF GIRLS HANGING AROUND HIM! WHO IS THIS GUY?
YEAH, AND CHECK THE CHICK WITH THE BRAID. SHE'S HUGE!
!!

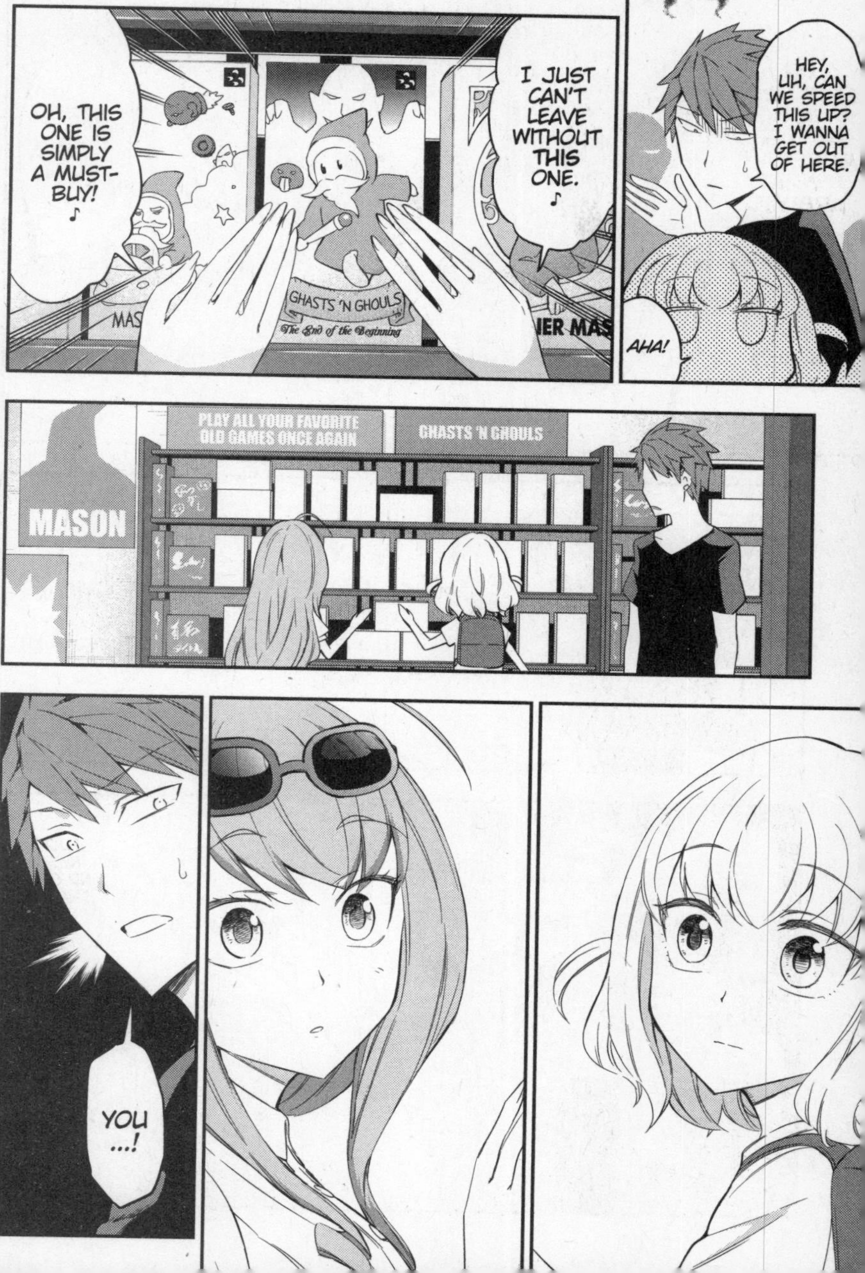
HEY, UH, CAN WE SPEED THIS UP? I WANNA GET OUT OF HERE.
AHA!
I JUST CAN'T LEAVE WITHOUT THIS ONE. ♪
GHASTS 'N GHOULS
The End of the Beginning
OH, THIS ONE IS SIMPLY A MUST-BUY! ♪
GHASTS 'N GHOULS
PLAY ALL YOUR FAVORITE OLD GAMES ONCE AGAIN
MASON
YOU ...!

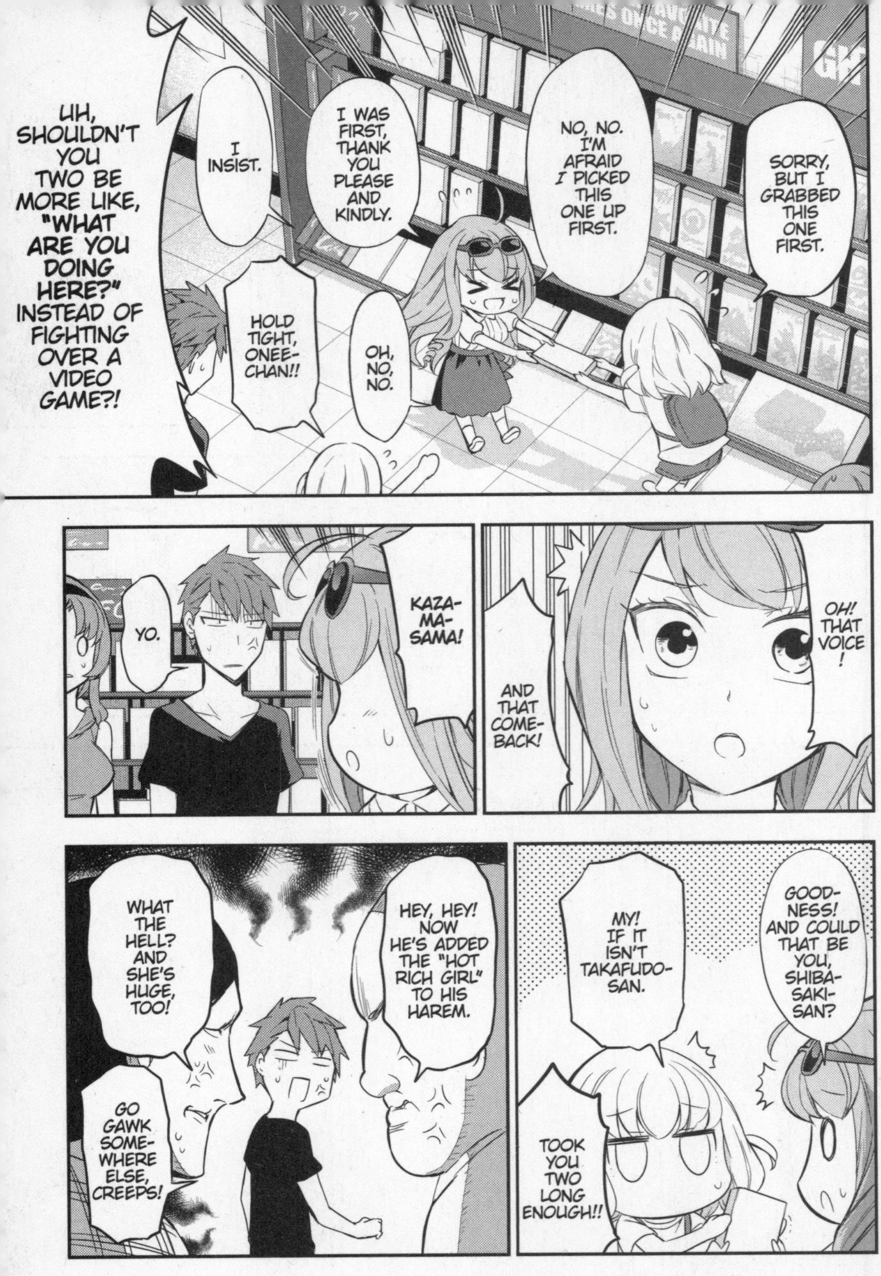
SORRY, BUT I GRABBED THIS ONE FIRST.
NO, NO. I'M AFRAID I PICKED THIS ONE UP FIRST.
I WAS FIRST, THANK YOU PLEASE AND KINDLY.
I INSIST.
OH, NO, NO.
HOLD TIGHT, ONEE-CHAN!!
UH, SHOULDN'T YOU TWO BE MORE LIKE, "WHAT ARE YOU DOING HERE?" INSTEAD OF FIGHTING OVER A VIDEO GAME?!
OH! THAT VOICE!
AND THAT COMEBACK!
KAZAMA-SAMA!
YO.
GOODNESS! AND COULD THAT BE YOU, SHIBASAKI-SAN?
MY! IF IT ISN'T TAKAFUDO-SAN.
TOOK YOU TWO LONG ENOUGH!!
HEY, HEY! NOW HE'S ADDED THE "HOT RICH GIRL" TO HIS HAREM.
WHAT THE HELL? AND SHE'S HUGE, TOO!
GO GAWK SOMEWHERE ELSE, CREEPS!

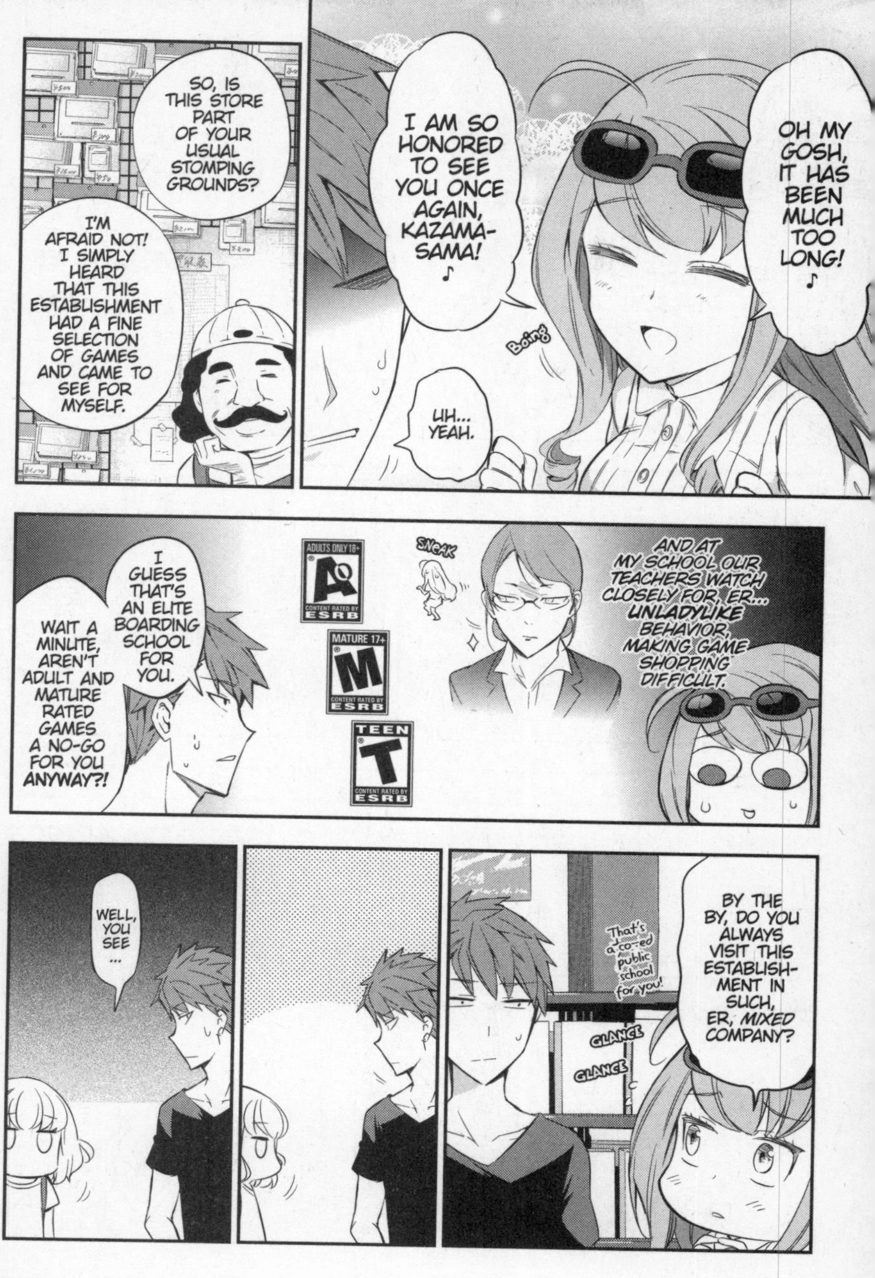
OH MY GOSH, IT HAS BEEN MUCH TOO LONG! ♪
I AM SO HONORED TO SEE YOU ONCE AGAIN, KAZAMA-SAMA! ♪
Boing
UH... YEAH.
SO, IS THIS STORE PART OF YOUR USUAL STOMPING GROUNDS?
I'M AFRAID NOT! I SIMPLY HEARD THAT THIS ESTABLISHMENT HAD A FINE SELECTION OF GAMES AND CAME TO SEE FOR MYSELF.
AND AT MY SCHOOL OUR TEACHERS WATCH CLOSELY FOR, ER... UNLADYLIKE BEHAVIOR, MAKING GAME SHOPPING DIFFICULT.
SNEAK
ADULTS ONLY 18+ AO CONTENT RATED BY ESRB
MATURE 17+ M CONTENT RATED BY ESRB
TEEN T CONTENT RATED BY ESRB
I GUESS THAT'S AN ELITE BOARDING SCHOOL FOR YOU.
WAIT A MINUTE, AREN'T ADULT AND MATURE RATED GAMES A NO-GO FOR YOU ANYWAY?!
BY THE BY, DO YOU ALWAYS VISIT THIS ESTABLISHMENT IN SUCH, ER, *MIXED* COMPANY?
That's a co-ed public school for you!
GLANCE
GLANCE
WELL, YOU SEE ...

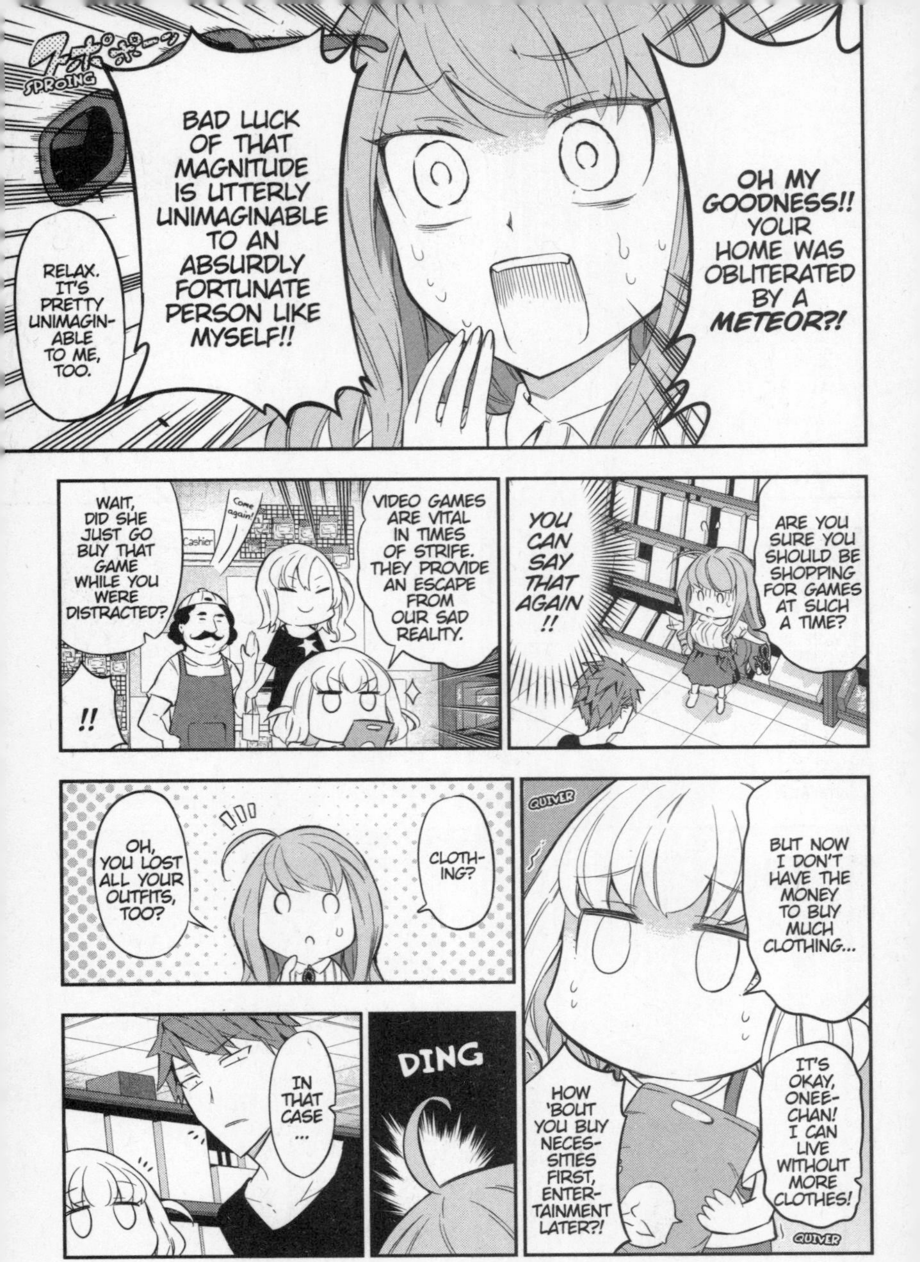
OH MY GOODNESS!! YOUR HOME WAS OBLITERATED BY A *METEOR?!*
BAD LUCK OF THAT MAGNITUDE IS UTTERLY UNIMAGINABLE TO AN ABSURDLY FORTUNATE PERSON LIKE MYSELF!!
SPROING
RELAX. IT'S PRETTY UNIMAGINABLE TO ME, TOO.
ARE YOU SURE YOU SHOULD BE SHOPPING FOR GAMES AT SUCH A TIME?
YOU CAN SAY THAT AGAIN!!
VIDEO GAMES ARE VITAL IN TIMES OF STRIFE. THEY PROVIDE AN ESCAPE FROM OUR SAD REALITY.
Come again!
Cashier
WAIT, DID SHE JUST GO BUY THAT GAME WHILE YOU WERE DISTRACTED?
!!
QUIVER
BUT NOW I DON'T HAVE THE MONEY TO BUY MUCH CLOTHING...
CLOTHING?
OH, YOU LOST ALL YOUR OUTFITS, TOO?
IT'S OKAY, ONEE-CHAN! I CAN LIVE WITHOUT MORE CLOTHES!
QUIVER
HOW 'BOUT YOU BUY NECESSITIES FIRST, ENTERTAINMENT LATER?!
DING
IN THAT CASE...

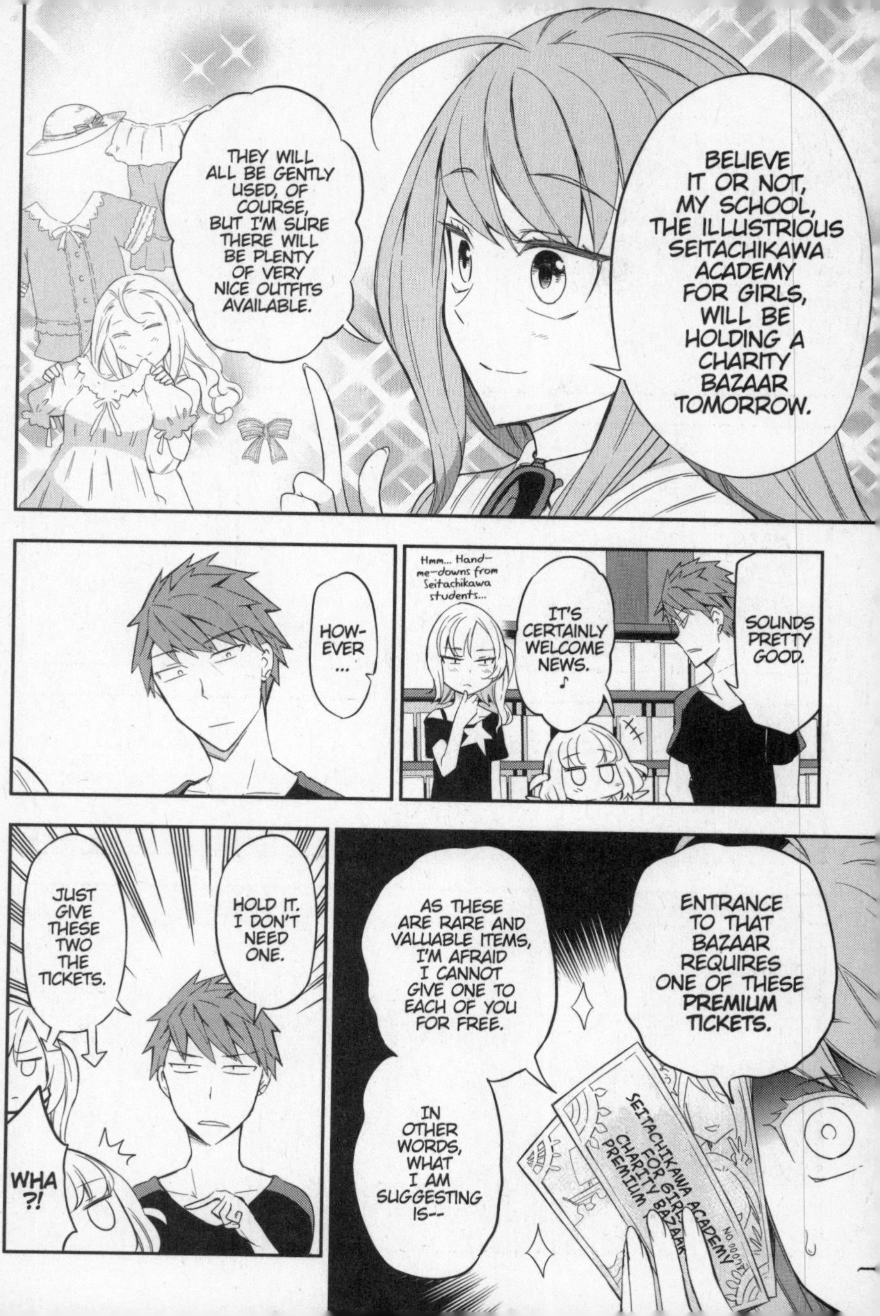
BELIEVE IT OR NOT, MY SCHOOL, THE ILLUSTRIOUS SEITACHIKAWA ACADEMY FOR GIRLS, WILL BE HOLDING A CHARITY BAZAAR TOMORROW.
THEY WILL ALL BE GENTLY USED, OF COURSE, BUT I'M SURE THERE WILL BE PLENTY OF VERY NICE OUTFITS AVAILABLE.
SOUNDS PRETTY GOOD.
IT'S CERTAINLY WELCOME NEWS. ♪
Hmm... Hand-me-downs from Seitachikawa students...
HOW-EVER...
ENTRANCE TO THAT BAZAAR REQUIRES ONE OF THESE PREMIUM TICKETS.
SEITACHIKAWA ACADEMY
FOR GIRL
CHARITY BAZAAR
PREMIUM
AS THESE ARE RARE AND VALUABLE ITEMS, I'M AFRAID I CANNOT GIVE ONE TO EACH OF YOU FOR FREE.
IN OTHER WORDS, WHAT I AM SUGGESTING IS--
HOLD IT. I DON'T NEED ONE.
JUST GIVE THESE TWO THE TICKETS.
WHA?!

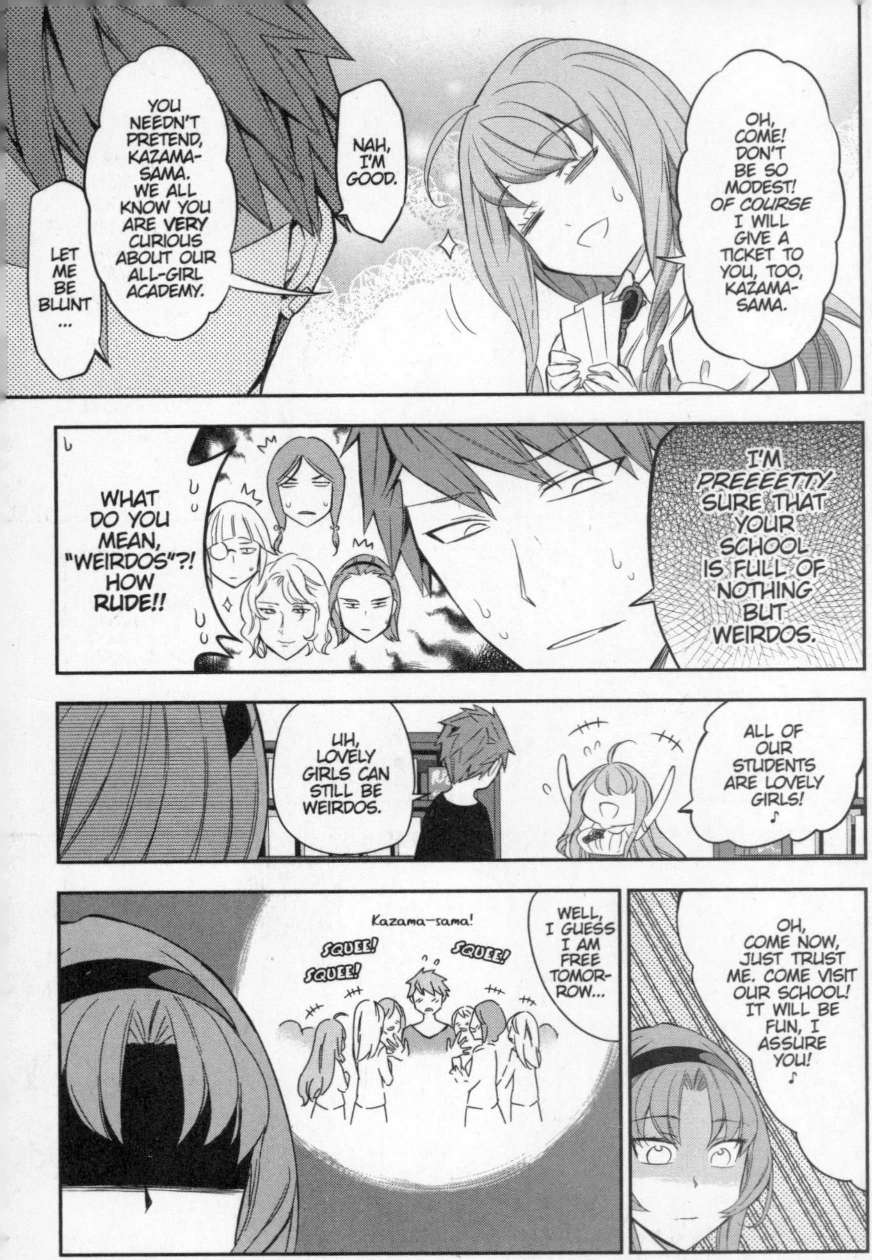
OH, COME! DON'T BE SO MODEST! OF COURSE I WILL GIVE A TICKET TO YOU, TOO, KAZAMA-SAMA.
NAH, I'M GOOD.
YOU NEEDN'T PRETEND, KAZAMA-SAMA. WE ALL KNOW YOU ARE VERY CURIOUS ABOUT OUR ALL-GIRL ACADEMY.
LET ME BE BLUNT...
I'M PREEEETTY SURE THAT YOUR SCHOOL IS FULL OF NOTHING BUT WEIRDOS.
WHAT DO YOU MEAN, "WEIRDOS"?! HOW RUDE!!
ALL OF OUR STUDENTS ARE LOVELY GIRLS! ♪
UH, LOVELY GIRLS CAN STILL BE WEIRDOS.
OH, COME NOW, JUST TRUST ME. COME VISIT OUR SCHOOL! IT WILL BE FUN, I ASSURE YOU! ♪
WELL, I GUESS I AM FREE TOMORROW...
Kazama-sama!
SQUEE!
SQUEE!
SQUEE!

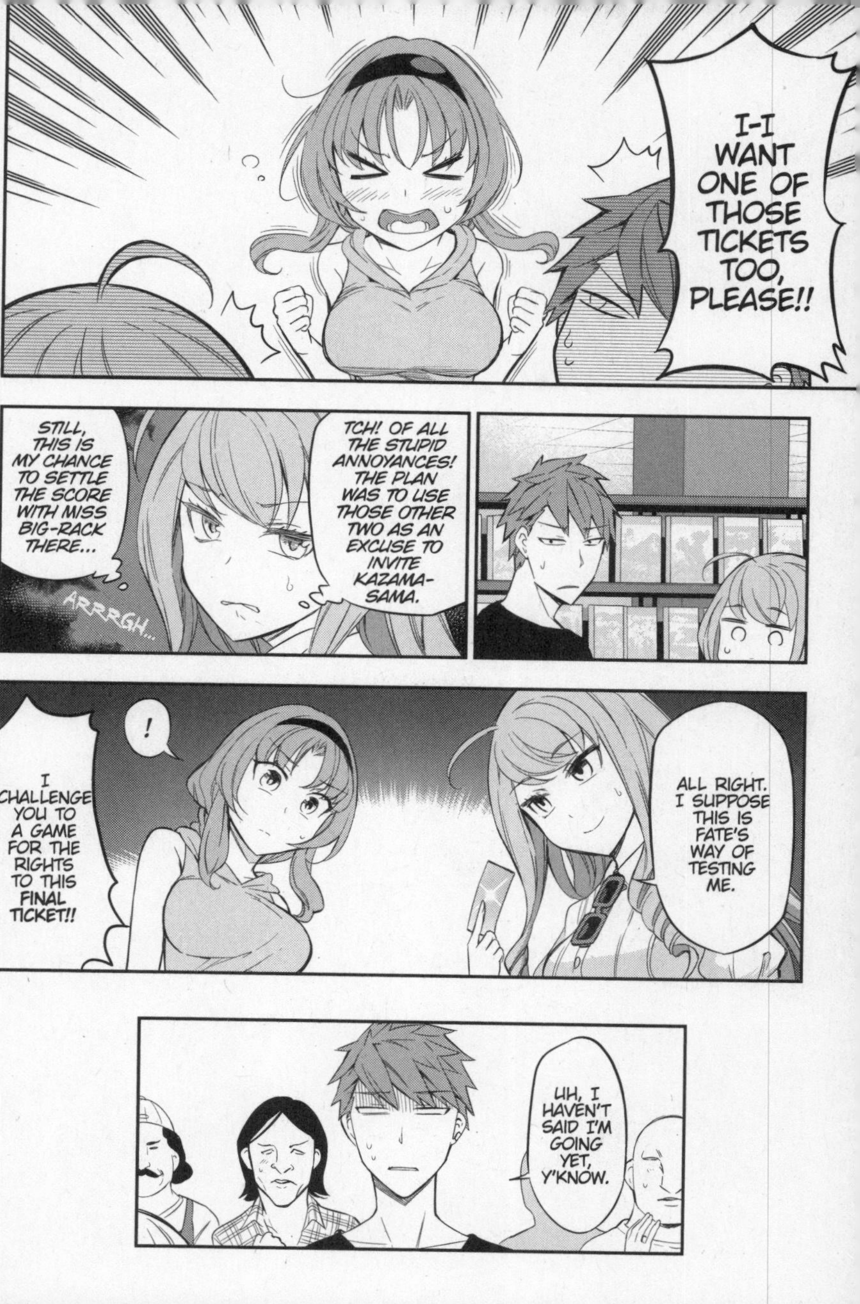
I-I WANT ONE OF THOSE TICKETS TOO, PLEASE!!
TCH! OF ALL THE STUPID ANNOYANCES! THE PLAN WAS TO USE THOSE OTHER TWO AS AN EXCUSE TO INVITE KAZAMA-SAMA.
STILL, THIS IS MY CHANCE TO SETTLE THE SCORE WITH MISS BIG-RACK THERE...
ARRRGH...
ALL RIGHT. I SUPPOSE THIS IS FATE'S WAY OF TESTING ME.
!
I CHALLENGE YOU TO A GAME FOR THE RIGHTS TO THIS FINAL TICKET!!
UH, I HAVEN'T SAID I'M GOING YET, Y'KNOW.

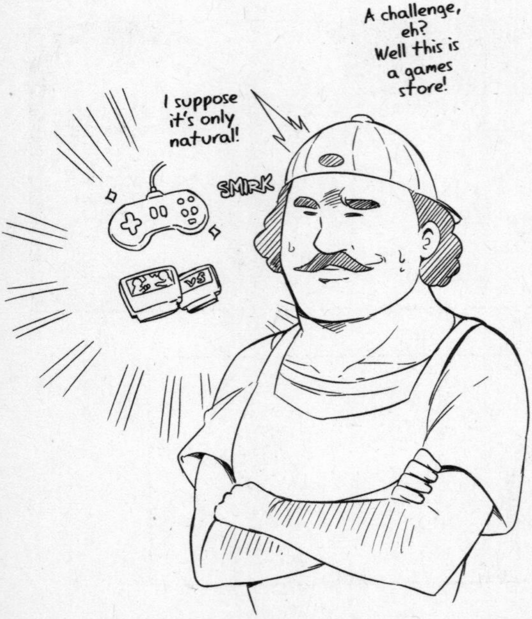
A challenge, eh? Well this is a games store!
I suppose it's only natural!
SMIRK
VS

D-FRAGMENTS
ディーふらぐ!

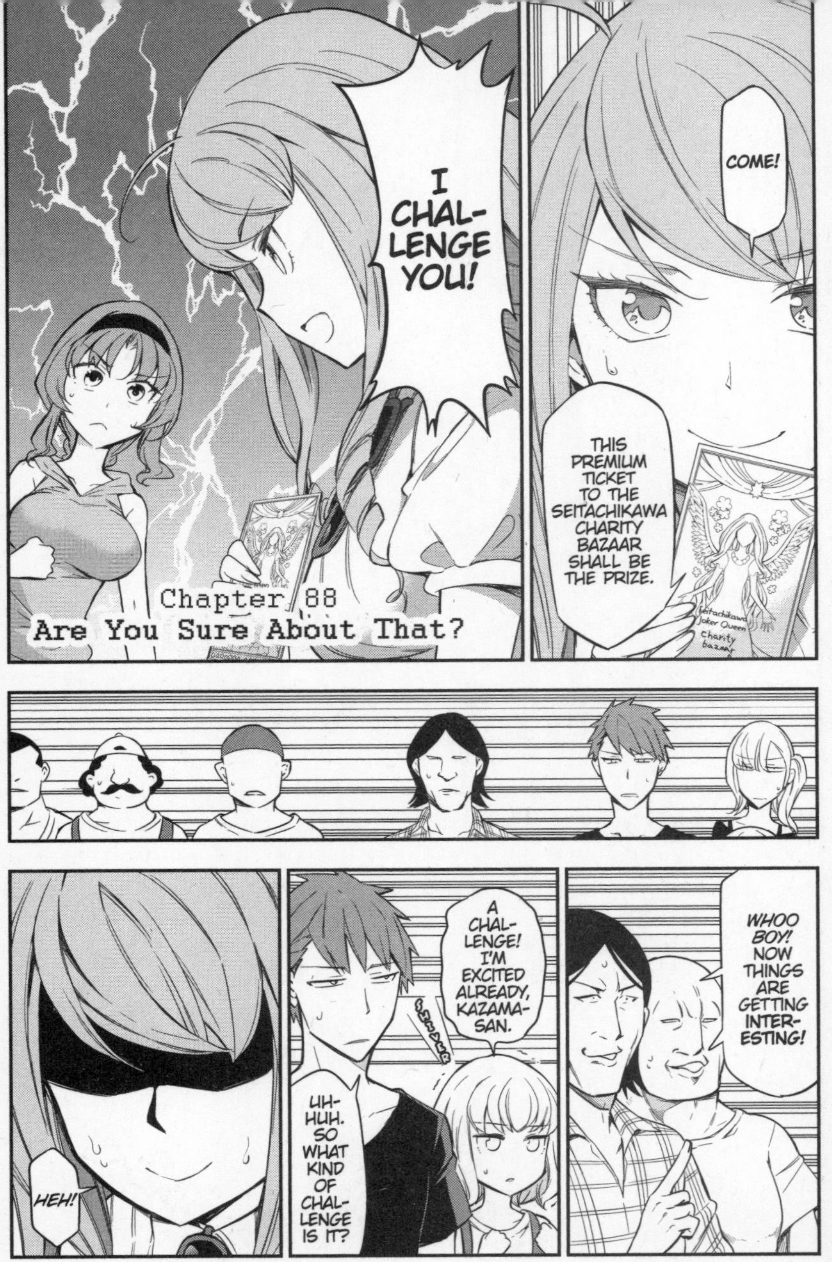
COME!
THIS PREMIUM TICKET TO THE SEITACHIKAWA CHARITY BAZAAR SHALL BE THE PRIZE.
Seitachikawa Joker Queen Charity bazaar
I CHAL-LENGE YOU!
Chapter 88
Are You Sure About That?
WHOO BOY! NOW THINGS ARE GETTING INTER-ESTING!
A CHAL-LENGE! I'M EXCITED ALREADY, KAZAMA-SAN.
SHIVER
UH-HUH. SO WHAT KIND OF CHAL-LENGE IS IT?
HEH!

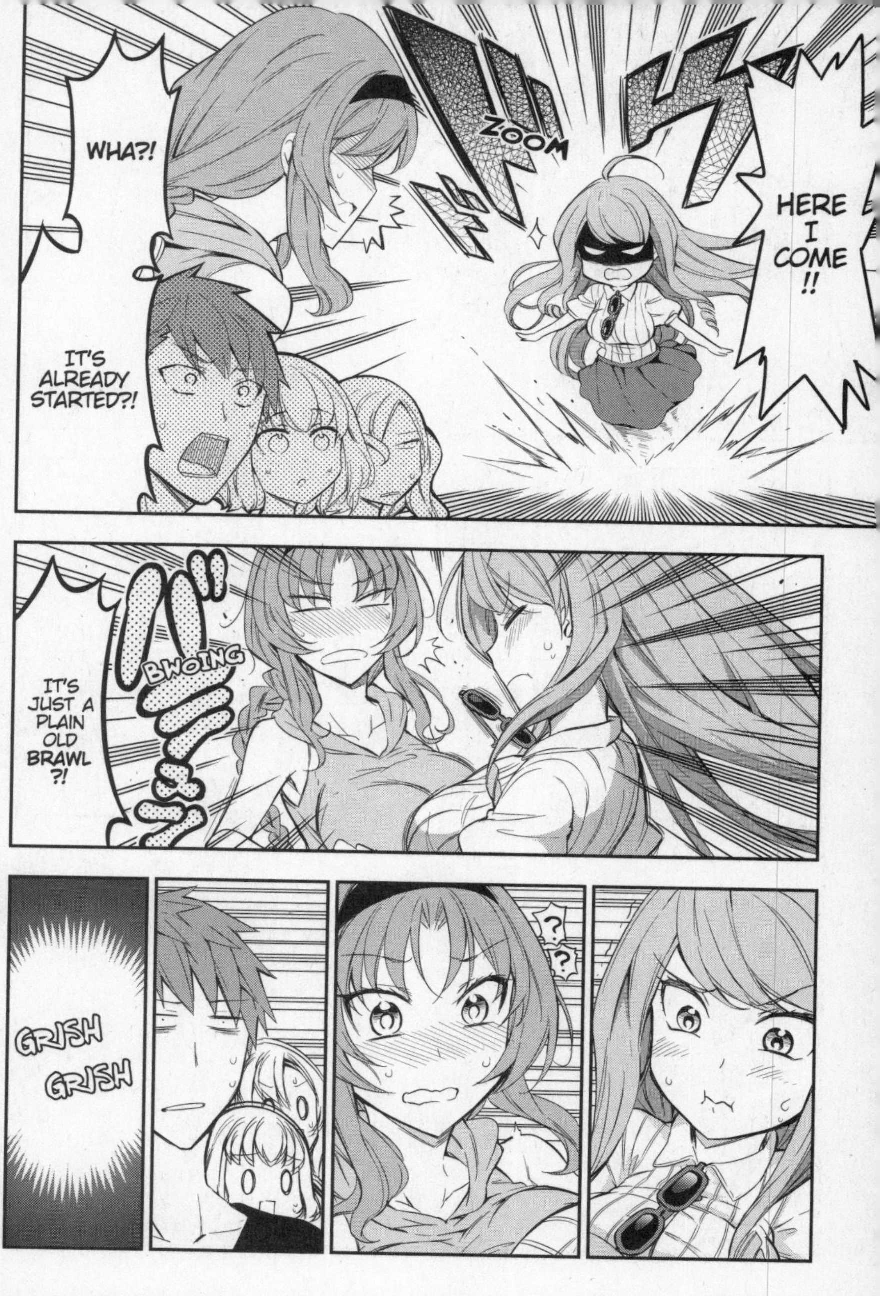
HERE I COME!!
ZOOM
WHA?!
IT'S ALREADY STARTED?!
BWOING
IT'S JUST A PLAIN OLD BRAWL?!
? ?
GRISH GRISH

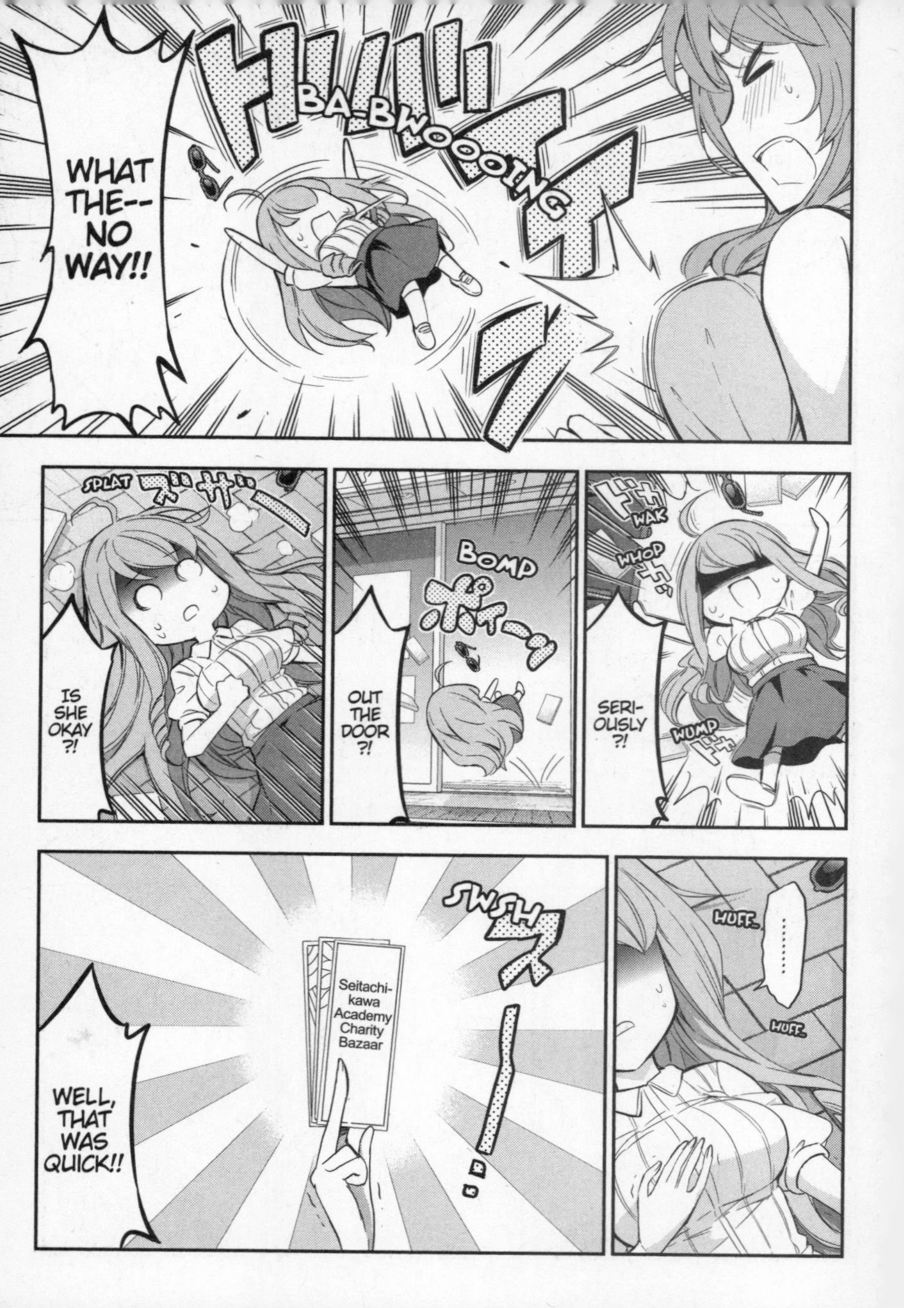
BA-BWOOOING
WHAT THE-- NO WAY!!
WAK
WHOP
WUMP
SERI-OUSLY ?!
BOMP
OUT THE DOOR ?!
SPLAT
IS SHE OKAY ?!
HUFF...
....
HUFF...
SWSH
Seitachi-kawa Academy Charity Bazaar
WELL, THAT WAS QUICK!!

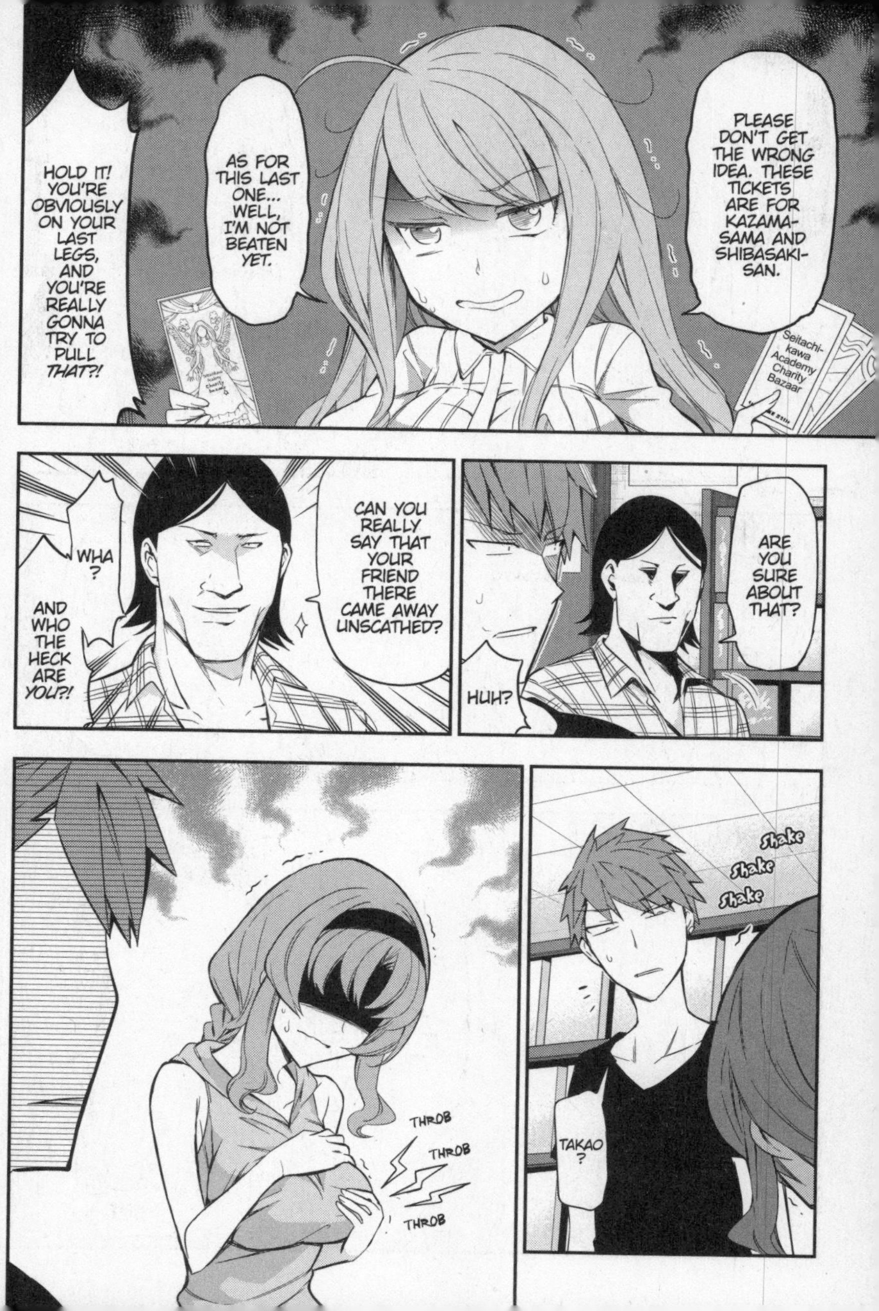
PLEASE DON'T GET THE WRONG IDEA. THESE TICKETS ARE FOR KAZAMA-SAMA AND SHIBASAKI-SAN.
Seitachikawa Academy Charity Bazaar
AS FOR THIS LAST ONE... WELL, I'M NOT BEATEN YET.
HOLD IT! YOU'RE OBVIOUSLY ON YOUR LAST LEGS, AND YOU'RE REALLY GONNA TRY TO PULL *THAT?!*
ARE YOU SURE ABOUT THAT?
HUH?
CAN YOU REALLY SAY THAT YOUR FRIEND THERE CAME AWAY UNSCATHED?
WHA?
AND WHO THE HECK ARE *YOU?!*
Shake
Shake
Shake
TAKAO?
THROB
THROB
THROB

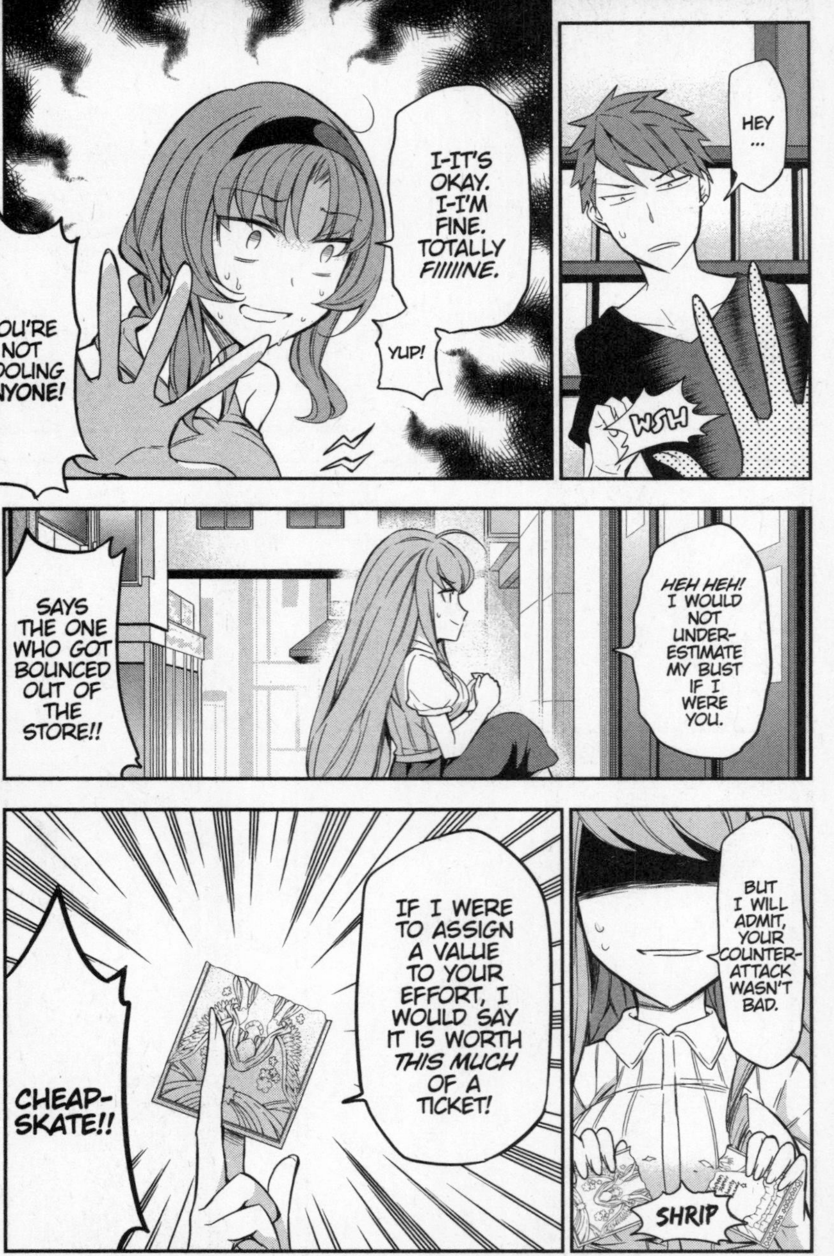
HEY ...
WSH
I-IT'S OKAY. I-I'M FINE. TOTALLY *FIIIIINE.*
YUP!
YOU'RE NOT FOOLING ANYONE!
HEH HEH! I WOULD NOT UNDER-ESTIMATE MY BUST IF I WERE YOU.
SAYS THE ONE WHO GOT BOUNCED OUT OF THE STORE!!
BUT I WILL ADMIT, YOUR COUNTER-ATTACK WASN'T BAD.
SHRIP
IF I WERE TO ASSIGN A VALUE TO YOUR EFFORT, I WOULD SAY IT IS WORTH *THIS MUCH* OF A TICKET!
CHEAP-SKATE!!

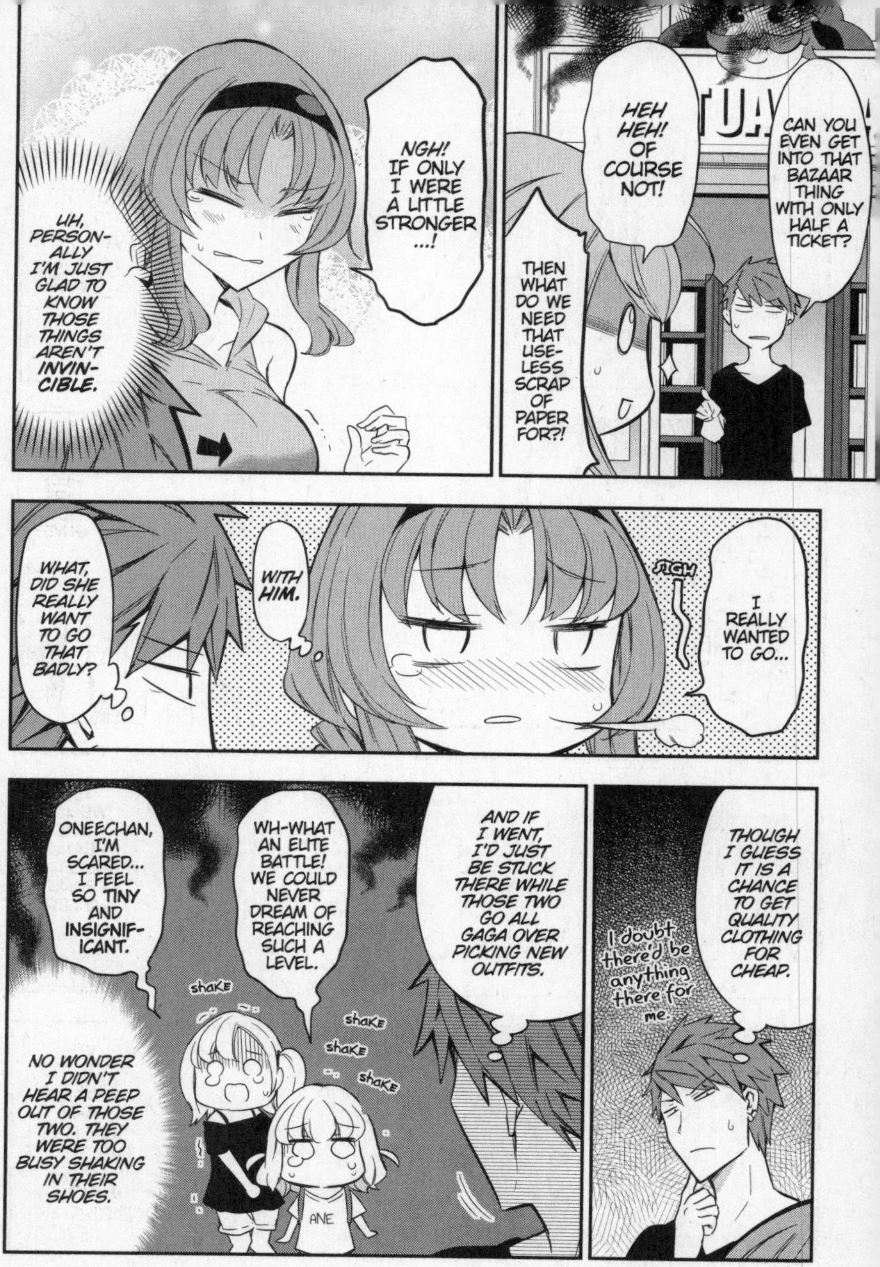
CAN YOU EVEN GET INTO THAT BAZAAR THING WITH ONLY HALF A TICKET?
HEH HEH! OF COURSE NOT!
THEN WHAT DO WE NEED THAT USELESS SCRAP OF PAPER FOR?!
NGH! IF ONLY I WERE A LITTLE STRONGER ...!
UH, PERSONALLY I'M JUST GLAD TO KNOW THOSE THINGS AREN'T INVINCIBLE.
I REALLY WANTED TO GO...
SIGH
WITH HIM.
WHAT, DID SHE REALLY WANT TO GO THAT BADLY?
THOUGH I GUESS IT IS A CHANCE TO GET QUALITY CLOTHING FOR CHEAP.
I doubt there'd be anything there for me.
AND IF I WENT, I'D JUST BE STUCK THERE WHILE THOSE TWO GO ALL GAGA OVER PICKING NEW OUTFITS.
WH-WHAT AN ELITE BATTLE! WE COULD NEVER DREAM OF REACHING SUCH A LEVEL.
ONEECHAN, I'M SCARED... I FEEL SO TINY AND INSIGNIFICANT.
shake
shake
shake
shake
NO WONDER I DIDN'T HEAR A PEEP OUT OF THOSE TWO. THEY WERE TOO BUSY SHAKING IN THEIR SHOES.
ANE

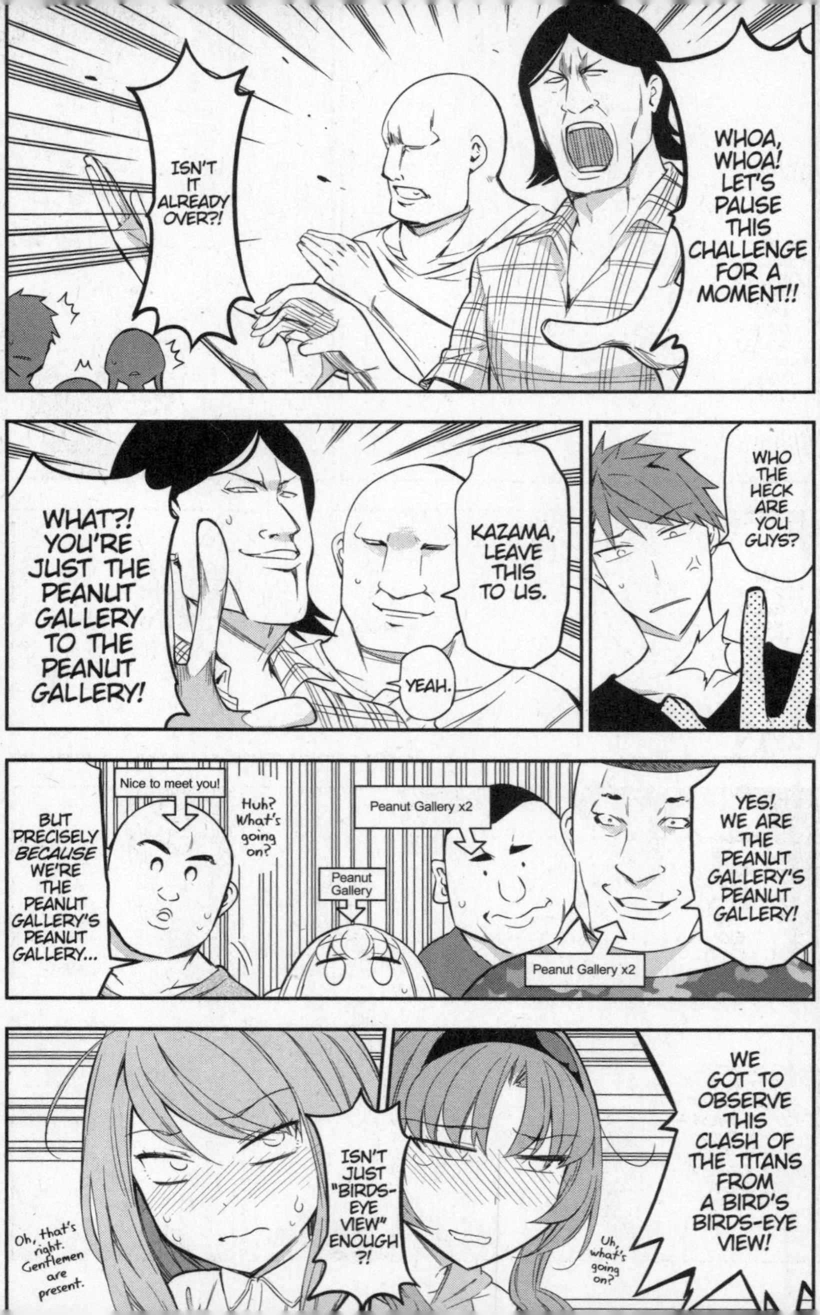

WHOA, WHOA! LET'S PAUSE THIS CHALLENGE FOR A MOMENT!!
ISN'T IT ALREADY OVER?!
WHO THE HECK ARE YOU GUYS?
KAZAMA, LEAVE THIS TO US.
WHAT?! YOU'RE JUST THE PEANUT GALLERY TO THE PEANUT GALLERY!
YEAH.
YES! WE ARE THE PEANUT GALLERY'S PEANUT GALLERY!
Peanut Gallery x2
Peanut Gallery x2
Peanut Gallery
Huh? What's going on?
Nice to meet you!
BUT PRECISELY *BECAUSE* WE'RE THE PEANUT GALLERY'S PEANUT GALLERY...
WE GOT TO OBSERVE THIS CLASH OF THE TITANS FROM A BIRD'S BIRDS-EYE VIEW!
Uh, what's going on?
ISN'T JUST "BIRDS-EYE VIEW" ENOUGH?!
Oh, that's right. Gentlemen are present.

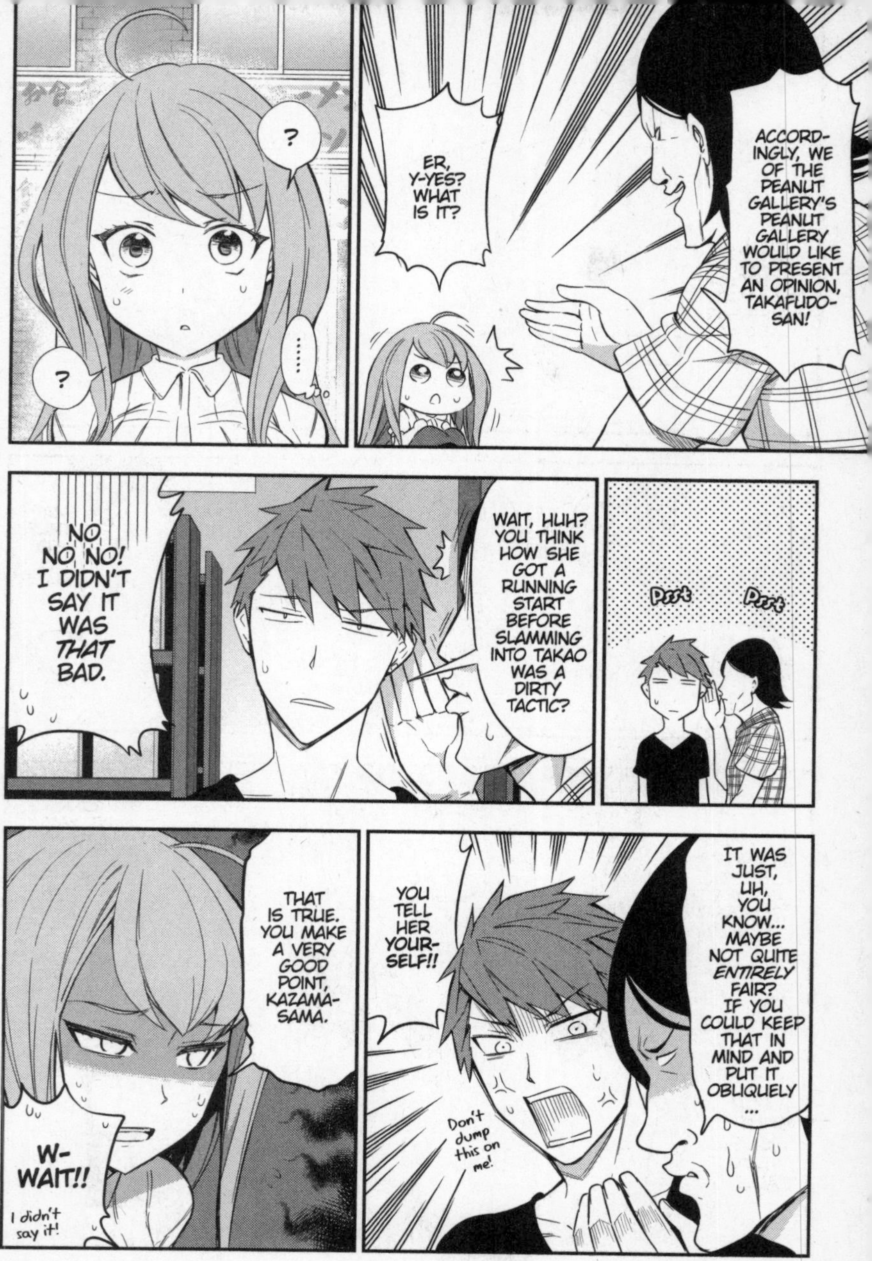
ACCORD-INGLY, WE OF THE PEANUT GALLERY'S PEANUT GALLERY WOULD LIKE TO PRESENT AN OPINION, TAKAFUDO-SAN!
ER, Y-YES? WHAT IS IT?
?
......
?
Psst
Psst
WAIT, HUH? YOU THINK HOW SHE GOT A RUNNING START BEFORE SLAMMING INTO TAKAO WAS A DIRTY TACTIC?
NO NO, NO! I DIDN'T SAY IT WAS *THAT* BAD.
IT WAS JUST, UH, YOU KNOW... MAYBE NOT QUITE *ENTIRELY* FAIR? IF YOU COULD KEEP THAT IN MIND AND PUT IT OBLIQUELY ...
YOU TELL HER YOUR-SELF!!
Don't dump this on me!
THAT IS TRUE. YOU MAKE A VERY GOOD POINT, KAZAMA-SAMA.
W-WAIT!!
I didn't say it!

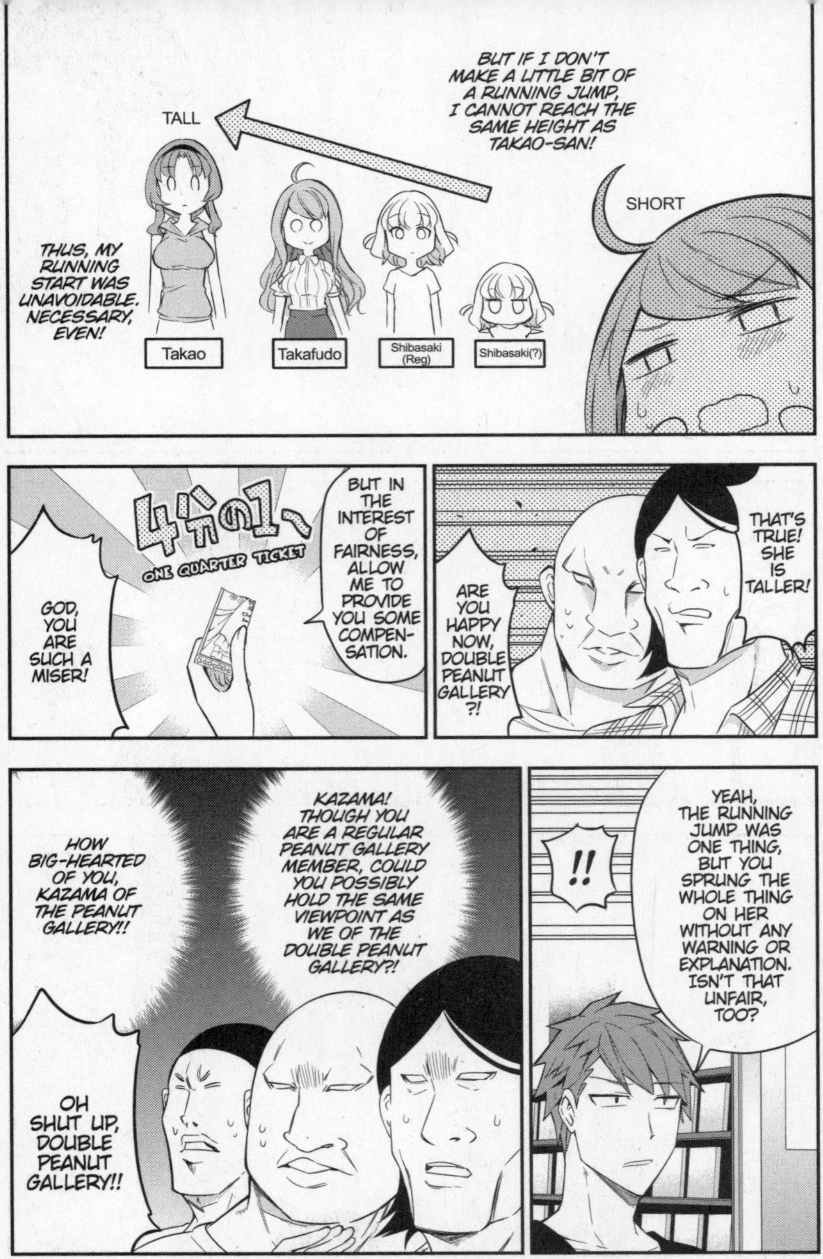
BUT IF I DON'T MAKE A LITTLE BIT OF A RUNNING JUMP, I CANNOT REACH THE SAME HEIGHT AS TAKAO-SAN!
SHORT
TALL
THUS, MY RUNNING START WAS UNAVOIDABLE. NECESSARY, EVEN!
Takao
Takafudo
Shibasaki (Reg)
Shibasaki(?)
THAT'S TRUE! SHE IS TALLER!
ARE YOU HAPPY NOW, DOUBLE PEANUT GALLERY?!
BUT IN THE INTEREST OF FAIRNESS, ALLOW ME TO PROVIDE YOU SOME COMPEN-SATION.
4分の1、
ONE QUARTER TICKET
GOD, YOU ARE SUCH A MISER!
YEAH, THE RUNNING JUMP WAS ONE THING, BUT YOU SPRUNG THE WHOLE THING ON HER WITHOUT ANY WARNING OR EXPLANATION. ISN'T THAT UNFAIR, TOO?
!!
KAZAMA! THOUGH YOU ARE A REGULAR PEANUT GALLERY MEMBER, COULD YOU POSSIBLY HOLD THE SAME VIEWPOINT AS WE OF THE DOUBLE PEANUT GALLERY?!
HOW BIG-HEARTED OF YOU, KAZAMA OF THE PEANUT GALLERY!!
OH SHUT UP, DOUBLE PEANUT GALLERY!!

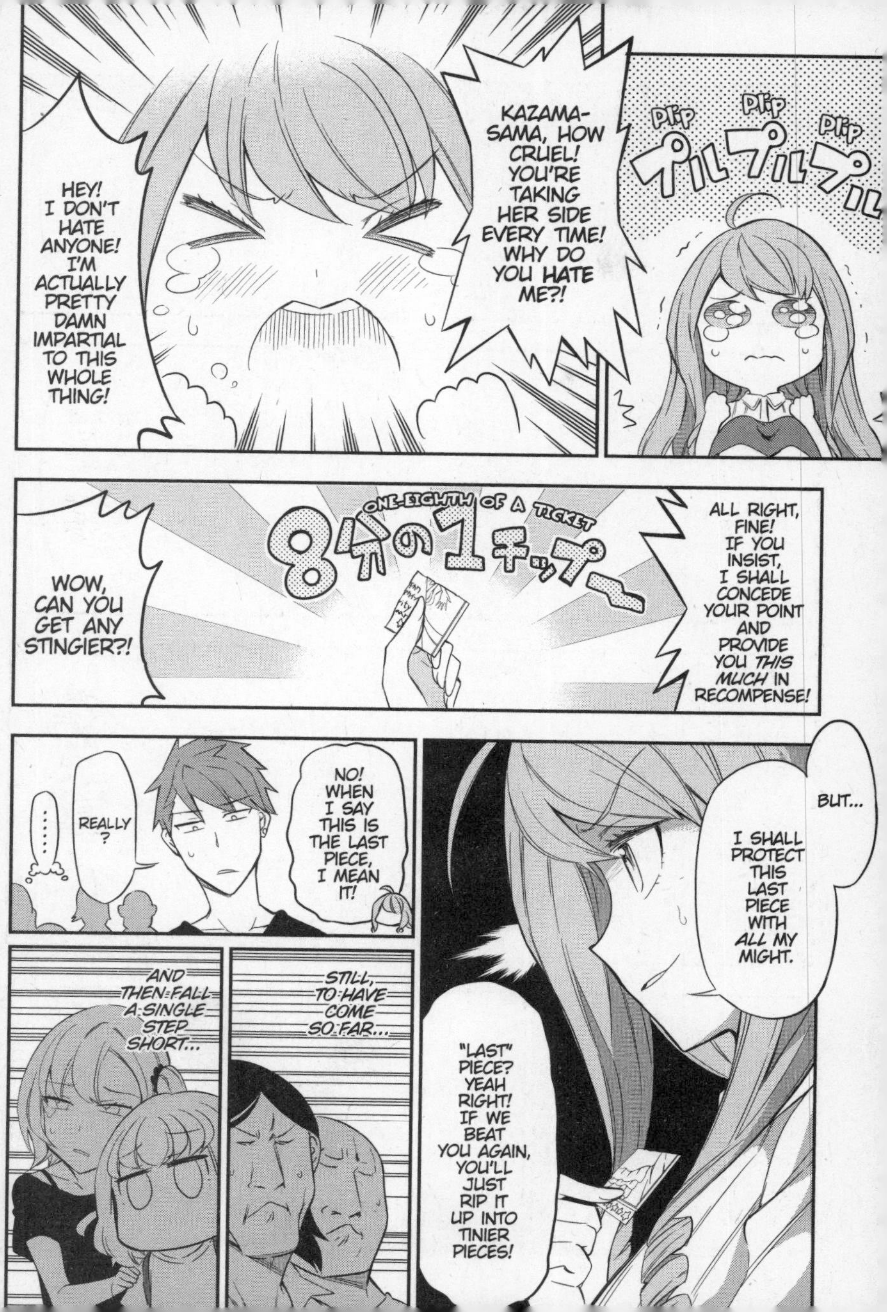
plip plip plip
プルプルプル
KAZAMA-SAMA, HOW CRUEL! YOU'RE TAKING HER SIDE EVERY TIME! WHY DO YOU HATE ME?!
HEY! I DON'T HATE ANYONE! I'M ACTUALLY PRETTY DAMN IMPARTIAL TO THIS WHOLE THING!
ALL RIGHT, FINE! IF YOU INSIST, I SHALL CONCEDE YOUR POINT AND PROVIDE YOU *THIS MUCH* IN RECOMPENSE!
ONE-EIGHTH OF A TICKET
8分の1チップ～
WOW, CAN YOU GET ANY STINGIER?!
BUT...
I SHALL PROTECT THIS LAST PIECE WITH *ALL MY* MIGHT.
"LAST" PIECE? YEAH RIGHT! IF WE BEAT YOU AGAIN, YOU'LL JUST RIP IT UP INTO TINIER PIECES!
NO! WHEN I SAY THIS IS THE LAST PIECE, I MEAN IT!
REALLY?
......
STILL, TO HAVE COME SO FAR...
AND THEN FALL A SINGLE STEP SHORT...

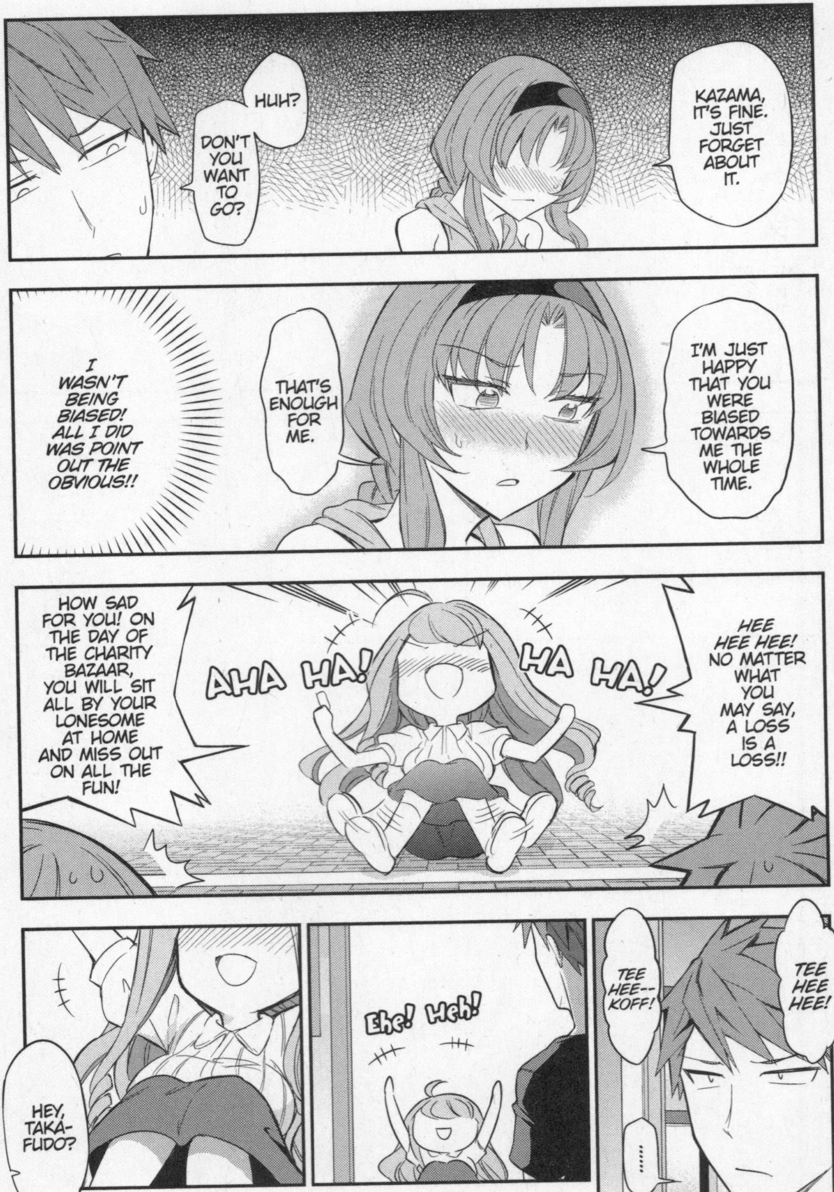
KAZAMA, IT'S FINE. JUST FORGET ABOUT IT.
HUH?
DON'T YOU WANT TO GO?
I'M JUST HAPPY THAT YOU WERE BIASED TOWARDS ME THE WHOLE TIME.
THAT'S ENOUGH FOR ME.
I WASN'T BEING BIASED! ALL I DID WAS POINT OUT THE OBVIOUS!!
HEE HEE HEE! NO MATTER WHAT YOU MAY SAY, A LOSS IS A LOSS!!
HA HA!
AHA HA!
HOW SAD FOR YOU! ON THE DAY OF THE CHARITY BAZAAR, YOU WILL SIT ALL BY YOUR LONESOME AT HOME AND MISS OUT ON ALL THE FUN!
TEE HEE HEE!
TEE HEE--KOFF!
......
Ehe! Heh!
HEY, TAKA-FUDO?

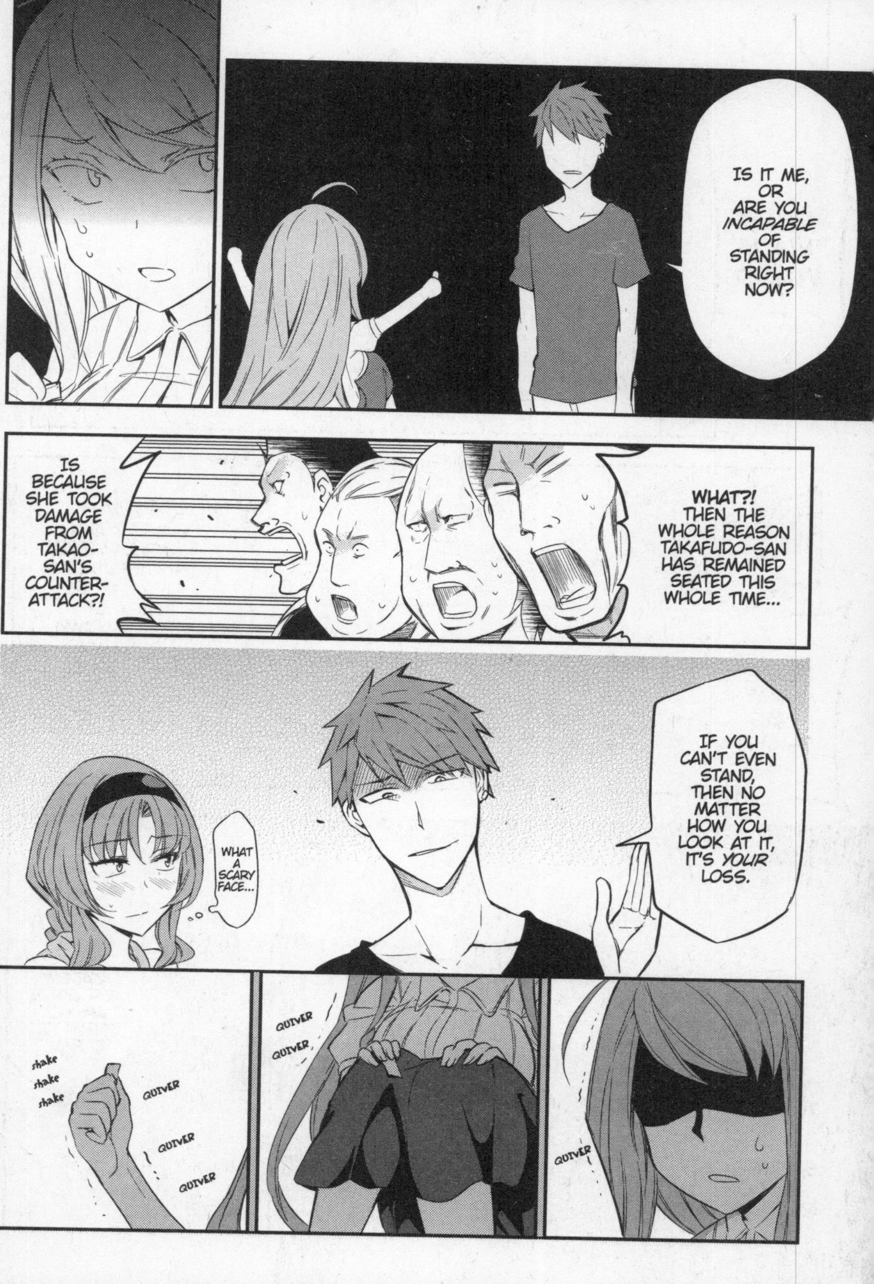
IS IT ME, OR ARE YOU INCAPABLE OF STANDING RIGHT NOW?
WHAT?! THEN THE WHOLE REASON TAKAFUDO-SAN HAS REMAINED SEATED THIS WHOLE TIME...
IS BECAUSE SHE TOOK DAMAGE FROM TAKAO-SAN'S COUNTER-ATTACK?!
IF YOU CAN'T EVEN STAND, THEN NO MATTER HOW YOU LOOK AT IT, IT'S YOUR LOSS.
WHAT A SCARY FACE...
QUIVER
QUIVER
QUIVER
shake
shake
shake
QUIVER
QUIVER
QUIVER

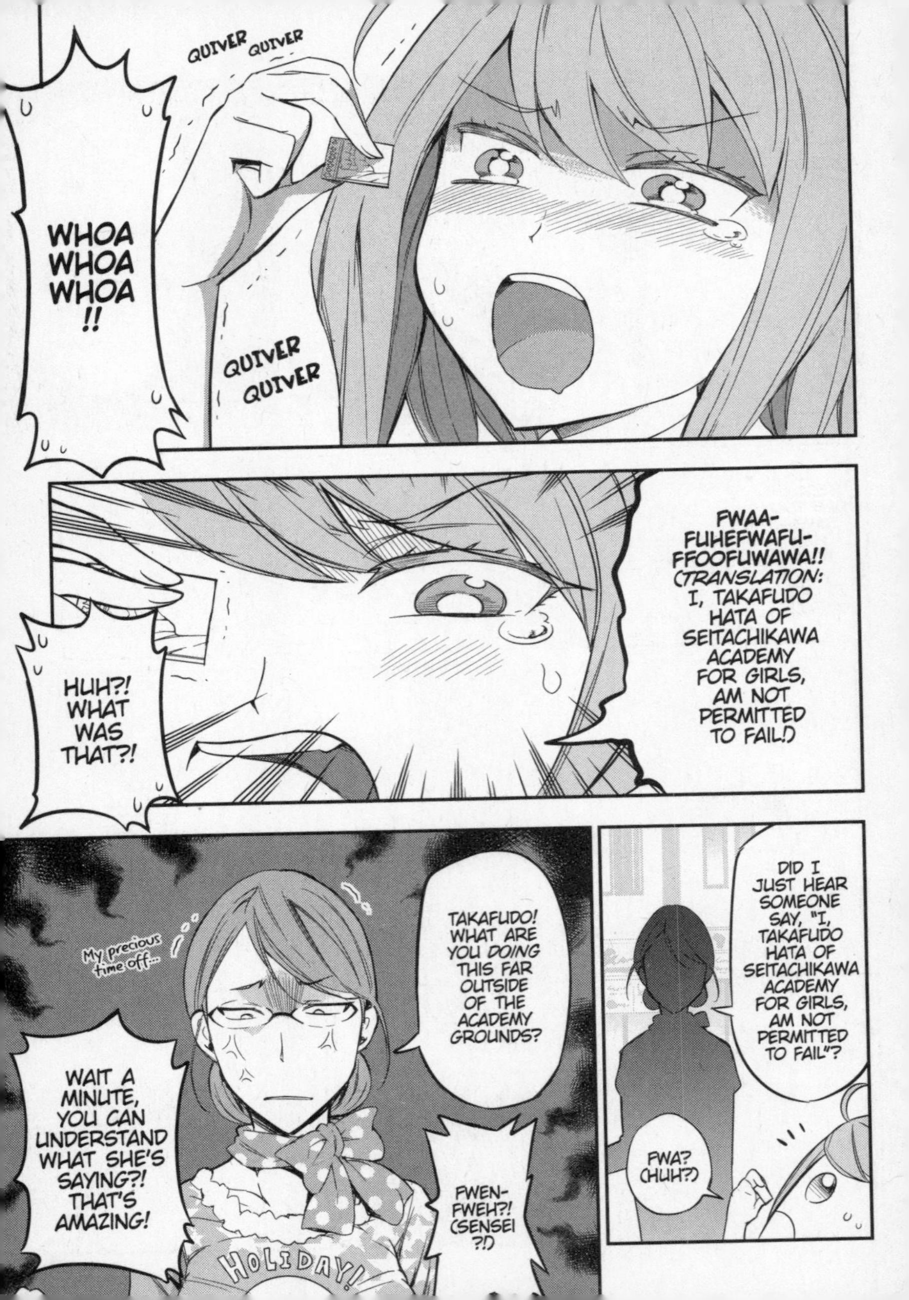
QUIVER QUIVER
WHOA WHOA WHOA!!
QUIVER QUIVER
FWAA-FUHEFWAFU-FFOOFUWAWA!! (TRANSLATION: I, TAKAFUDO HATA OF SEITACHIKAWA ACADEMY FOR GIRLS, AM NOT PERMITTED TO FAIL!)
HUH?! WHAT WAS THAT?!
DID I JUST HEAR SOMEONE SAY, "I, TAKAFUDO HATA OF SEITACHIKAWA ACADEMY FOR GIRLS, AM NOT PERMITTED TO FAIL"?
FWA? (HUH?)
TAKAFUDO! WHAT ARE YOU DOING THIS FAR OUTSIDE OF THE ACADEMY GROUNDS?
My precious time off...
WAIT A MINUTE, YOU CAN UNDERSTAND WHAT SHE'S SAYING?! THAT'S AMAZING!
FWEN-FWEH?! (SENSEI?!)
HOLIDAY!

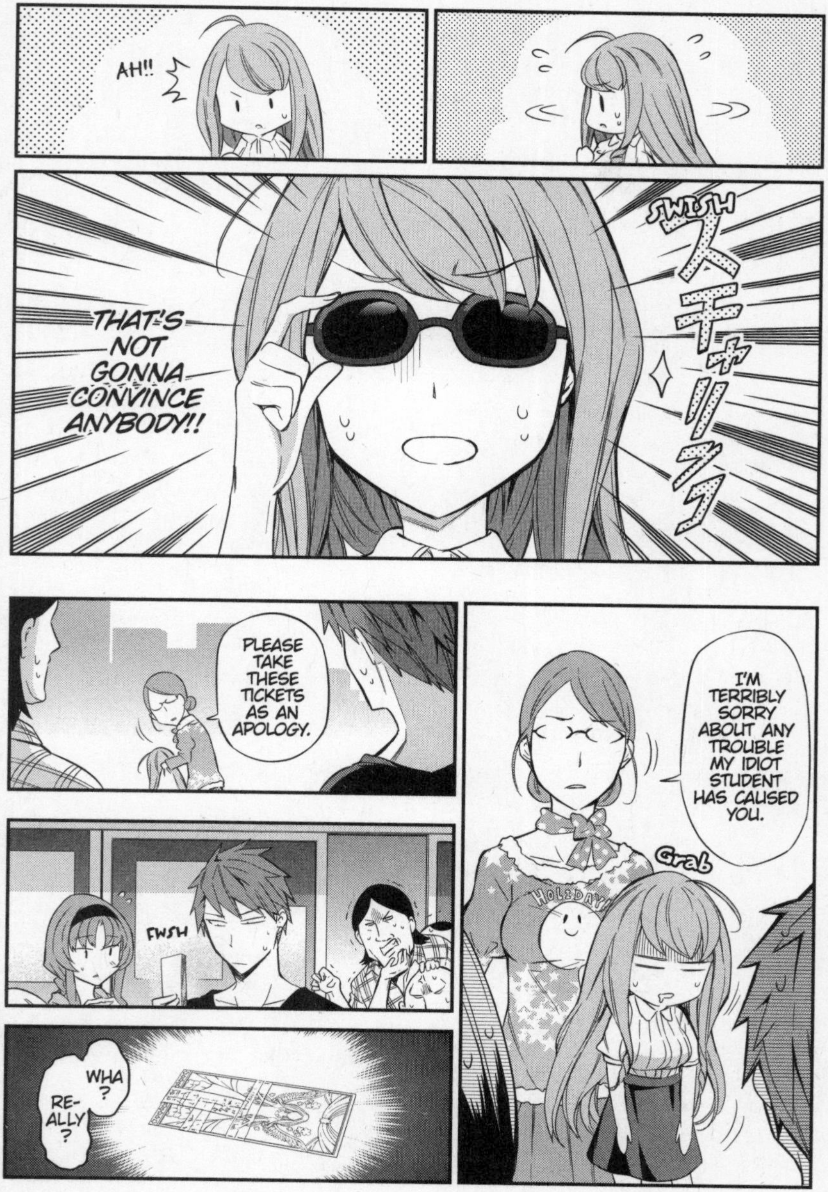
AH!!
SWISH
THAT'S NOT GONNA CONVINCE ANYBODY!!
I'M TERRIBLY SORRY ABOUT ANY TROUBLE MY IDIOT STUDENT HAS CAUSED YOU.
Grab
PLEASE TAKE THESE TICKETS AS AN APOLOGY.
FWSH
WHA?
RE-ALLY?

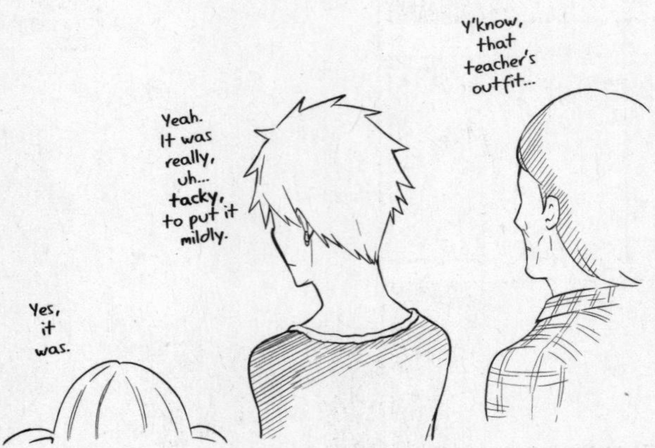
y'know, that teacher's outfit...
Yeah. It was really, uh... tacky, to put it mildly.
Yes, it was.

D-FRAGMENTS
ディーふらぐ!

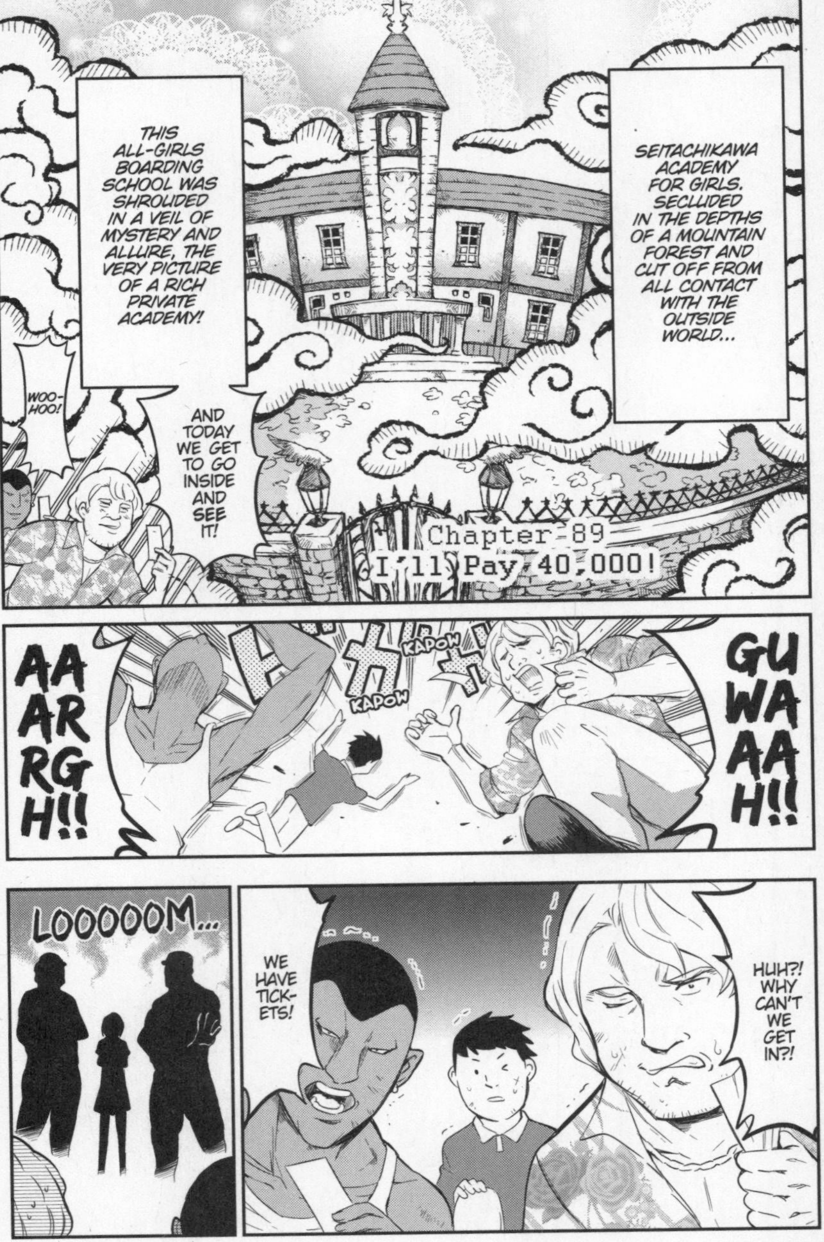
SEITACHIKAWA ACADEMY FOR GIRLS. SECLUDED IN THE DEPTHS OF A MOUNTAIN FOREST AND CUT OFF FROM ALL CONTACT WITH THE OUTSIDE WORLD...
THIS ALL-GIRLS BOARDING SCHOOL WAS SHROUDED IN A VEIL OF MYSTERY AND ALLURE, THE VERY PICTURE OF A RICH PRIVATE ACADEMY!
AND TODAY WE GET TO GO INSIDE AND SEE IT!
WOO-HOO!
Chapter 89
I'll Pay 40,000!
GUWAAAH!!
KAPOW
KAPOW
AAARGH!!
HUH?! WHY CAN'T WE GET IN?!
WE HAVE TICK-ETS!
LOOOOOM...

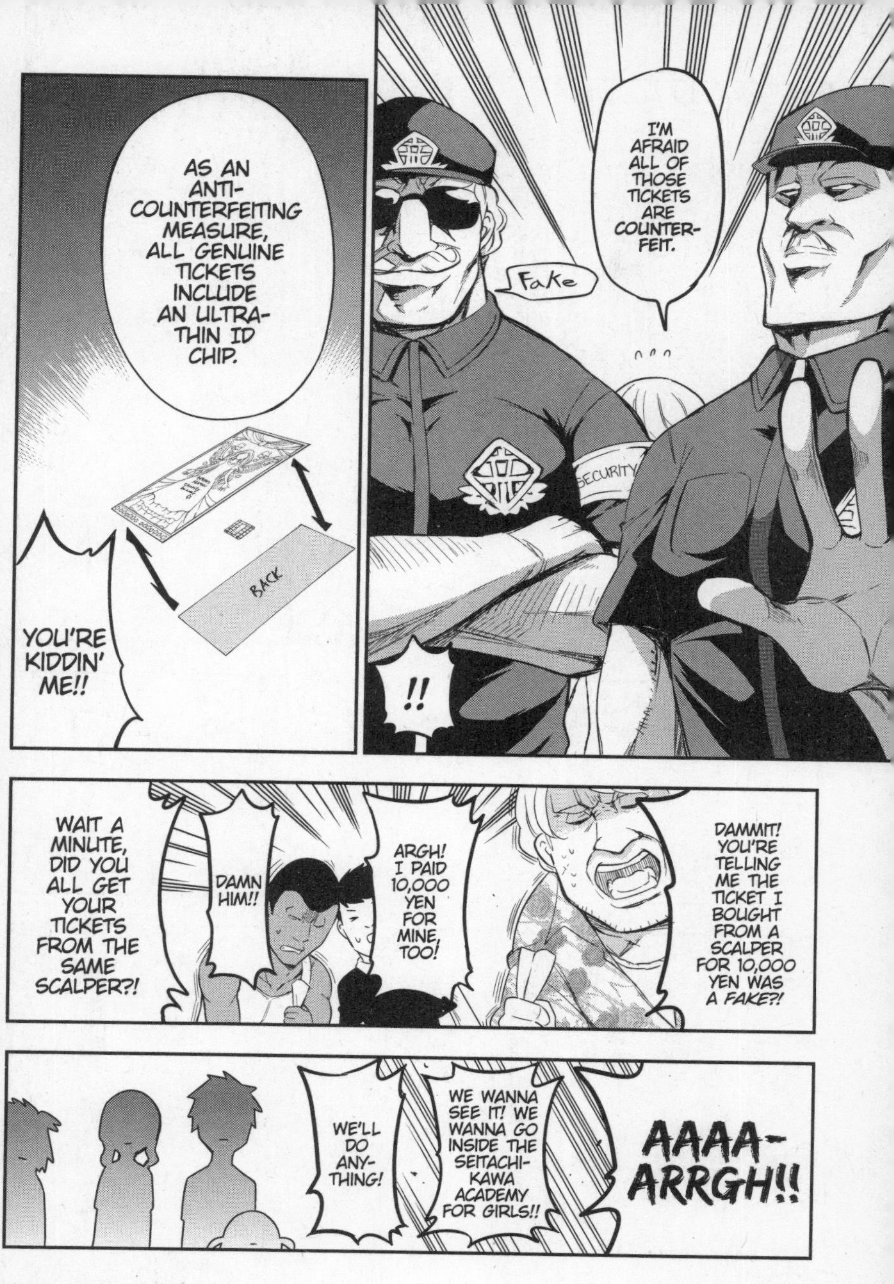
I'M AFRAID ALL OF THOSE TICKETS ARE COUNTER-FEIT.
Fake
SECURITY
!!
AS AN ANTI-COUNTERFEITING MEASURE, ALL GENUINE TICKETS INCLUDE AN ULTRA-THIN ID CHIP.
BACK
YOU'RE KIDDIN' ME!!
DAMMIT! YOU'RE TELLING ME THE TICKET I BOUGHT FROM A SCALPER FOR 10,000 YEN WAS A *FAKE*?!
ARGH! I PAID 10,000 YEN FOR MINE, TOO!
DAMN HIM!!
WAIT A MINUTE, DID YOU ALL GET YOUR TICKETS FROM THE SAME SCALPER?!
AAAA-ARRGH!!
WE WANNA SEE IT! WE WANNA GO INSIDE THE SEITACHI-KAWA ACADEMY FOR GIRLS!!
WE'LL DO ANYTHING!

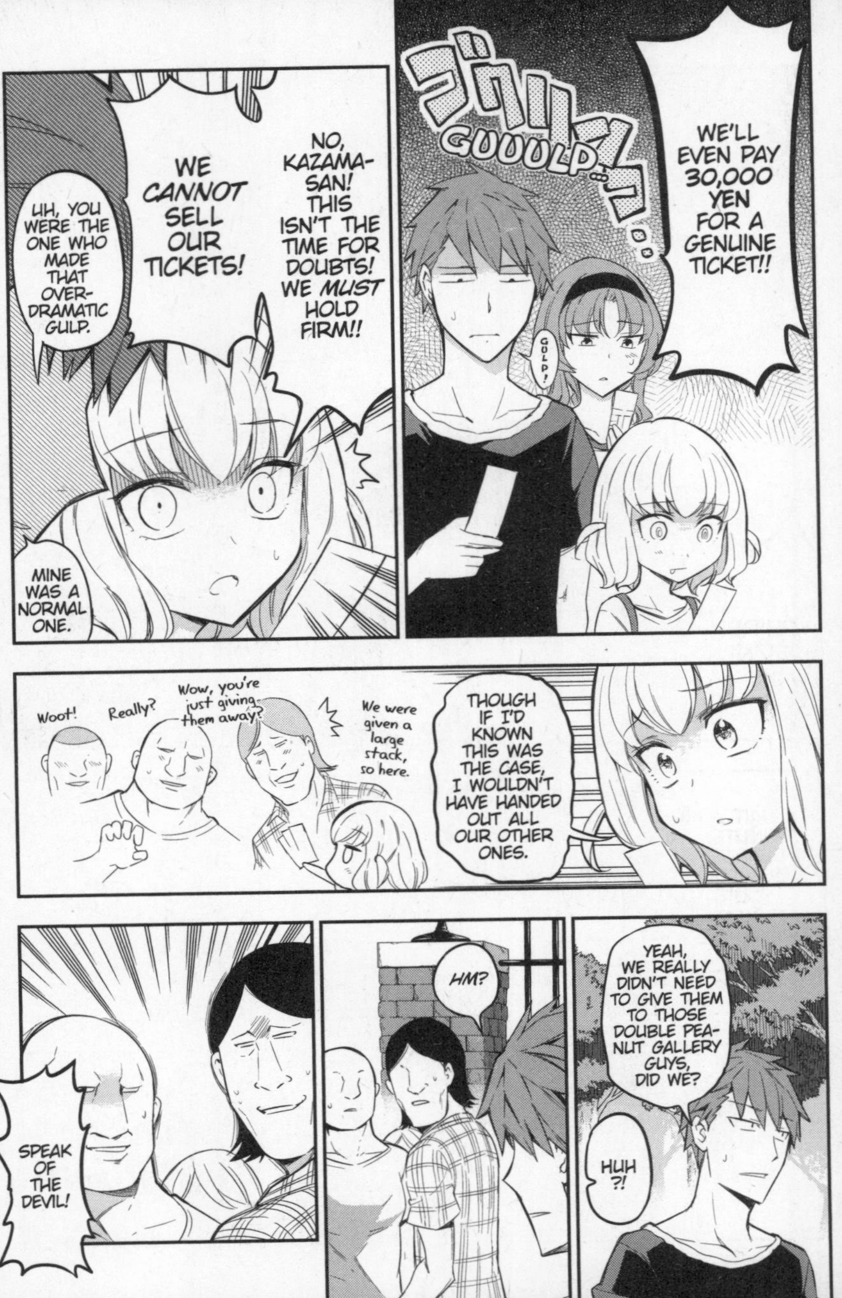
WE'LL EVEN PAY 30,000 YEN FOR A GENUINE TICKET!!
GUUULP...
GULP!
NO, KAZAMA-SAN! THIS ISN'T THE TIME FOR DOUBTS! WE MUST HOLD FIRM!!
WE CANNOT SELL OUR TICKETS!
UH, YOU WERE THE ONE WHO MADE THAT OVER-DRAMATIC GULP.
MINE WAS A NORMAL ONE.
THOUGH IF I'D KNOWN THIS WAS THE CASE, I WOULDN'T HAVE HANDED OUT ALL OUR OTHER ONES.
We were given a large stack, so here.
Wow, you're just giving them away?
Really?
Woot!
YEAH, WE REALLY DIDN'T NEED TO GIVE THEM TO THOSE DOUBLE PEA-NUT GALLERY GUYS, DID WE?
HUH?!
HM?
SPEAK OF THE DEVIL!

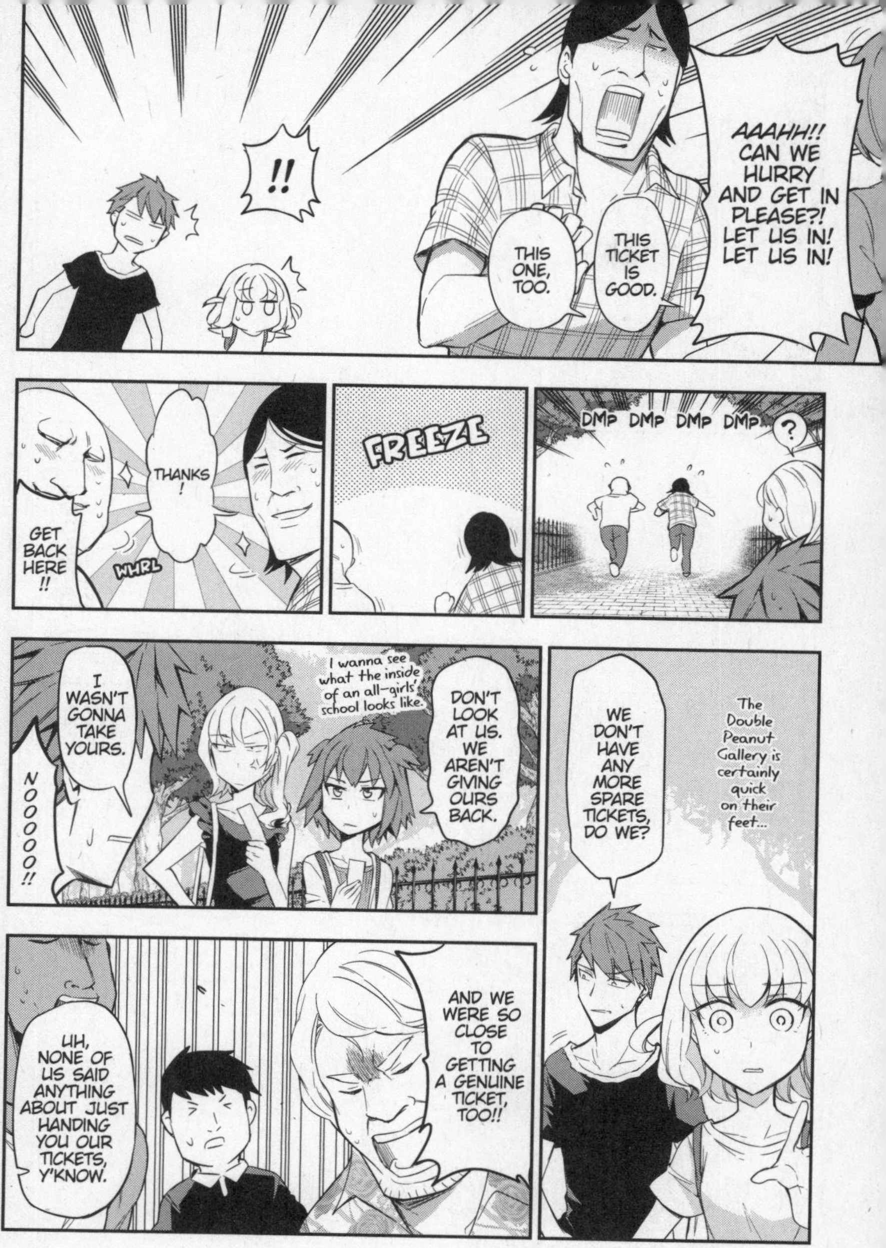
AAAHH!! CAN WE HURRY AND GET IN PLEASE?! LET US IN! LET US IN!
THIS TICKET IS GOOD.
THIS ONE, TOO.
!!
DMP DMP DMP DMP
?
FREEZE
THANKS!
WHRL
GET BACK HERE!!
The Double Peanut Gallery is certainly quick on their feet...
WE DON'T HAVE ANY MORE SPARE TICKETS, DO WE?
DON'T LOOK AT US. WE AREN'T GIVING OURS BACK.
I wanna see what the inside of an all-girls' school looks like.
I WASN'T GONNA TAKE YOURS.
NOOOOOO!!
AND WE WERE SO CLOSE TO GETTING A GENUINE TICKET, TOO!!
UH, NONE OF US SAID ANYTHING ABOUT JUST HANDING YOU OUR TICKETS, Y'KNOW.

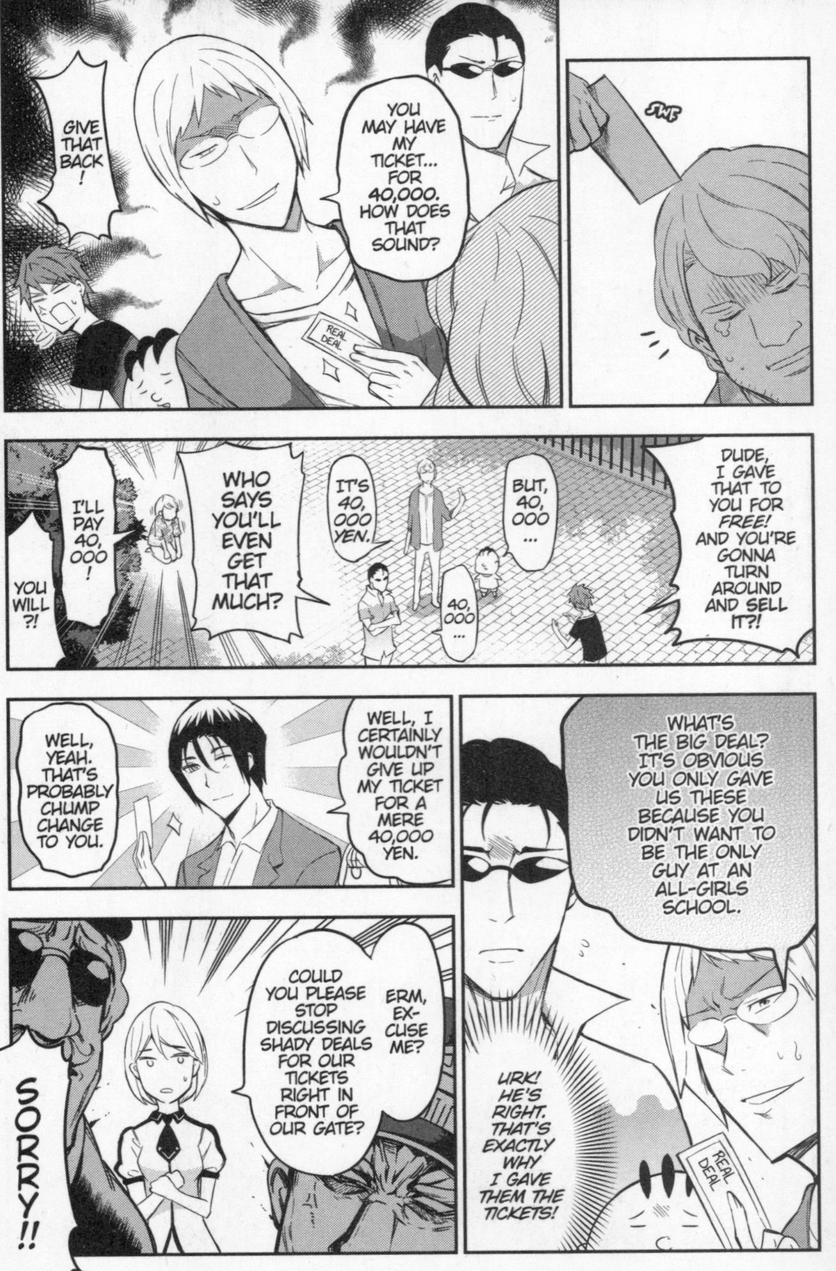
SWF
YOU MAY HAVE MY TICKET... FOR 40,000. HOW DOES THAT SOUND?
REAL DEAL
GIVE THAT BACK!
DUDE, I GAVE THAT TO YOU FOR FREE! AND YOU'RE GONNA TURN AROUND AND SELL IT?!
BUT, 40,000...
IT'S 40,000 YEN.
40,000...
WHO SAYS YOU'LL EVEN GET THAT MUCH?
I'LL PAY 40,000!
YOU WILL?!
WHAT'S THE BIG DEAL? IT'S OBVIOUS YOU ONLY GAVE US THESE BECAUSE YOU DIDN'T WANT TO BE THE ONLY GUY AT AN ALL-GIRLS SCHOOL.
URK! HE'S RIGHT. THAT'S EXACTLY WHY I GAVE THEM THE TICKETS!
REAL DEAL
WELL, I CERTAINLY WOULDN'T GIVE UP MY TICKET FOR A MERE 40,000 YEN.
WELL, YEAH. THAT'S PROBABLY CHUMP CHANGE TO YOU.
ERM, EX-CUSE ME?
COULD YOU PLEASE STOP DISCUSSING SHADY DEALS FOR OUR TICKETS RIGHT IN FRONT OF OUR GATE?
SORRY!!

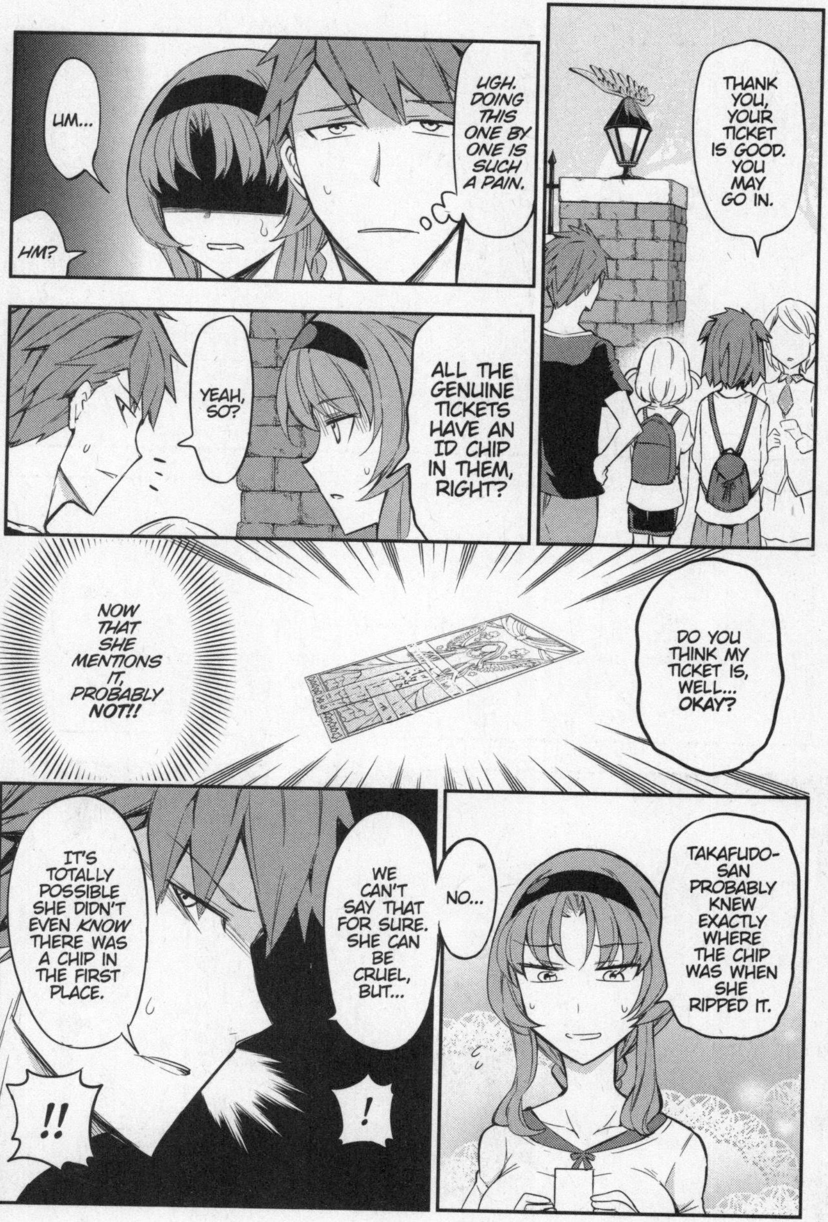
THANK YOU, YOUR TICKET IS GOOD. YOU MAY GO IN.
UGH. DOING THIS ONE BY ONE IS SUCH A PAIN.
UM...
HM?
ALL THE GENUINE TICKETS HAVE AN ID CHIP IN THEM, RIGHT?
YEAH, SO?
DO YOU THINK MY TICKET IS, WELL... OKAY?
NOW THAT SHE MENTIONS IT, PROBABLY NOT!!
TAKAFUDO-SAN PROBABLY KNEW EXACTLY WHERE THE CHIP WAS WHEN SHE RIPPED IT.
NO...
WE CAN'T SAY THAT FOR SURE. SHE CAN BE CRUEL, BUT...
IT'S TOTALLY POSSIBLE SHE DIDN'T EVEN KNOW THERE WAS A CHIP IN THE FIRST PLACE.
!
!!

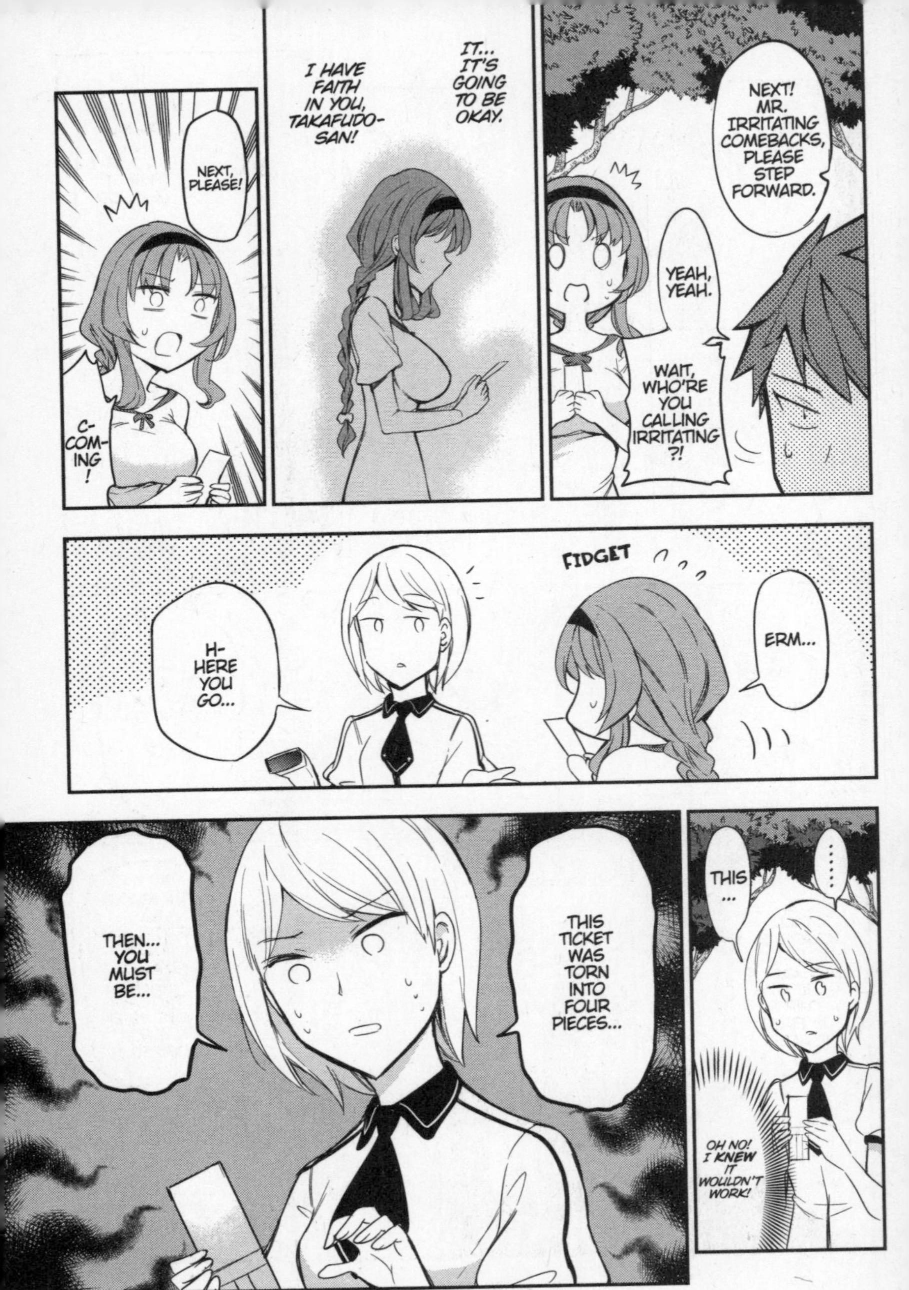
NEXT! MR. IRRITATING COMEBACKS, PLEASE STEP FORWARD.
YEAH, YEAH.
WAIT, WHO'RE YOU CALLING IRRITATING?!
IT... IT'S GOING TO BE OKAY.
I HAVE FAITH IN YOU, TAKAFUDO-SAN!
NEXT, PLEASE!
C-COMING!
FIDGET
ERM...
H-HERE YOU GO...
......
THIS...
OH NO! I KNEW IT WOULDN'T WORK!
THIS TICKET WAS TORN INTO FOUR PIECES...
THEN... YOU MUST BE...

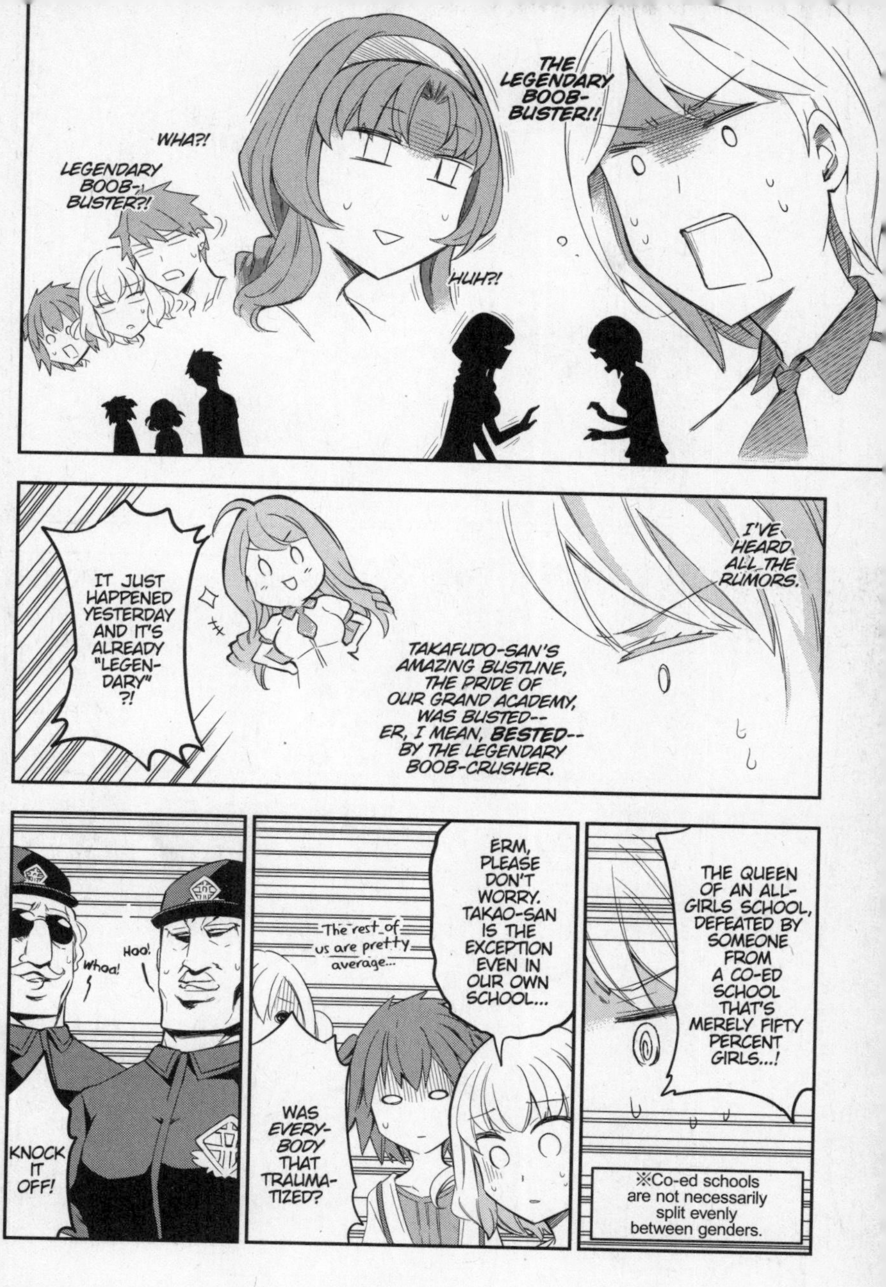
THE LEGENDARY BOOB-BUSTER!!
HUH?!
WHA?!
LEGENDARY BOOB-BUSTER?!
I'VE HEARD ALL THE RUMORS.
TAKAFUDO-SAN'S AMAZING BUSTLINE, THE PRIDE OF OUR GRAND ACADEMY, WAS BUSTED-- ER, I MEAN, BESTED-- BY THE LEGENDARY BOOB-CRUSHER.
IT JUST HAPPENED YESTERDAY AND IT'S ALREADY "LEGENDARY"?!
THE QUEEN OF AN ALL-GIRLS SCHOOL, DEFEATED BY SOMEONE FROM A CO-ED SCHOOL THAT'S MERELY FIFTY PERCENT GIRLS...!
※Co-ed schools are not necessarily split evenly between genders.
ERM, PLEASE DON'T WORRY. TAKAO-SAN IS THE EXCEPTION EVEN IN OUR OWN SCHOOL...
The rest of us are pretty average...
WAS EVERYBODY THAT TRAUMATIZED?
Hoo!
Whoa!
KNOCK IT OFF!

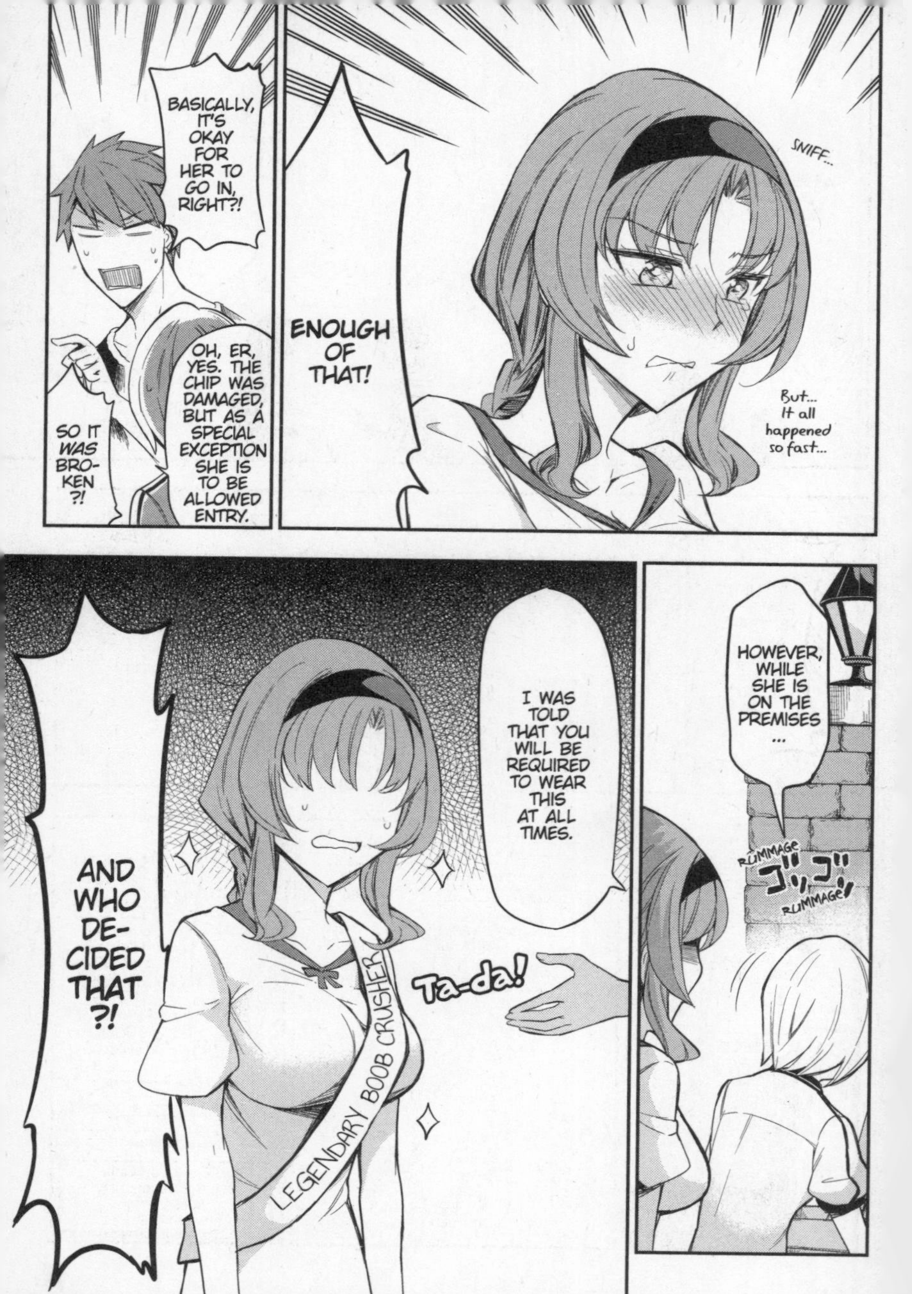
SNIFF...
But... It all happened so fast...
ENOUGH OF THAT!
BASICALLY, IT'S OKAY FOR HER TO GO IN, RIGHT?!
OH, ER, YES. THE CHIP WAS DAMAGED, BUT AS A SPECIAL EXCEPTION SHE IS TO BE ALLOWED ENTRY.
SO IT *WAS* BROKEN?!
HOWEVER, WHILE SHE IS ON THE PREMISES...
RUMMAGE
ゴソゴソ
RUMMAGE
I WAS TOLD THAT YOU WILL BE REQUIRED TO WEAR THIS AT ALL TIMES.
Ta-da!
LEGENDARY BOOB CRUSHER
AND WHO DECIDED THAT?!

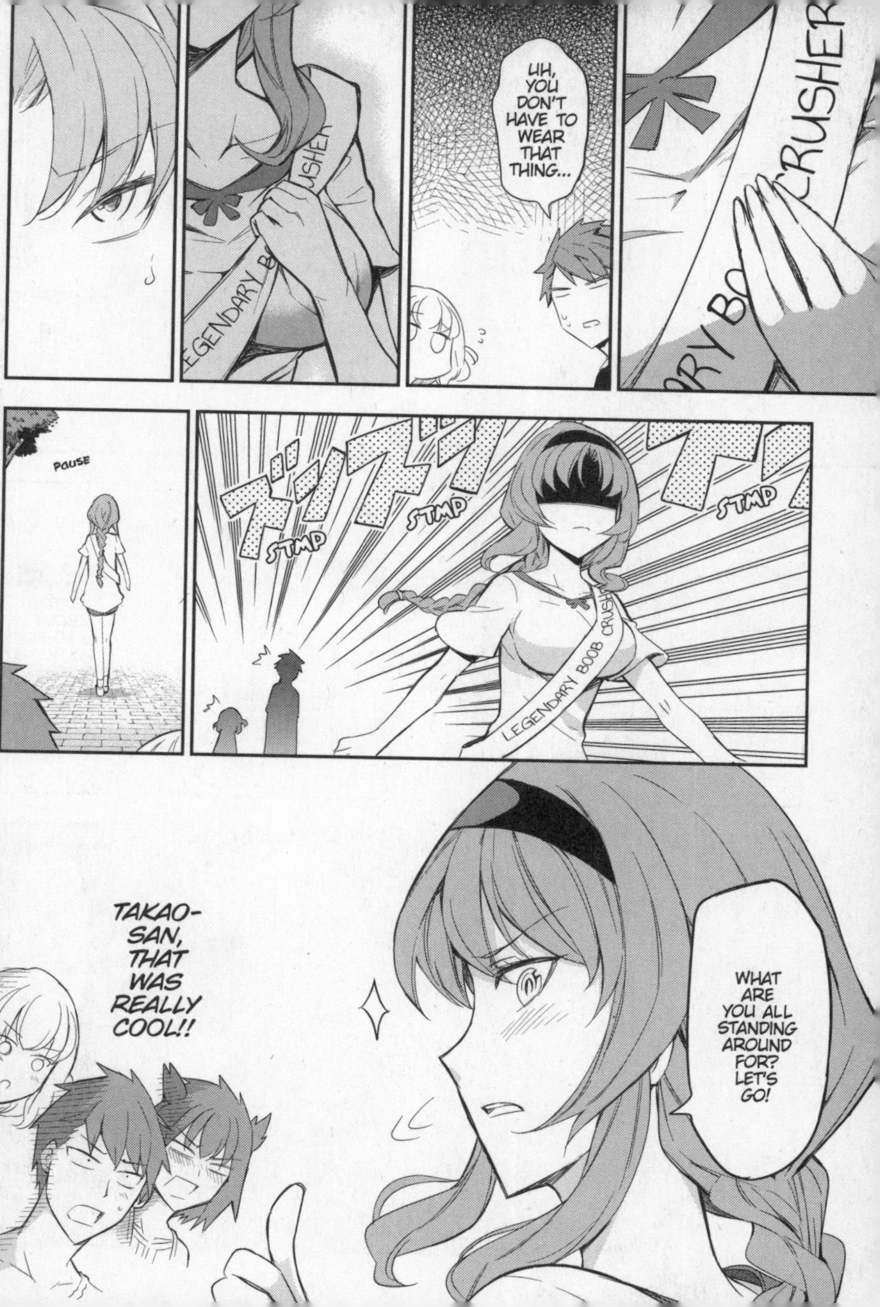
CRUSHER
UH, YOU DON'T HAVE TO WEAR THAT THING...
LEGENDARY
CRUSHER
STMP
STMP
STMP
LEGENDARY BOOB CRUSH
PAUSE
WHAT ARE YOU ALL STANDING AROUND FOR? LET'S GO!
TAKAO-SAN, THAT WAS REALLY COOL!!

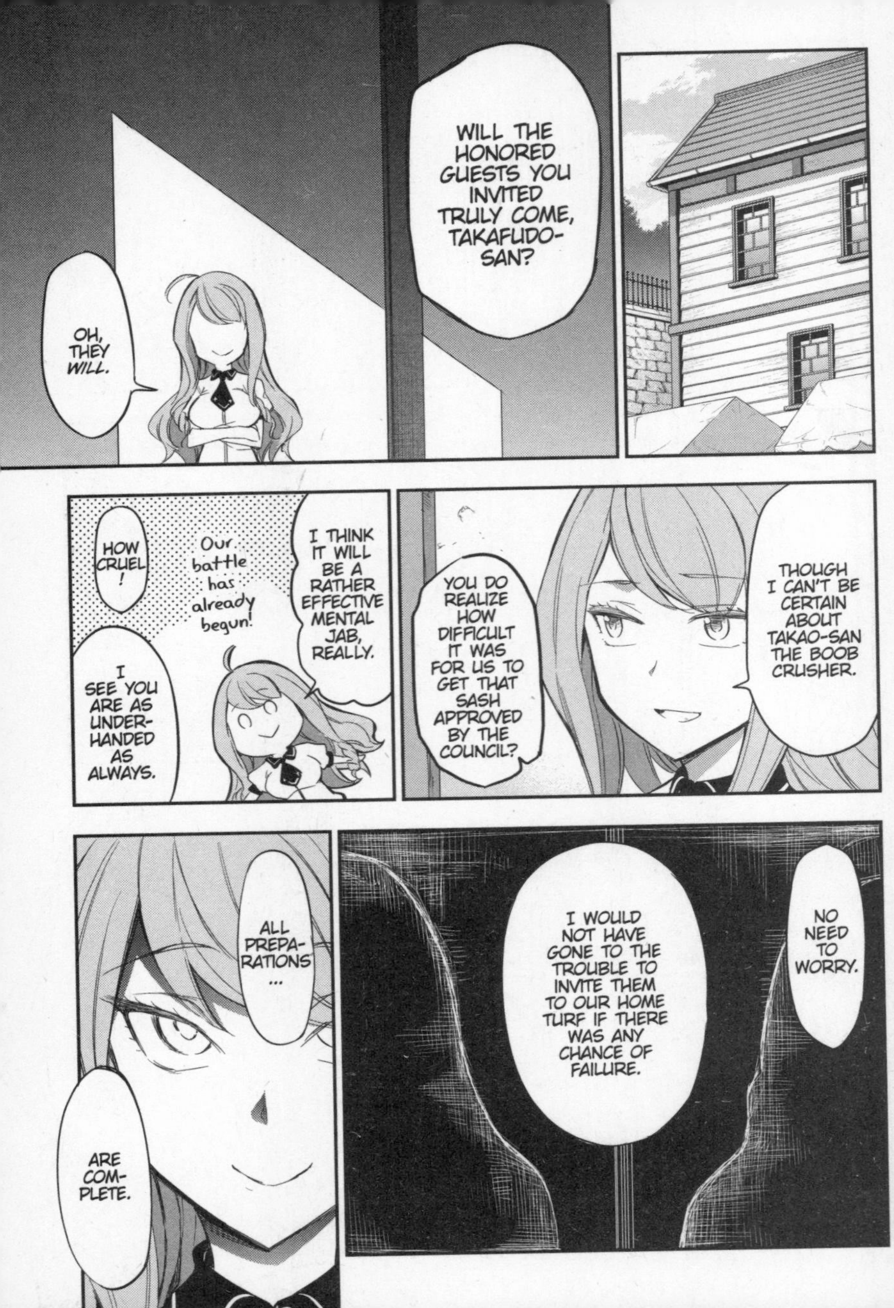
WILL THE HONORED GUESTS YOU INVITED TRULY COME, TAKAFUDO-SAN?
OH, THEY *WILL*.
THOUGH I CAN'T BE CERTAIN ABOUT TAKAO-SAN THE BOOB CRUSHER.
YOU DO REALIZE HOW DIFFICULT IT WAS FOR US TO GET THAT SASH APPROVED BY THE COUNCIL?
I THINK IT WILL BE A RATHER EFFECTIVE MENTAL JAB, REALLY.
Our battle has already begun!
HOW CRUEL!
I SEE YOU ARE AS UNDER-HANDED AS ALWAYS.
NO NEED TO WORRY.
I WOULD NOT HAVE GONE TO THE TROUBLE TO INVITE THEM TO OUR HOME TURF IF THERE WAS ANY CHANCE OF FAILURE.
ALL PREPA-RATIONS...
ARE COM-PLETE.

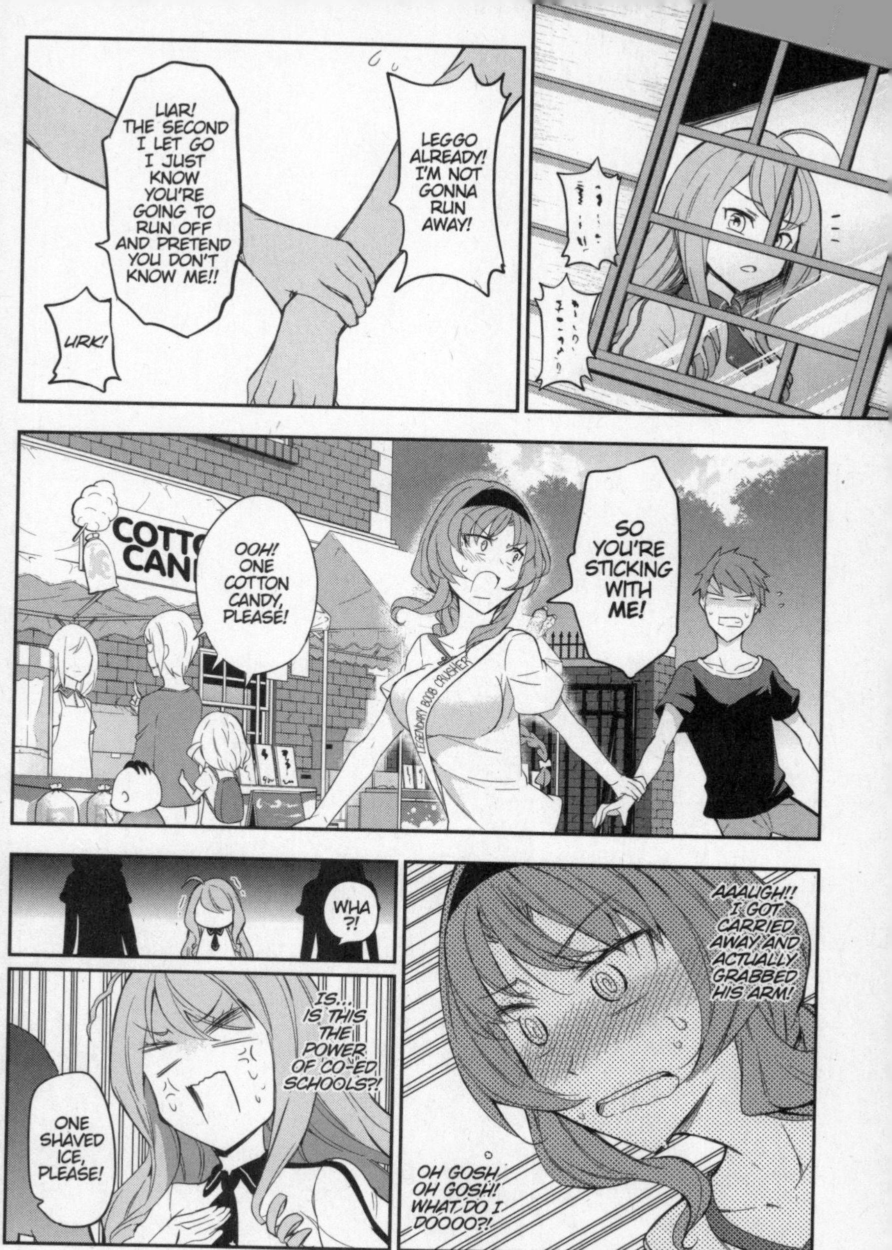

LEGGO ALREADY! I'M NOT GONNA RUN AWAY!
LIAR! THE SECOND I LET GO I JUST KNOW YOU'RE GOING TO RUN OFF AND PRETEND YOU DON'T KNOW ME!!
URK!
SO YOU'RE STICKING WITH ME!
LEGENDARY BOOB CRUSHER
OOH! ONE COTTON CANDY, PLEASE!
AAAUGH!! I GOT CARRIED AWAY AND ACTUALLY GRABBED HIS ARM!
OH GOSH OH GOSH! WHAT DO I DOOOO?!
WHA?!
IS... IS THIS THE POWER OF CO-ED SCHOOLS?!
ONE SHAVED ICE, PLEASE!

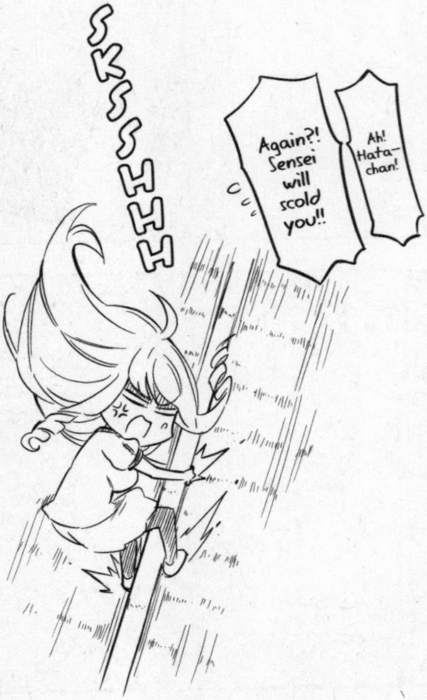
Ah! Hata-chan!
Again?! Sensei will scold you!!
SKSSHHH

D-FRAGMENTS
ディーふらぐめんつ!

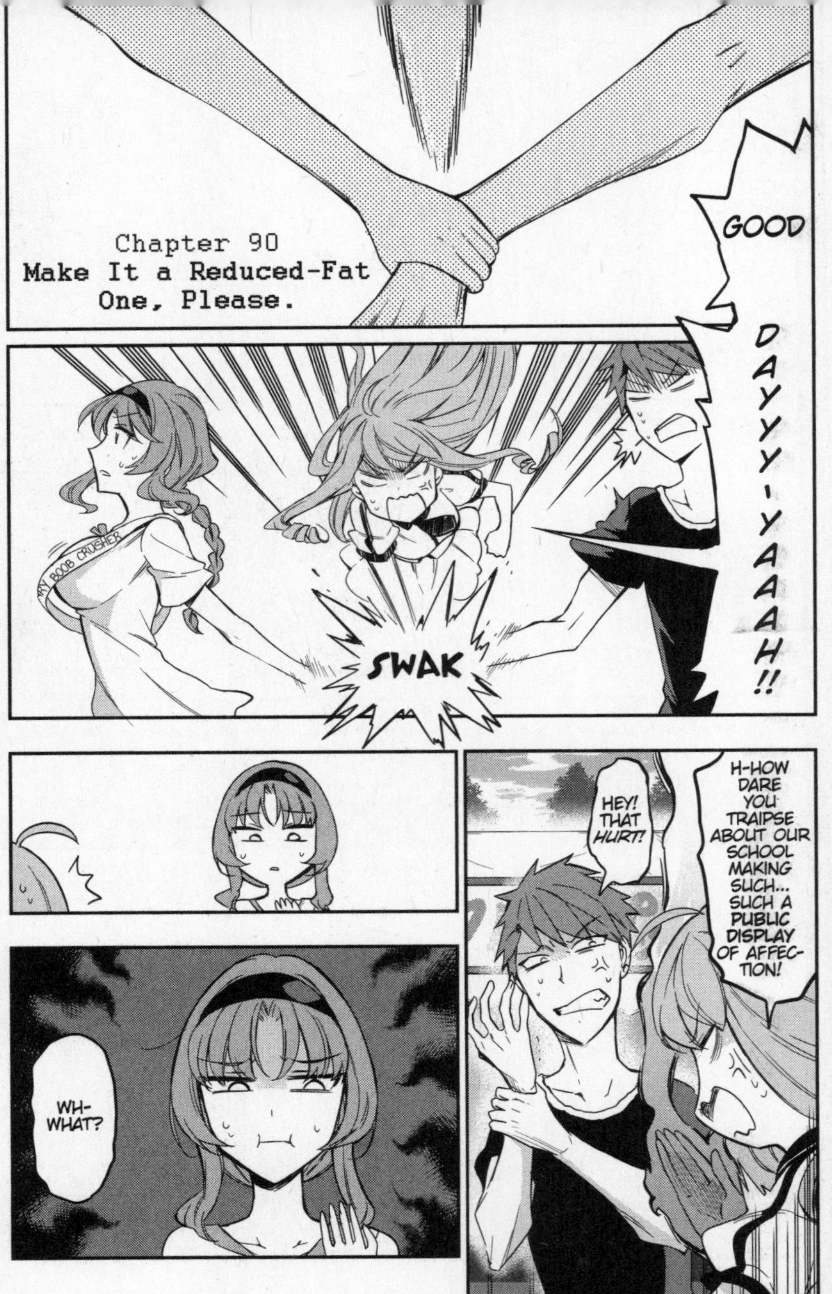
Chapter 90
Make It a Reduced-Fat One, Please.
GOOD
DAYYY-YAAAAH!!
BOOB CRUSHER
SWAK
H-HOW DARE YOU TRAIPSE ABOUT OUR SCHOOL MAKING SUCH... SUCH A PUBLIC DISPLAY OF AFFECTION!
HEY! THAT HURT!
WH-WHAT?

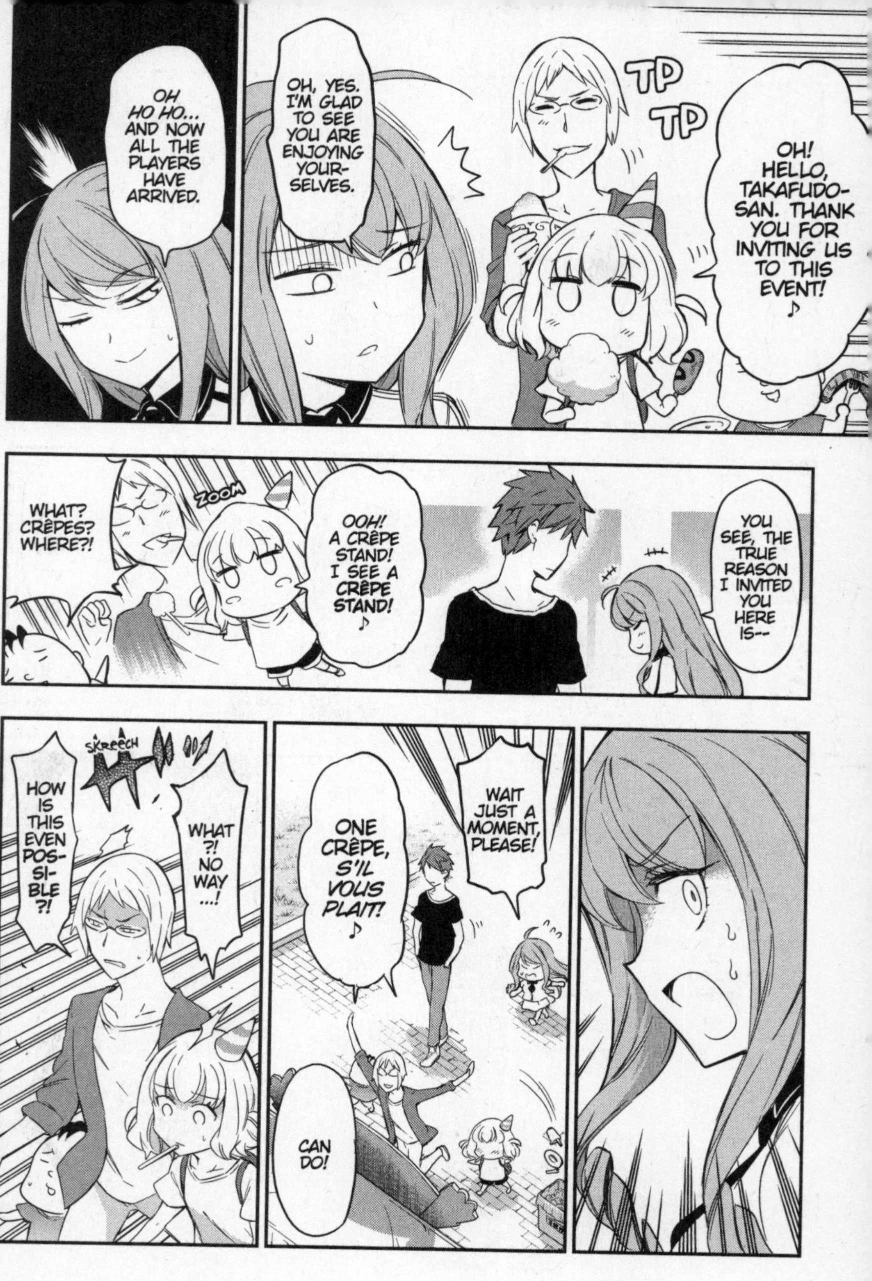
TP
TP
OH! HELLO, TAKAFUDO-SAN. THANK YOU FOR INVITING US TO THIS EVENT! ♪
OH, YES. I'M GLAD TO SEE YOU ARE ENJOYING YOUR-SELVES.
OH HO HO... AND NOW ALL THE PLAYERS HAVE ARRIVED.
YOU SEE, THE TRUE REASON I INVITED YOU HERE IS--
OOH! A CRÊPE STAND! I SEE A CRÊPE STAND! ♪
ZOOM
WHAT? CRÊPES? WHERE?!
WAIT JUST A MOMENT, PLEASE!
ONE CRÊPE, S'IL VOUS PLAIT! ♪
CAN DO!
SKREECH
WHAT?! NO WAY...!
HOW IS THIS EVEN POS-SI-BLE?!

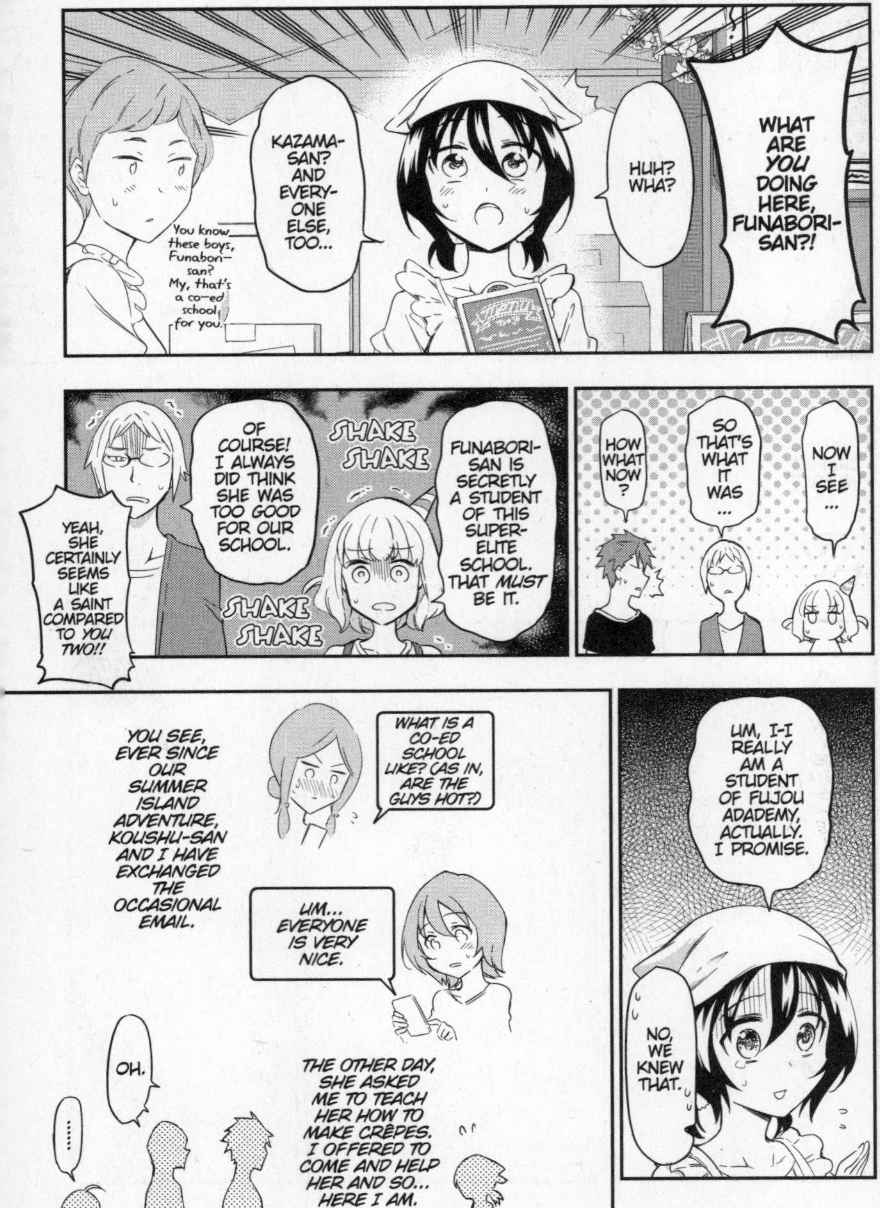
WHAT ARE YOU DOING HERE, FUNABORI-SAN?!
HUH? WHA?
KAZAMA-SAN? AND EVERYONE ELSE, TOO...
You know these boys, Funabori-san? My, that's a co-ed school for you.
NOW I SEE...
SO THAT'S WHAT IT WAS...
HOW WHAT NOW?
FUNABORI-SAN IS SECRETLY A STUDENT OF THIS SUPER-ELITE SCHOOL. THAT MUST BE IT.
SHAKE SHAKE
OF COURSE! I ALWAYS DID THINK SHE WAS TOO GOOD FOR OUR SCHOOL.
SHAKE SHAKE
YEAH, SHE CERTAINLY SEEMS LIKE A SAINT COMPARED TO YOU TWO!!
UM, I-I REALLY AM A STUDENT OF FUJOU ADADEMY, ACTUALLY. I PROMISE.
NO, WE KNEW THAT.
YOU SEE, EVER SINCE OUR SUMMER ISLAND ADVENTURE, KOUSHU-SAN AND I HAVE EXCHANGED THE OCCASIONAL EMAIL.
WHAT IS A CO-ED SCHOOL LIKE? (AS IN, ARE THE GUYS HOT?)
UM... EVERYONE IS VERY NICE.
THE OTHER DAY, SHE ASKED ME TO TEACH HER HOW TO MAKE CRÊPES. I OFFERED TO COME AND HELP HER AND SO... HERE I AM.
OH.
......

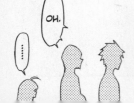

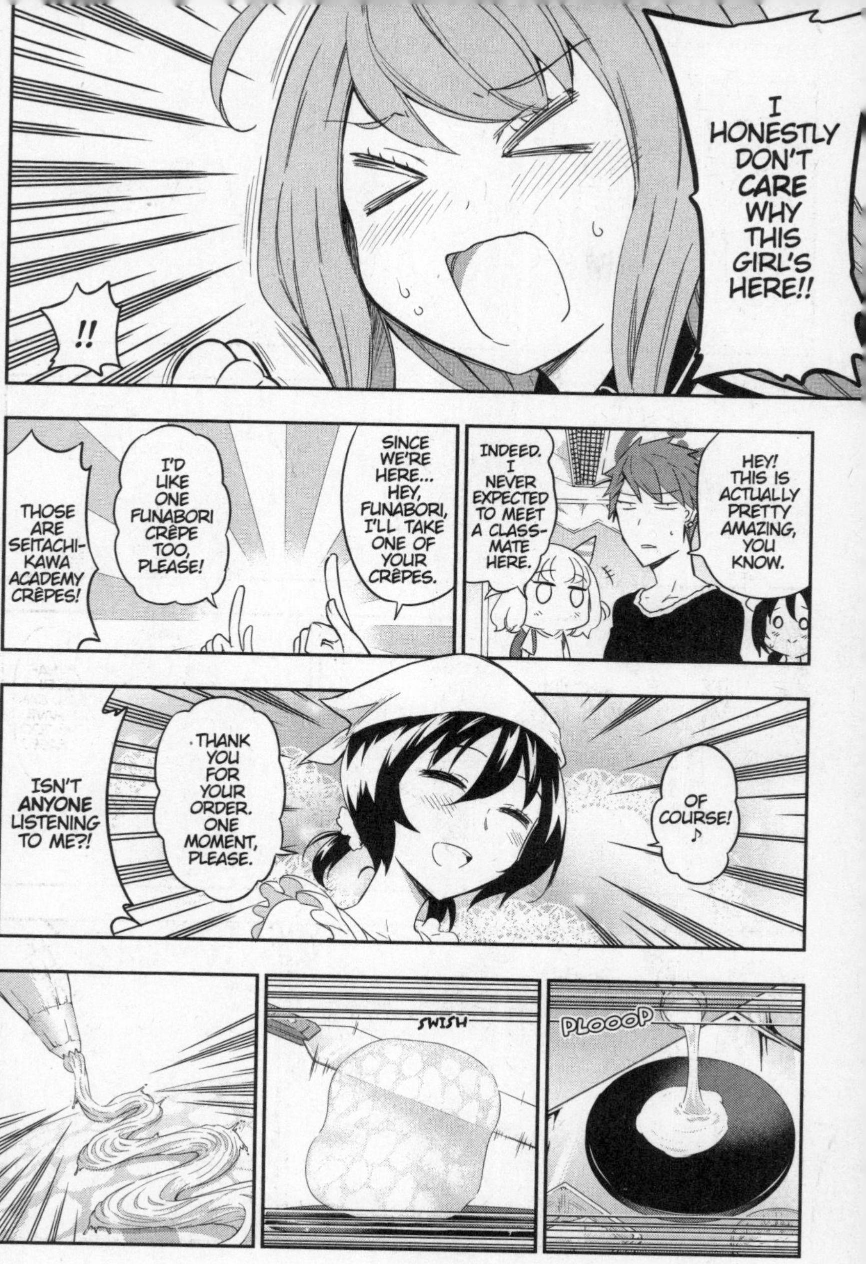
I HONESTLY DON'T CARE WHY THIS GIRL'S HERE!!
!!
HEY! THIS IS ACTUALLY PRETTY AMAZING, YOU KNOW.
INDEED. I NEVER EXPECTED TO MEET A CLASSMATE HERE.
SINCE WE'RE HERE... HEY, FUNABORI, I'LL TAKE ONE OF YOUR CRÊPES.
I'D LIKE ONE FUNABORI CRÊPE TOO, PLEASE!
THOSE ARE SEITACHIKAWA ACADEMY CRÊPES!
OF COURSE! ♪
THANK YOU FOR YOUR ORDER. ONE MOMENT, PLEASE.
ISN'T ANYONE LISTENING TO ME?!
PLOOOP
SWISH

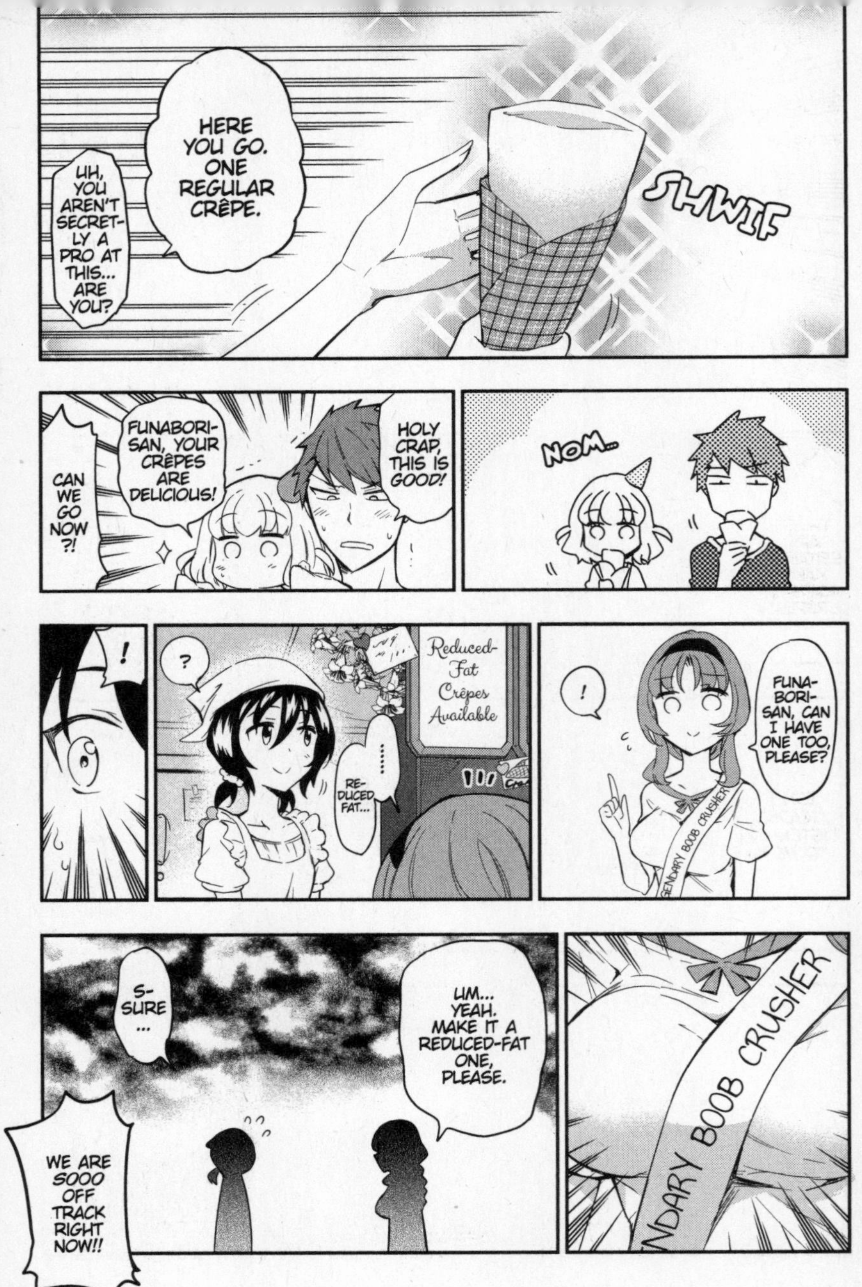
SHWIF
HERE YOU GO. ONE REGULAR CRÊPE.
UH, YOU AREN'T SECRET-LY A PRO AT THIS... ARE YOU?
NOM...
HOLY CRAP, THIS IS GOOD!
FUNABORI-SAN, YOUR CRÊPES ARE DELICIOUS!
CAN WE GO NOW?!
FUNA-BORI-SAN, CAN I HAVE ONE TOO, PLEASE?
!
GENDARY BOOB CRUSHER
Reduced-Fat Crêpes Available
......
RE-DUCED FAT...
?
!
NDARY BOOB CRUSHER
UM... YEAH. MAKE IT A REDUCED-FAT ONE, PLEASE.
S-SURE...
WE ARE SOOO OFF TRACK RIGHT NOW!!

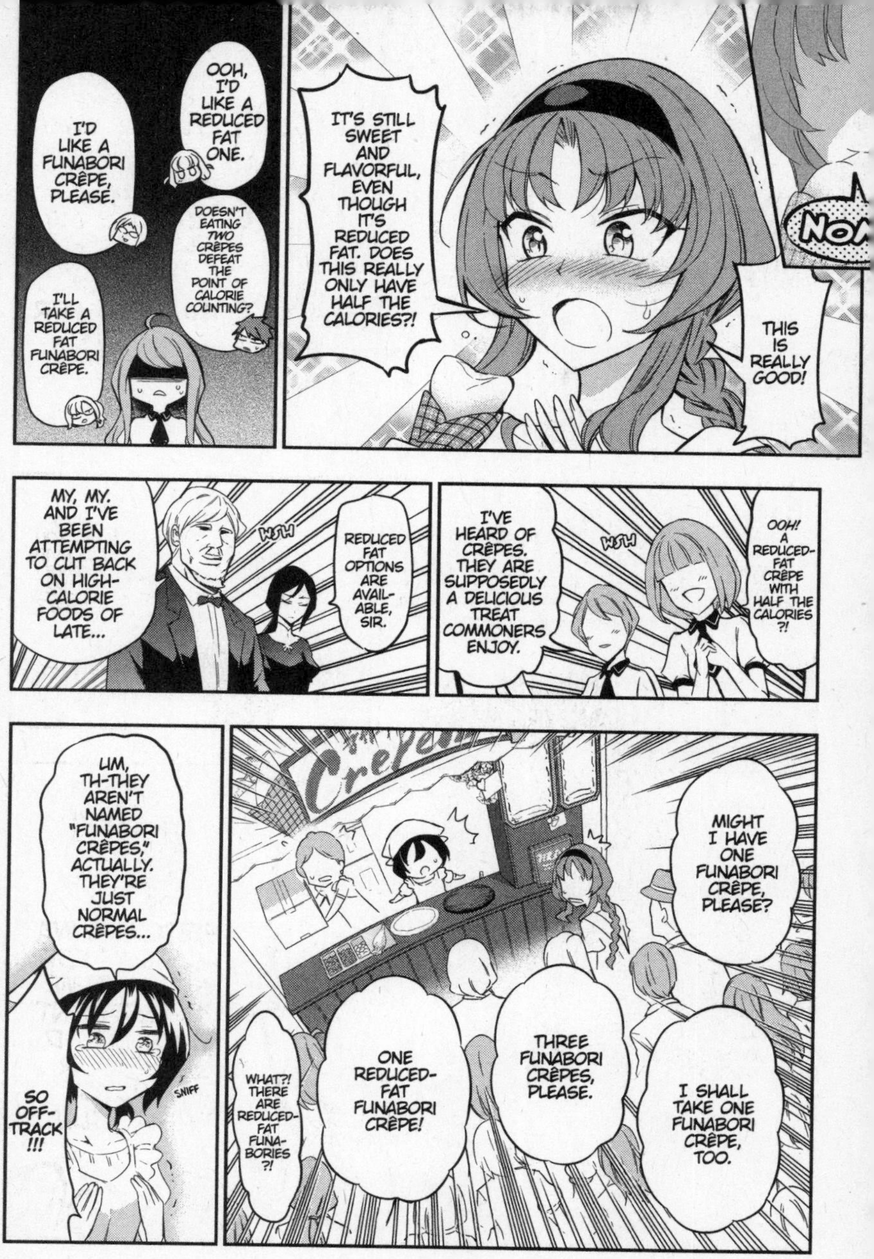
NOM
IT'S STILL SWEET AND FLAVORFUL, EVEN THOUGH IT'S REDUCED FAT. DOES THIS REALLY ONLY HAVE HALF THE CALORIES?!
THIS IS REALLY GOOD!
OOH, I'D LIKE A REDUCED FAT ONE.
I'D LIKE A FUNABORI CRÊPE, PLEASE.
DOESN'T EATING *TWO* CRÊPES DEFEAT THE POINT OF CALORIE COUNTING?
I'LL TAKE A REDUCED FAT FUNABORI CRÊPE.
OOH! A REDUCED-FAT CRÊPE WITH HALF THE CALORIES?!
I'VE HEARD OF CRÊPES. THEY ARE SUPPOSEDLY A DELICIOUS TREAT COMMONERS ENJOY.
WSH
REDUCED FAT OPTIONS ARE AVAIL-ABLE, SIR.
WSH
MY, MY. AND I'VE BEEN ATTEMPTING TO CUT BACK ON HIGH-CALORIE FOODS OF LATE...
Crepe
MIGHT I HAVE ONE FUNABORI CRÊPE, PLEASE?
I SHALL TAKE ONE FUNABORI CRÊPE, TOO.
THREE FUNABORI CRÊPES, PLEASE.
ONE REDUCED-FAT FUNABORI CRÊPE!
WHAT?! THERE ARE REDUCED-FAT FUNA-BORIES ?!
UM, TH-THEY AREN'T NAMED "FUNABORI CRÊPES," ACTUALLY. THEY'RE JUST NORMAL CRÊPES...
SNIFF
SO OFF-TRACK !!!

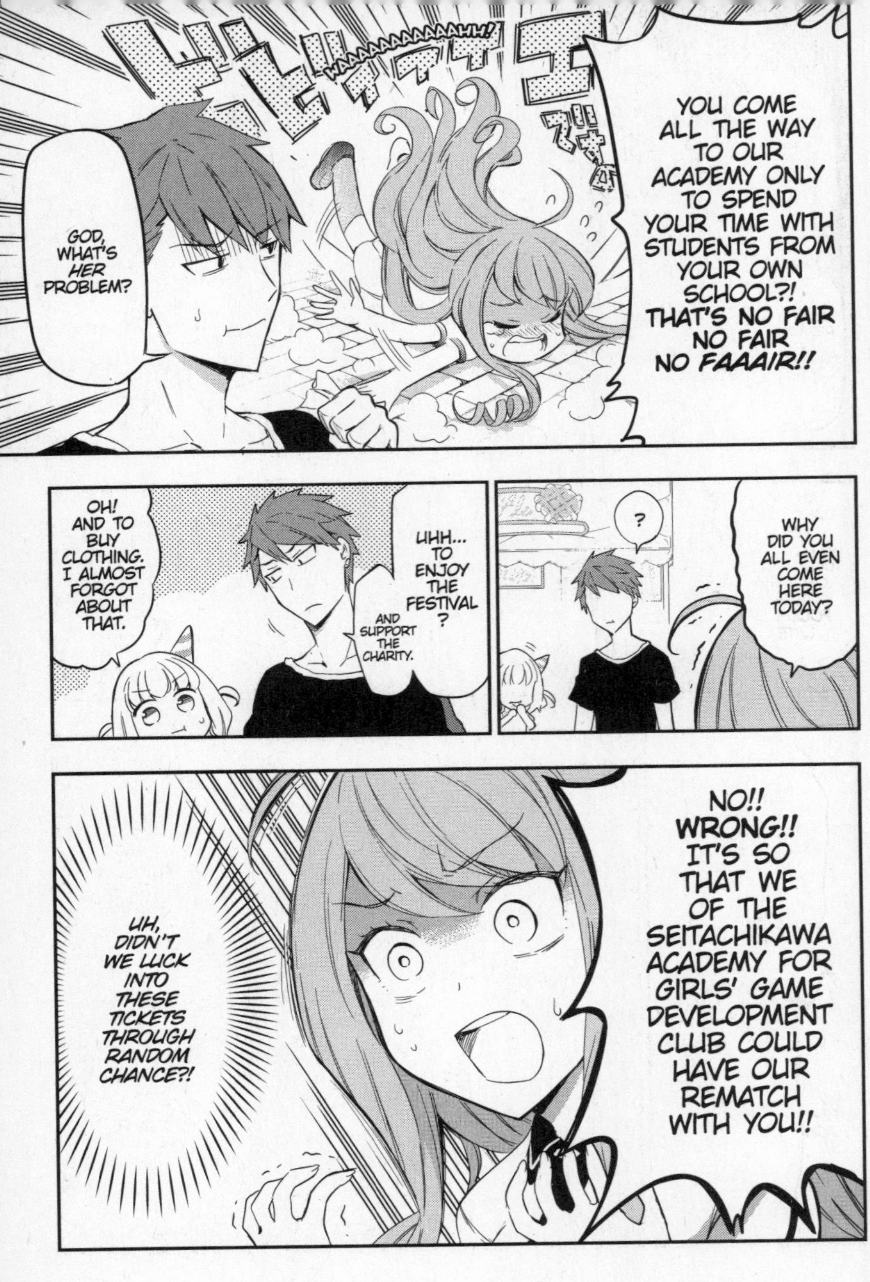
YOU COME ALL THE WAY TO OUR ACADEMY ONLY TO SPEND YOUR TIME WITH STUDENTS FROM YOUR OWN SCHOOL?! THAT'S NO FAIR NO FAIR NO *FAAAIR!!*
WAAAAAAAAAAAHH!
GOD, WHAT'S *HER* PROBLEM?
WHY DID YOU ALL EVEN COME HERE TODAY?
?
UHH... TO ENJOY THE FESTIVAL?
AND SUPPORT THE CHARITY.
OH! AND TO BUY CLOTHING. I ALMOST FORGOT ABOUT THAT.
NO!! WRONG!! IT'S SO THAT WE OF THE SEITACHIKAWA ACADEMY FOR GIRLS' GAME DEVELOPMENT CLUB COULD HAVE OUR REMATCH WITH YOU!!
UH, DIDN'T WE LUCK INTO THESE TICKETS THROUGH RANDOM CHANCE?!

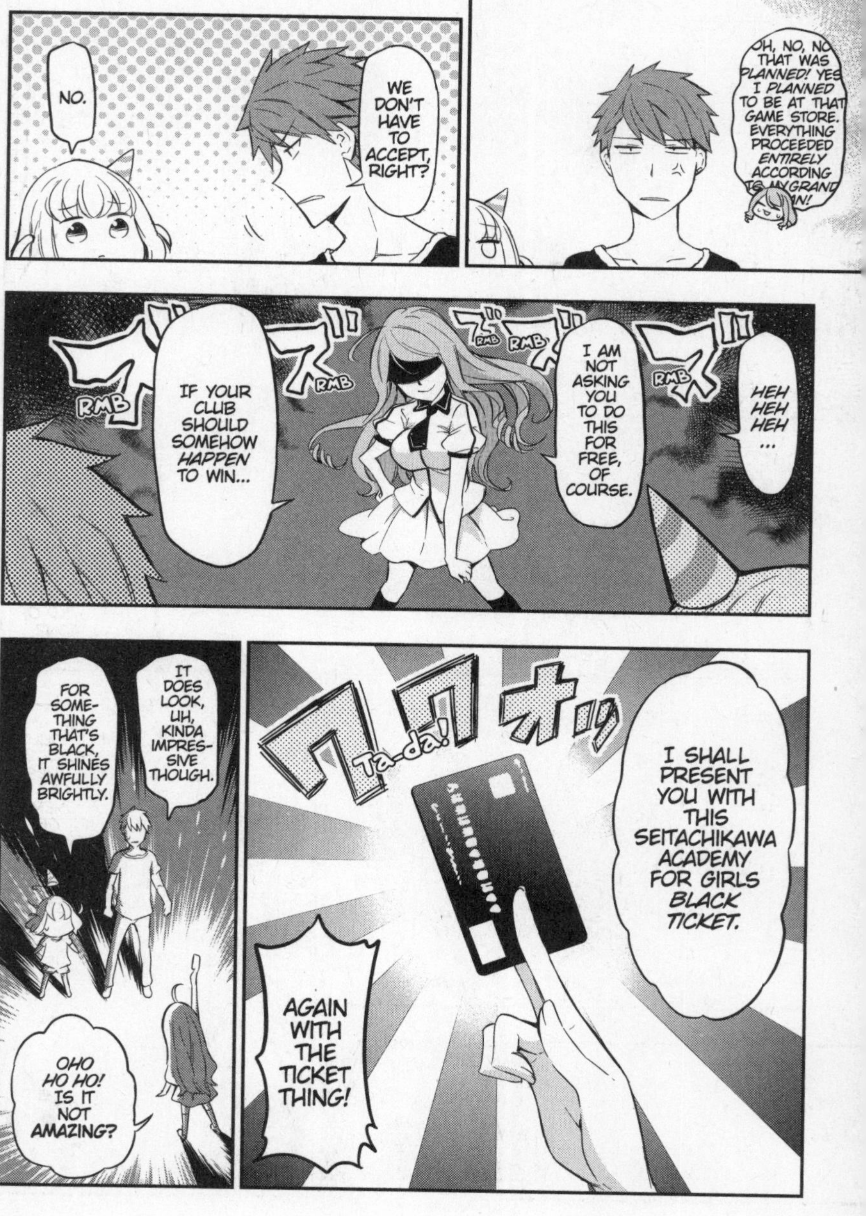
OH, NO, NO THAT WAS PLANNED! YES I PLANNED TO BE AT THAT GAME STORE. EVERYTHING PROCEEDED ENTIRELY ACCORDING TO MY GRAND PLAN!
WE DON'T HAVE TO ACCEPT, RIGHT?
NO.
RMB
HEH HEH HEH ...
RMB
I AM NOT ASKING YOU TO DO THIS FOR FREE, OF COURSE.
RMB
RMB
IF YOUR CLUB SHOULD SOMEHOW HAPPEN TO WIN...
RMB
Ta-da!
I SHALL PRESENT YOU WITH THIS SEITACHIKAWA ACADEMY FOR GIRLS BLACK TICKET.
AGAIN WITH THE TICKET THING!
IT DOES LOOK, UH, KINDA IMPRESSIVE THOUGH.
FOR SOMETHING THAT'S BLACK, IT SHINES AWFULLY BRIGHTLY.
OHO HO HO! IS IT NOT AMAZING?

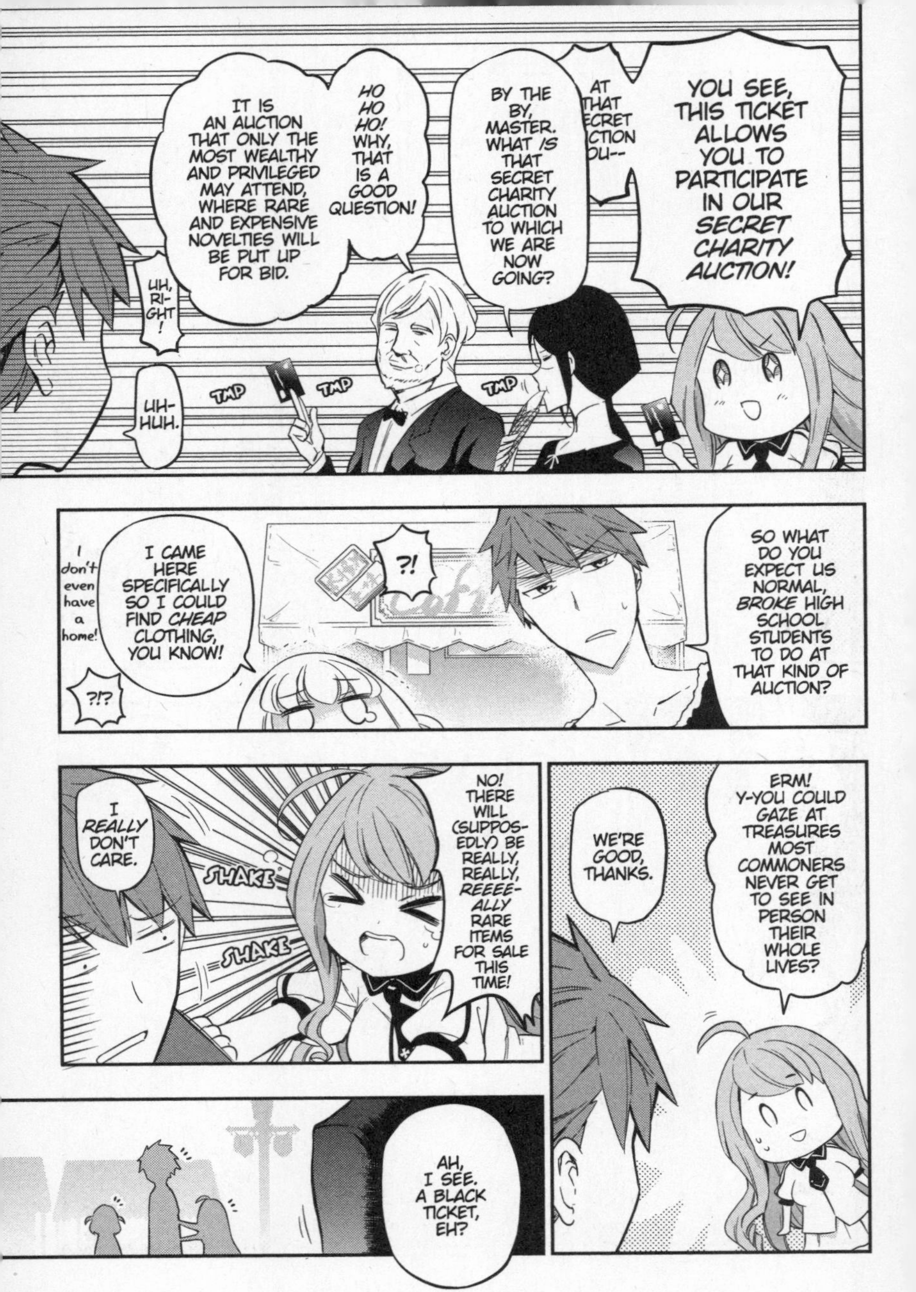

YOU SEE, THIS TICKET ALLOWS YOU TO PARTICIPATE IN OUR SECRET CHARITY AUCTION!
AT THAT SECRET AUCTION YOU--
BY THE BY, MASTER. WHAT IS THAT SECRET CHARITY AUCTION TO WHICH WE ARE NOW GOING?
HO HO HO! WHY, THAT IS A GOOD QUESTION!
IT IS AN AUCTION THAT ONLY THE MOST WEALTHY AND PRIVILEGED MAY ATTEND, WHERE RARE AND EXPENSIVE NOVELTIES WILL BE PUT UP FOR BID.
TMP
TMP
TMP
UH, RIGHT!
UH-HUH.
SO WHAT DO YOU EXPECT US NORMAL, BROKE HIGH SCHOOL STUDENTS TO DO AT THAT KIND OF AUCTION?
?!
I CAME HERE SPECIFICALLY SO I COULD FIND CHEAP CLOTHING, YOU KNOW!
I don't even have a home!
?!?
ERM! Y-YOU COULD GAZE AT TREASURES MOST COMMONERS NEVER GET TO SEE IN PERSON THEIR WHOLE LIVES?
WE'RE GOOD, THANKS.
NO! THERE WILL (SUPPOSEDLY) BE REALLY, REALLY, REEEE-ALLY RARE ITEMS FOR SALE THIS TIME!
SHAKE
SHAKE
I REALLY DON'T CARE.
AH, I SEE. A BLACK TICKET, EH?

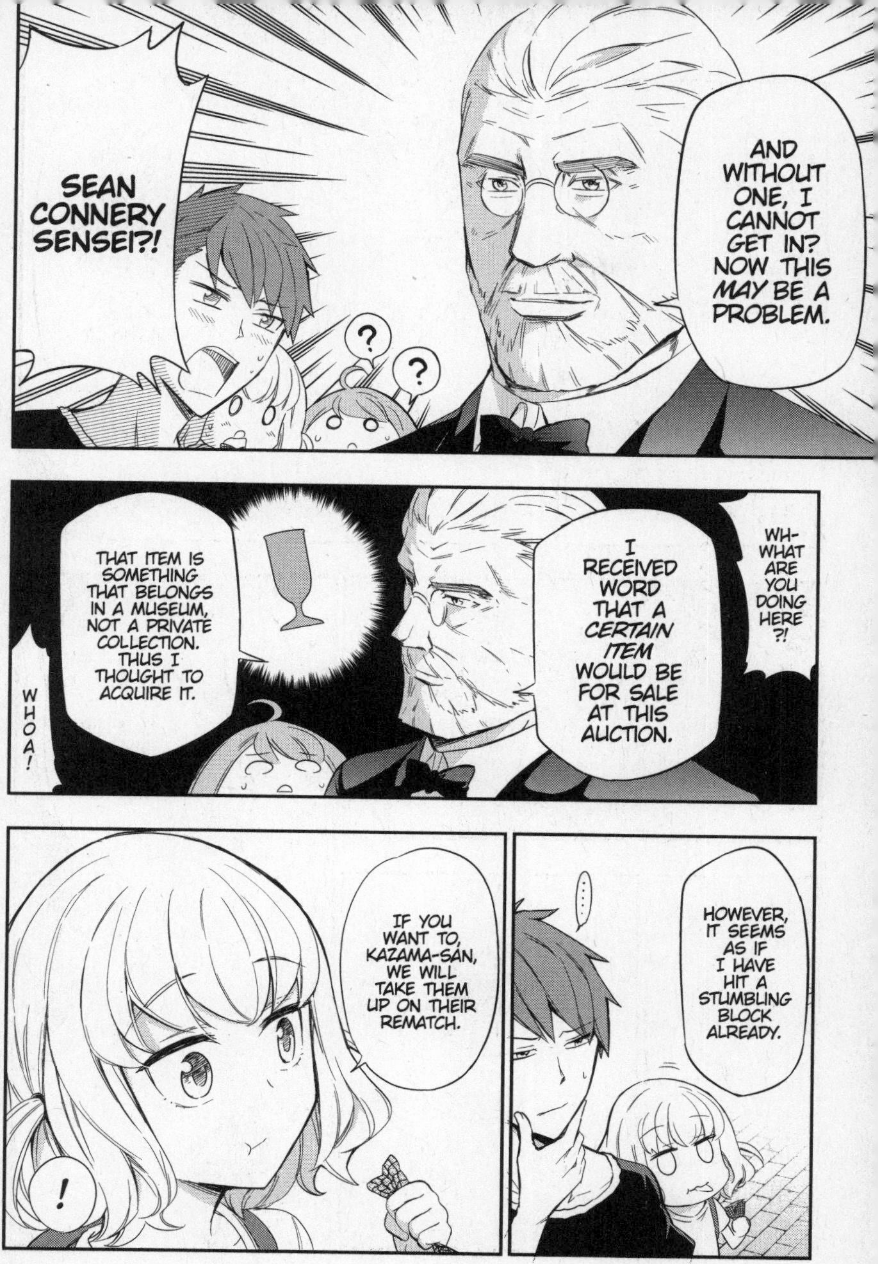
AND WITHOUT ONE, I CANNOT GET IN? NOW THIS *MAY* BE A PROBLEM.
?
?
SEAN CONNERY SENSEI?!
WH-WHAT ARE YOU DOING HERE?!
I RECEIVED WORD THAT A *CERTAIN ITEM* WOULD BE FOR SALE AT THIS AUCTION.
THAT ITEM IS SOMETHING THAT BELONGS IN A MUSEUM, NOT A PRIVATE COLLECTION. THUS I THOUGHT TO ACQUIRE IT.
WHOA!
HOWEVER, IT SEEMS AS IF I HAVE HIT A STUMBLING BLOCK ALREADY.
...
IF YOU WANT TO, KAZAMA-SAN, WE WILL TAKE THEM UP ON THEIR REMATCH.
!

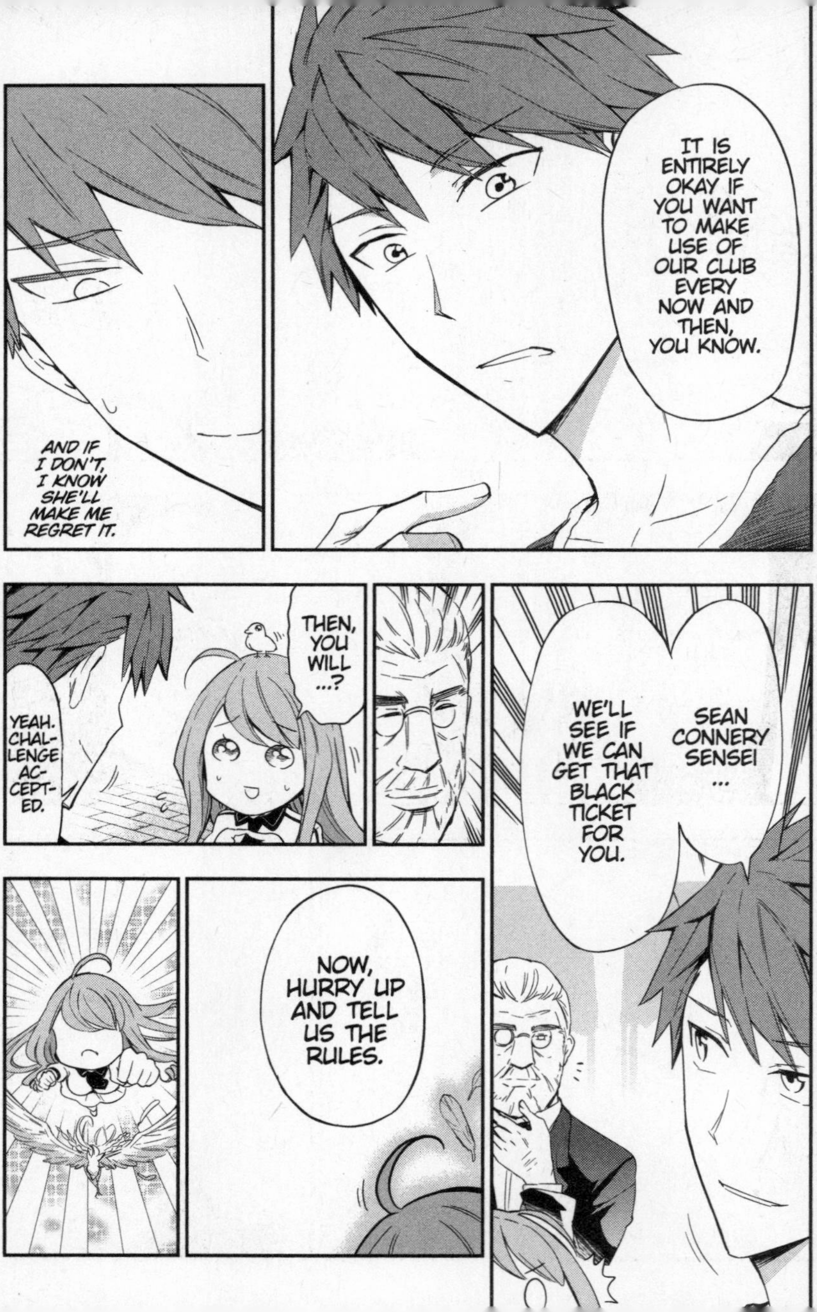
IT IS ENTIRELY OKAY IF YOU WANT TO MAKE USE OF OUR CLUB EVERY NOW AND THEN, YOU KNOW.
AND IF I DON'T, I KNOW SHE'LL MAKE ME REGRET IT.
SEAN CONNERY SENSEI ...
WE'LL SEE IF WE CAN GET THAT BLACK TICKET FOR YOU.
THEN, YOU WILL ...?
YEAH. CHALLENGE ACCEPTED.
NOW, HURRY UP AND TELL US THE RULES.

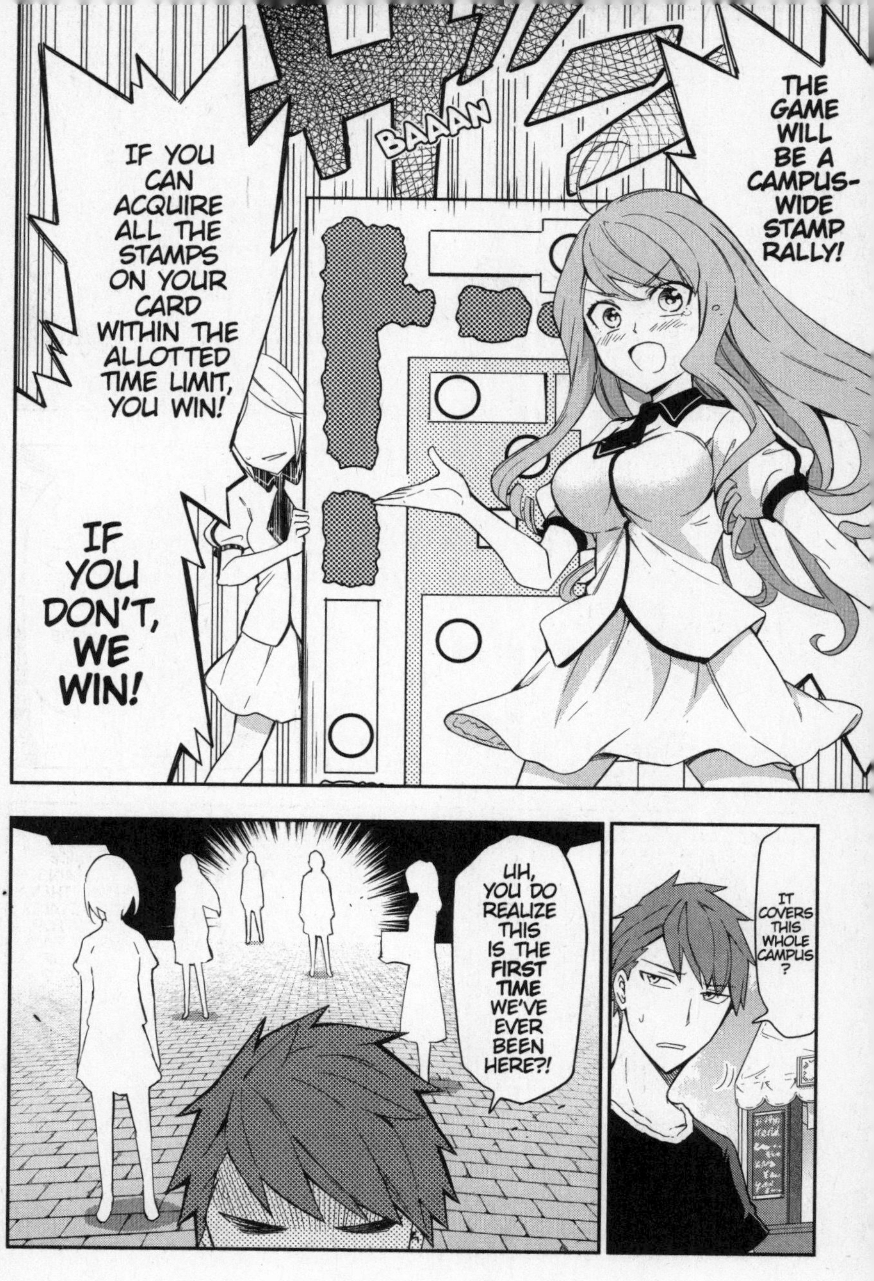
THE GAME WILL BE A CAMPUS-WIDE STAMP RALLY!
BAAAN
IF YOU CAN ACQUIRE ALL THE STAMPS ON YOUR CARD WITHIN THE ALLOTTED TIME LIMIT, YOU WIN!
IF YOU DON'T, WE WIN!
IT COVERS THIS WHOLE CAMPUS?
UH, YOU DO REALIZE THIS IS THE FIRST TIME WE'VE EVER BEEN HERE?!

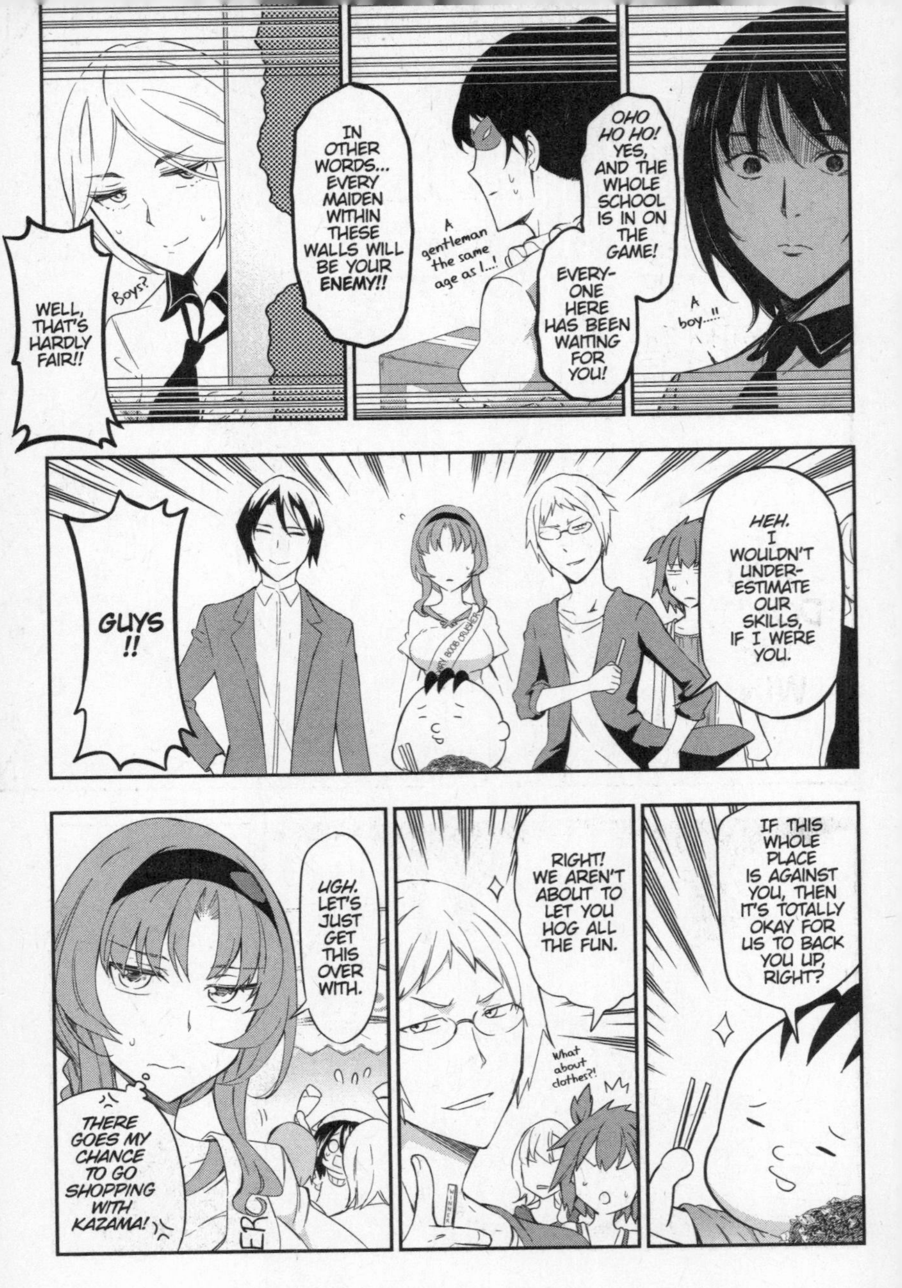
A boy...!!
OHO HO HO! YES, AND THE WHOLE SCHOOL IS IN ON THE GAME!
EVERY-ONE HERE HAS BEEN WAITING FOR YOU!
A gentleman the same age as I...!
IN OTHER WORDS... EVERY MAIDEN WITHIN THESE WALLS WILL BE YOUR ENEMY!!
Boys?
WELL, THAT'S HARDLY FAIR!!
HEH. I WOULDN'T UNDER-ESTIMATE OUR SKILLS, IF I WERE YOU.
GUYS!!
IF THIS WHOLE PLACE IS AGAINST YOU, THEN IT'S TOTALLY OKAY FOR US TO BACK YOU UP, RIGHT?
RIGHT! WE AREN'T ABOUT TO LET YOU HOG ALL THE FUN.
What about clothes?!
UGH. LET'S JUST GET THIS OVER WITH.
THERE GOES MY CHANCE TO GO SHOPPING WITH KAZAMA!

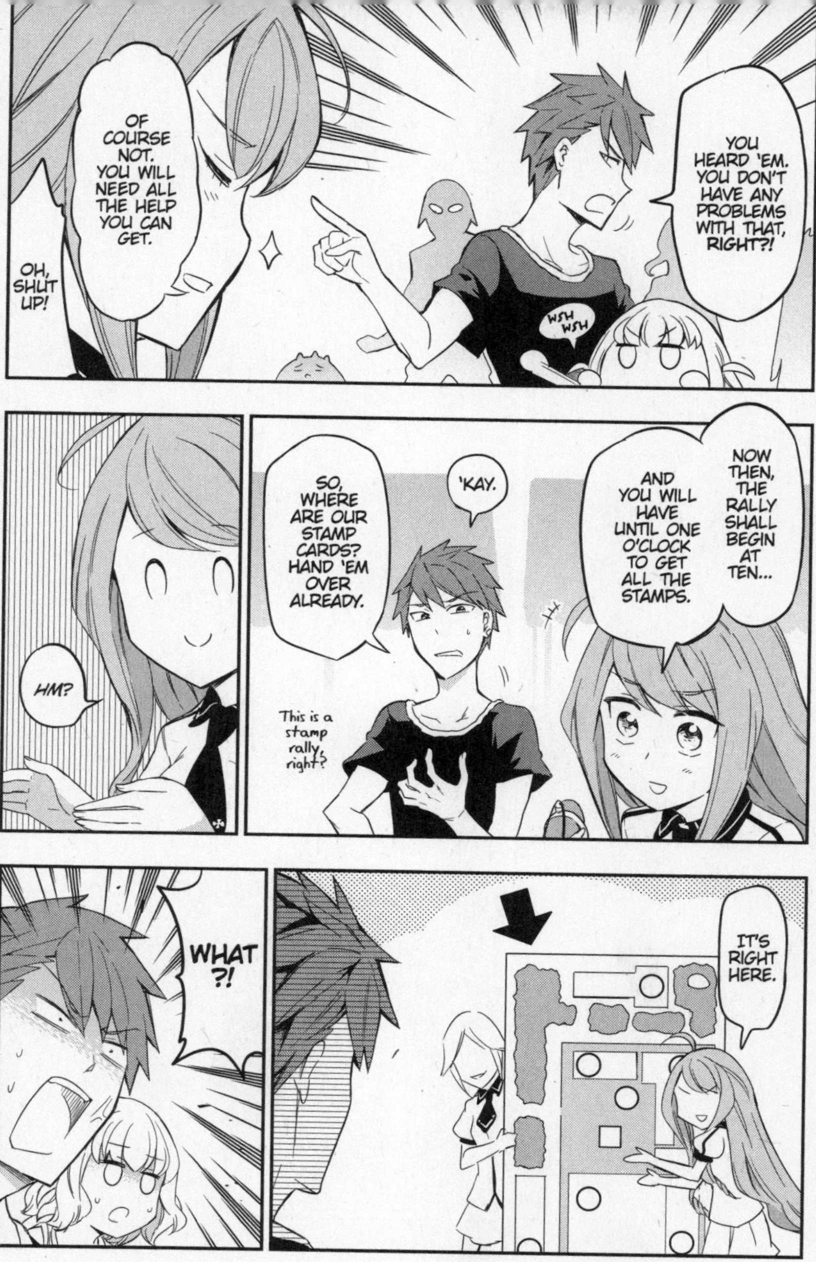
YOU HEARD 'EM. YOU DON'T HAVE ANY PROBLEMS WITH THAT, RIGHT?!
WSH WSH
OF COURSE NOT. YOU WILL NEED ALL THE HELP YOU CAN GET.
OH, SHUT UP!
NOW THEN, THE RALLY SHALL BEGIN AT TEN...
AND YOU WILL HAVE UNTIL ONE O'CLOCK TO GET ALL THE STAMPS.
'KAY.
SO, WHERE ARE OUR STAMP CARDS? HAND 'EM OVER ALREADY.
This is a stamp rally, right?
HM?
IT'S RIGHT HERE.
WHAT?!

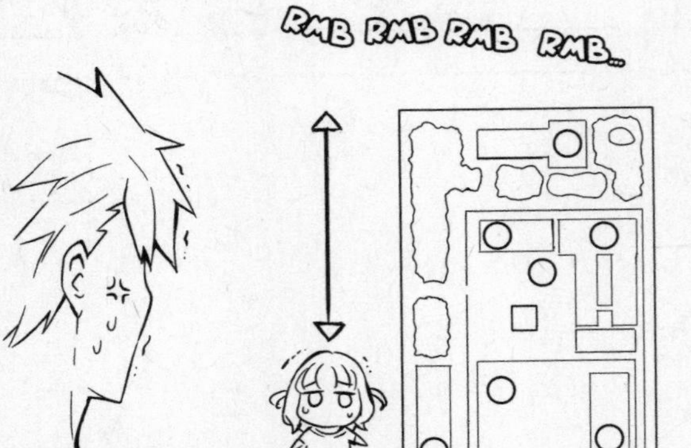
RMB RMB RMB RMB...

D-FRAGMENTS ディーふらぐ！

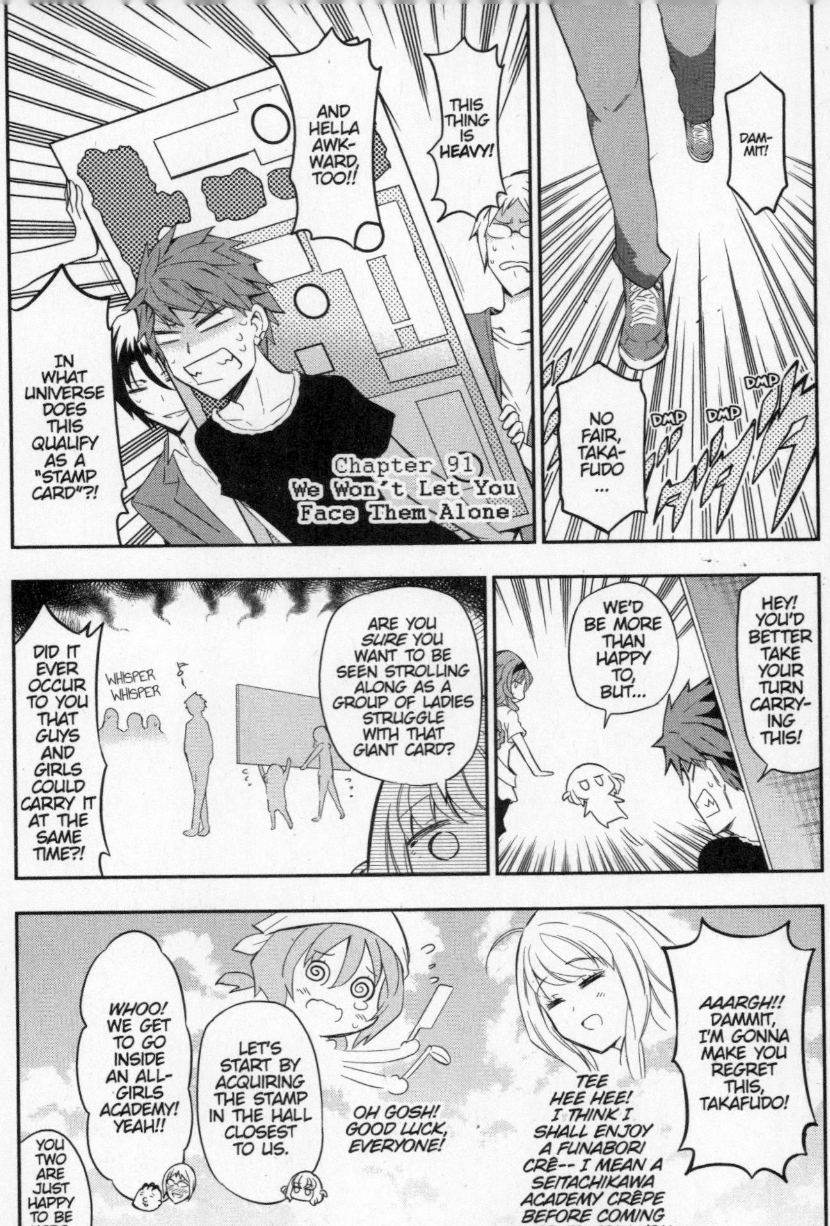
DAM-MIT!
NO FAIR, TAKA-FUDO ...
DMP DMP DMP
THIS THING IS HEAVY!
AND HELLA AWK-WARD, TOO!!
IN WHAT UNIVERSE DOES THIS QUALIFY AS A "STAMP CARD"?!
Chapter 91
We Won't Let You Face Them Alone
HEY! YOU'D BETTER TAKE YOUR TURN CARRY-ING THIS!
WE'D BE MORE THAN HAPPY TO, BUT...
ARE YOU SURE YOU WANT TO BE SEEN STROLLING ALONG AS A GROUP OF LADIES STRUGGLE WITH THAT GIANT CARD?
WHISPER WHISPER
DID IT EVER OCCUR TO YOU THAT GUYS AND GIRLS COULD CARRY IT AT THE SAME TIME?!
AAARGH!! DAMMIT, I'M GONNA MAKE YOU REGRET THIS, TAKAFUDO!
TEE HEE HEE! I THINK I SHALL ENJOY A FUNABORI CRÊ-- I MEAN A SEITACHIKAWA ACADEMY CRÊPE BEFORE COMING OVER TO JOIN YOU.
OH GOSH! GOOD LUCK, EVERYONE!
LET'S START BY ACQUIRING THE STAMP IN THE HALL CLOSEST TO US.
WHOO! WE GET TO GO INSIDE AN ALL-GIRLS ACADEMY! YEAH!!
YOU TWO ARE JUST HAPPY TO BE HERE, EH?

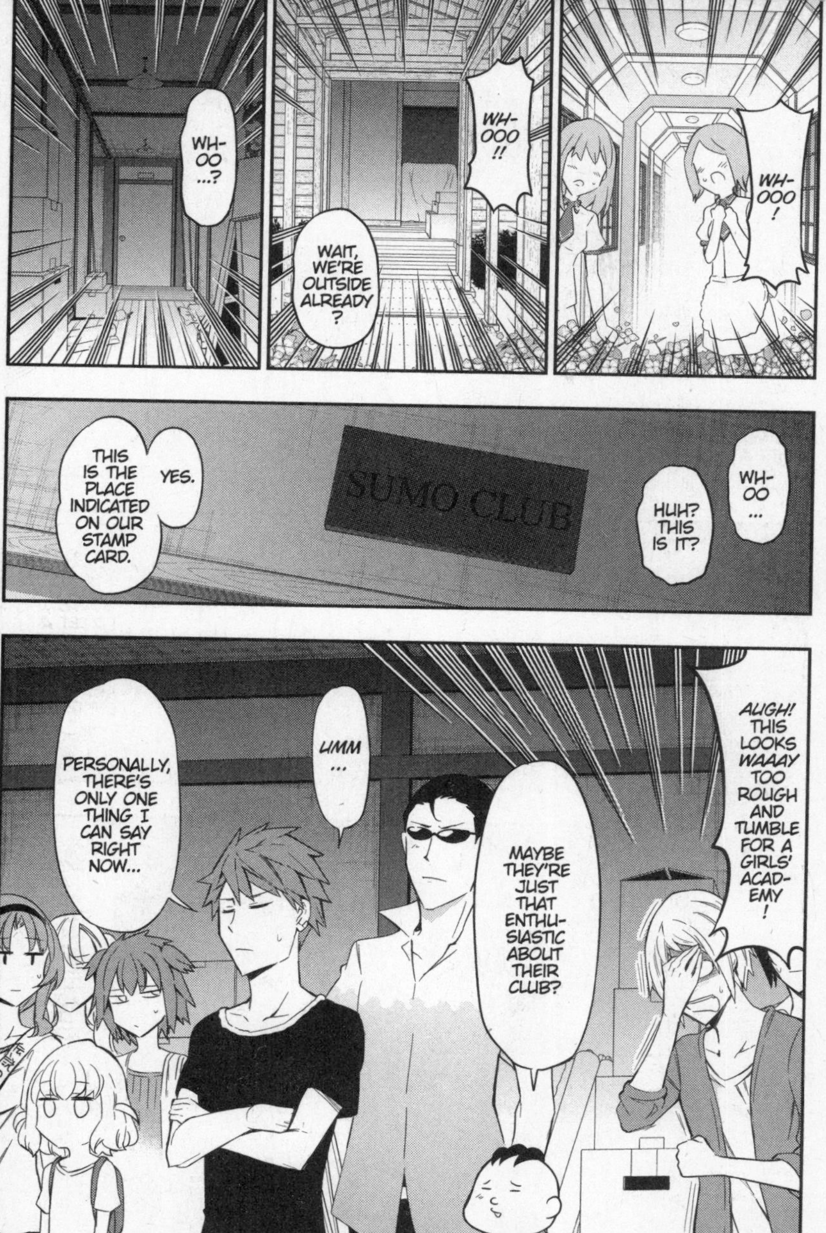
WH-OOO!
WH-OOO!!
WAIT, WE'RE OUTSIDE ALREADY?
WH-OO...?
WH-OO...
HUH? THIS IS IT?
SUMO CLUB
YES.
THIS IS THE PLACE INDICATED ON OUR STAMP CARD.
AUGH! THIS LOOKS WAAAY TOO ROUGH AND TUMBLE FOR A GIRLS' ACADEMY!
MAYBE THEY'RE JUST THAT ENTHUSIASTIC ABOUT THEIR CLUB?
UMM...
PERSONALLY, THERE'S ONLY ONE THING I CAN SAY RIGHT NOW...

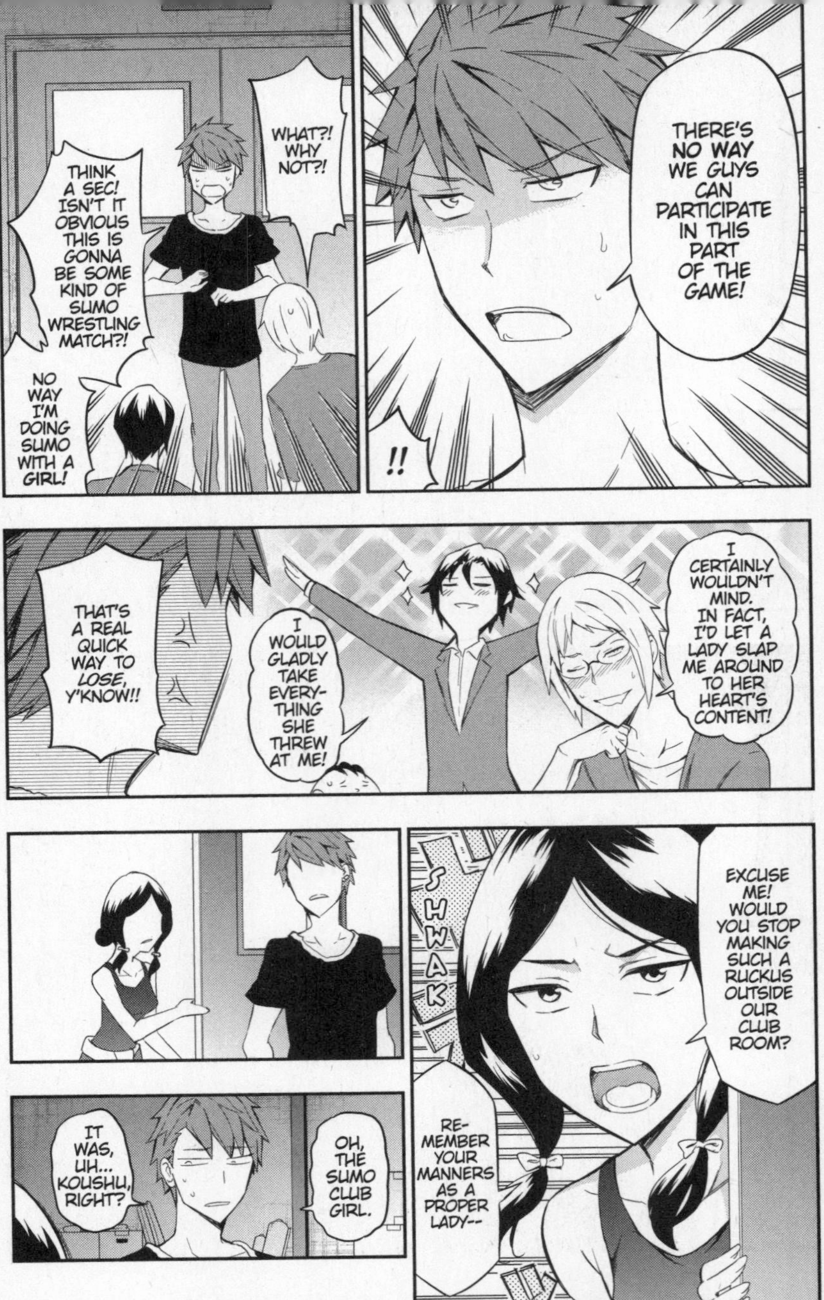
THERE'S NO WAY WE GUYS CAN PARTICIPATE IN THIS PART OF THE GAME!
!!
WHAT?! WHY NOT?!
THINK A SEC! ISN'T IT OBVIOUS THIS IS GONNA BE SOME KIND OF SUMO WRESTLING MATCH?!
NO WAY I'M DOING SUMO WITH A GIRL!
I CERTAINLY WOULDN'T MIND. IN FACT, I'D LET A LADY SLAP ME AROUND TO HER HEART'S CONTENT!
I WOULD GLADLY TAKE EVERYTHING SHE THREW AT ME!
THAT'S A REAL QUICK WAY TO *LOSE*, Y'KNOW!!
SHWAK
EXCUSE ME! WOULD YOU STOP MAKING SUCH A RUCKUS OUTSIDE OUR CLUB ROOM?
REMEMBER YOUR MANNERS AS A PROPER LADY--
OH, THE SUMO CLUB GIRL.
IT WAS, UH... KOUSHU, RIGHT?

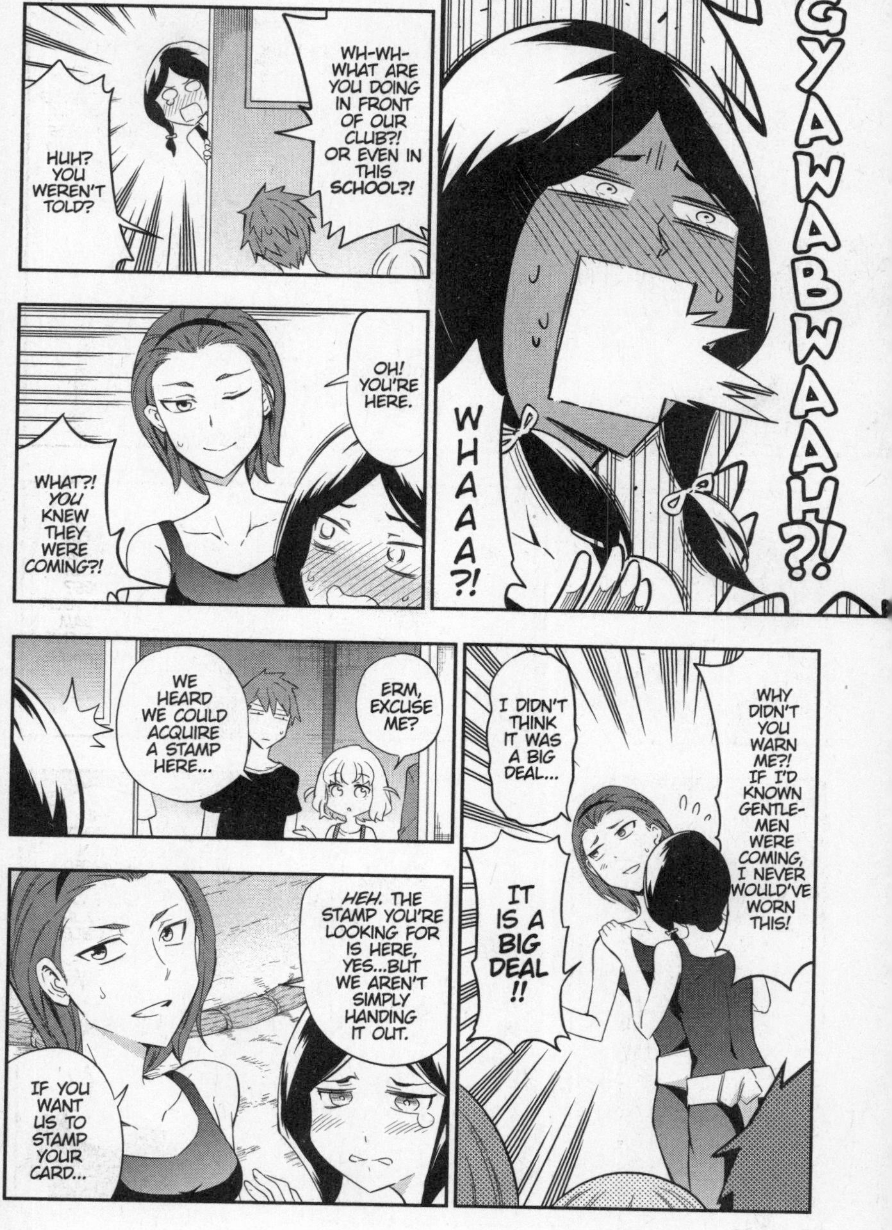
GYAWABWAAH?!
WHAAAA?!
WH-WH-WHAT ARE YOU DOING IN FRONT OF OUR CLUB?! OR EVEN IN THIS SCHOOL?!
HUH? YOU WEREN'T TOLD?
OH! YOU'RE HERE.
WHAT?! *YOU* KNEW THEY WERE COMING?!
WHY DIDN'T YOU WARN ME?! IF I'D KNOWN GENTLEMEN WERE COMING, I NEVER WOULD'VE WORN THIS!
I DIDN'T THINK IT WAS A BIG DEAL...
IT IS A BIG DEAL!!
ERM, EXCUSE ME?
WE HEARD WE COULD ACQUIRE A STAMP HERE...
HEH. THE STAMP YOU'RE LOOKING FOR IS HERE, YES...BUT WE AREN'T SIMPLY HANDING IT OUT.
IF YOU WANT US TO STAMP YOUR CARD...

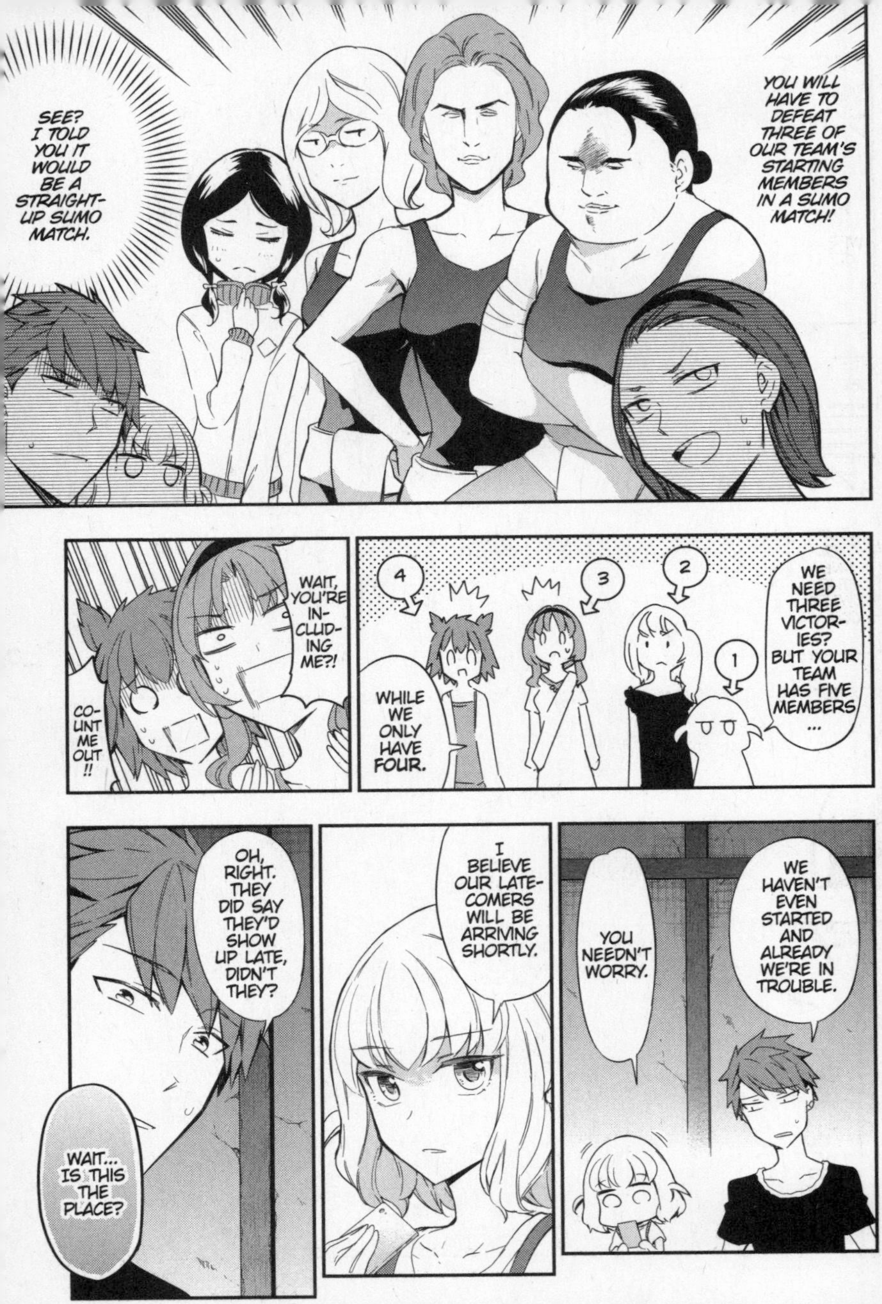
YOU WILL HAVE TO DEFEAT THREE OF OUR TEAM'S STARTING MEMBERS IN A SUMO MATCH!
SEE? I TOLD YOU IT WOULD BE A STRAIGHT-UP SUMO MATCH.
WE NEED THREE VICTORIES? BUT YOUR TEAM HAS FIVE MEMBERS...
2
1
3
4
WHILE WE ONLY HAVE FOUR.
WAIT, YOU'RE IN-CLUD-ING ME?!
CO-UNT ME OUT!!
WE HAVEN'T EVEN STARTED AND ALREADY WE'RE IN TROUBLE.
YOU NEEDN'T WORRY.
I BELIEVE OUR LATE-COMERS WILL BE ARRIVING SHORTLY.
OH, RIGHT. THEY DID SAY THEY'D SHOW UP LATE, DIDN'T THEY?
WAIT... IS THIS THE PLACE?

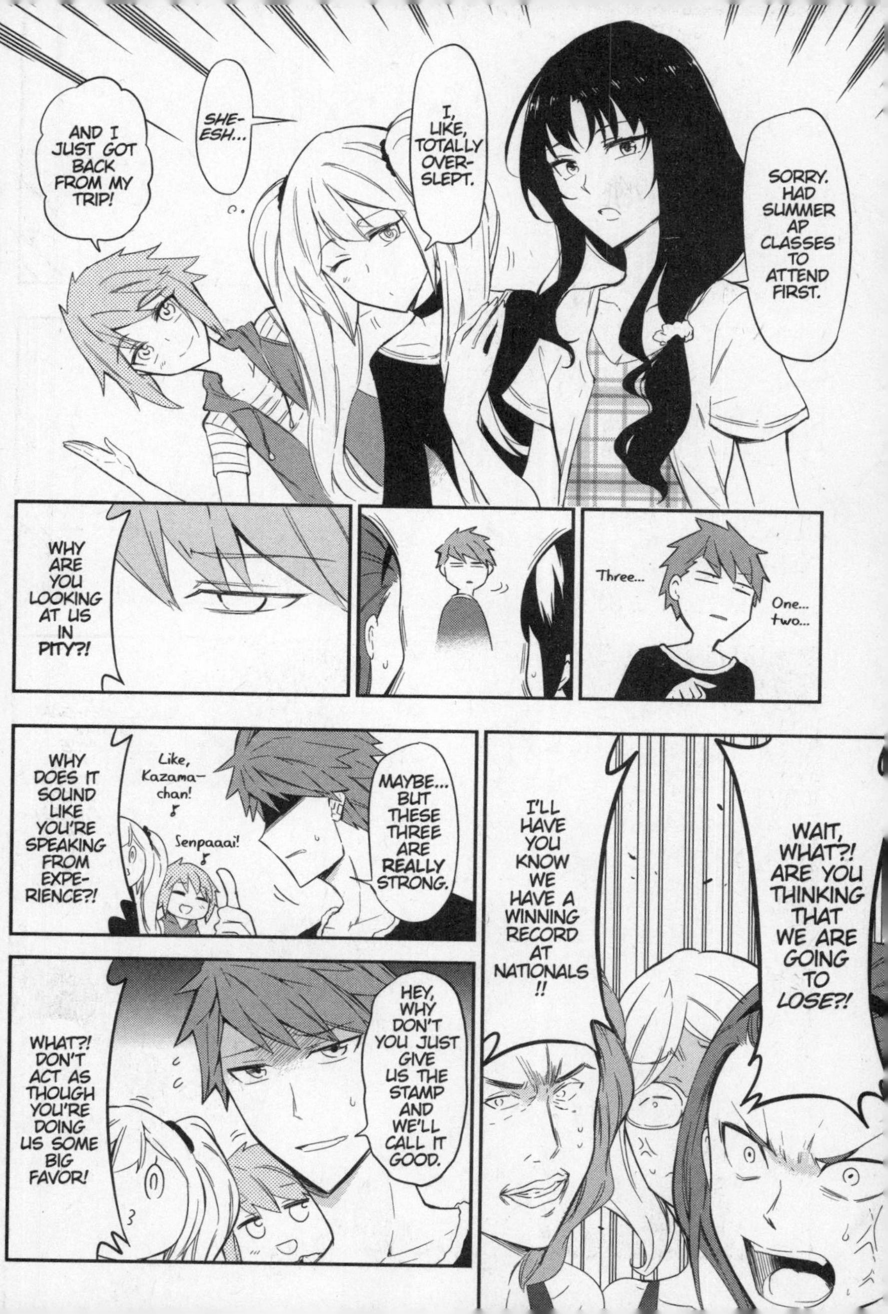
SORRY. HAD SUMMER AP CLASSES TO ATTEND FIRST.
I, LIKE, TOTALLY OVER-SLEPT.
SHE-ESH...
AND I JUST GOT BACK FROM MY TRIP!
One... two...
Three...
WHY ARE YOU LOOKING AT US IN PITY?!
WAIT, WHAT?! ARE YOU THINKING THAT WE ARE GOING TO LOSE?!
I'LL HAVE YOU KNOW WE HAVE A WINNING RECORD AT NATIONALS!!
MAYBE... BUT THESE THREE ARE REALLY STRONG.
Like, Kazama-chan!
Senpaaai!
WHY DOES IT SOUND LIKE YOU'RE SPEAKING FROM EXPE-RIENCE?!
HEY, WHY DON'T YOU JUST GIVE US THE STAMP AND WE'LL CALL IT GOOD.
WHAT?! DON'T ACT AS THOUGH YOU'RE DOING US SOME BIG FAVOR!

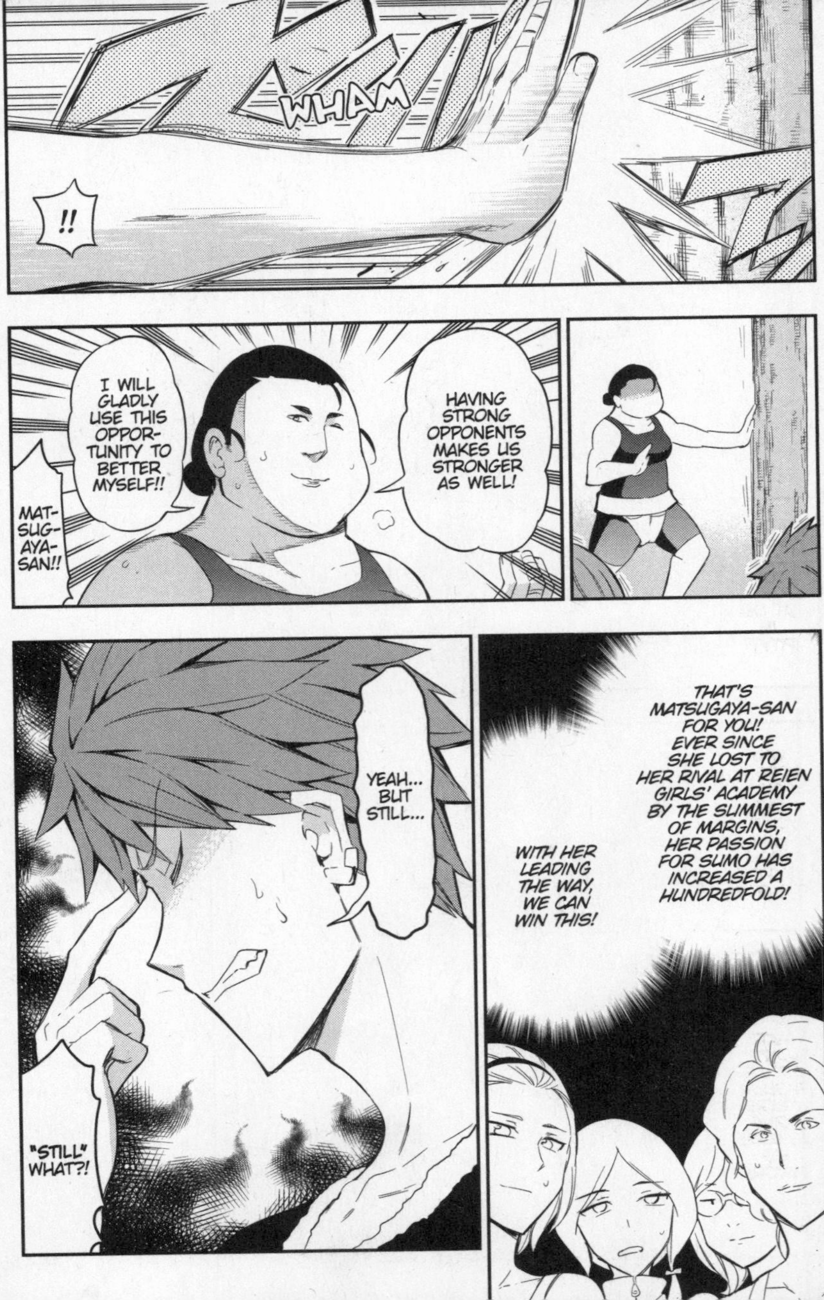
WHAM
!!
HAVING STRONG OPPONENTS MAKES US STRONGER AS WELL!
I WILL GLADLY USE THIS OPPORTUNITY TO BETTER MYSELF!!
MATSUGAYA-SAN!!
THAT'S MATSUGAYA-SAN FOR YOU! EVER SINCE SHE LOST TO HER RIVAL AT REIEN GIRLS' ACADEMY BY THE SLIMMEST OF MARGINS, HER PASSION FOR SUMO HAS INCREASED A HUNDREDFOLD!
WITH HER LEADING THE WAY, WE CAN WIN THIS!
YEAH... BUT STILL...
"STILL" WHAT?!

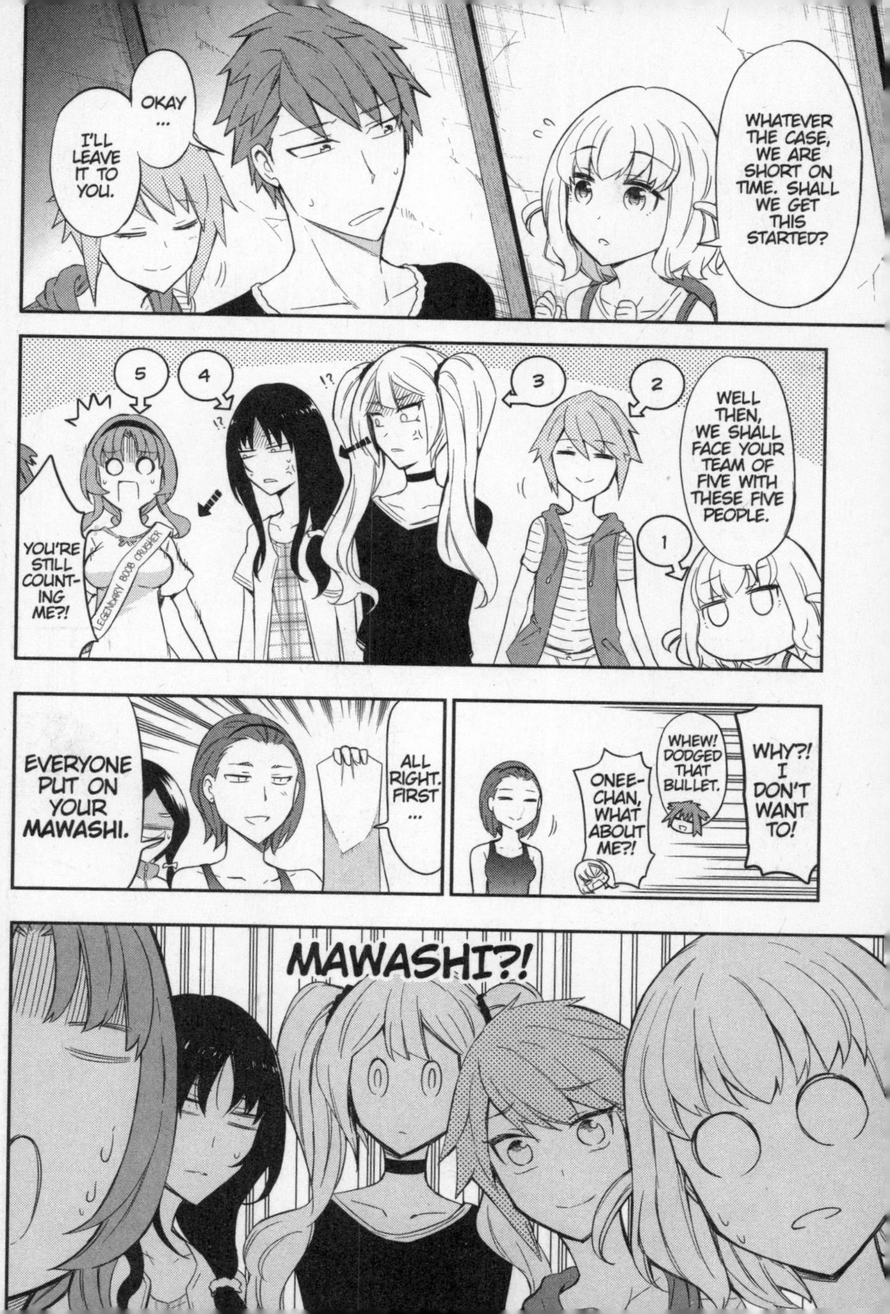

WHATEVER THE CASE, WE ARE SHORT ON TIME. SHALL WE GET THIS STARTED?
OKAY ...
I'LL LEAVE IT TO YOU.
WELL THEN, WE SHALL FACE YOUR TEAM OF FIVE WITH THESE FIVE PEOPLE.
1
2
3
!?
4
!?
5
YOU'RE STILL COUNTING ME?!
LEGENDARY BOOB CRUSHER
WHY?! I DON'T WANT TO!
WHEW! DODGED THAT BULLET.
ONEE-CHAN, WHAT ABOUT ME?!
ALL RIGHT. FIRST ...
EVERYONE PUT ON YOUR MAWASHI.
MAWASHI?!

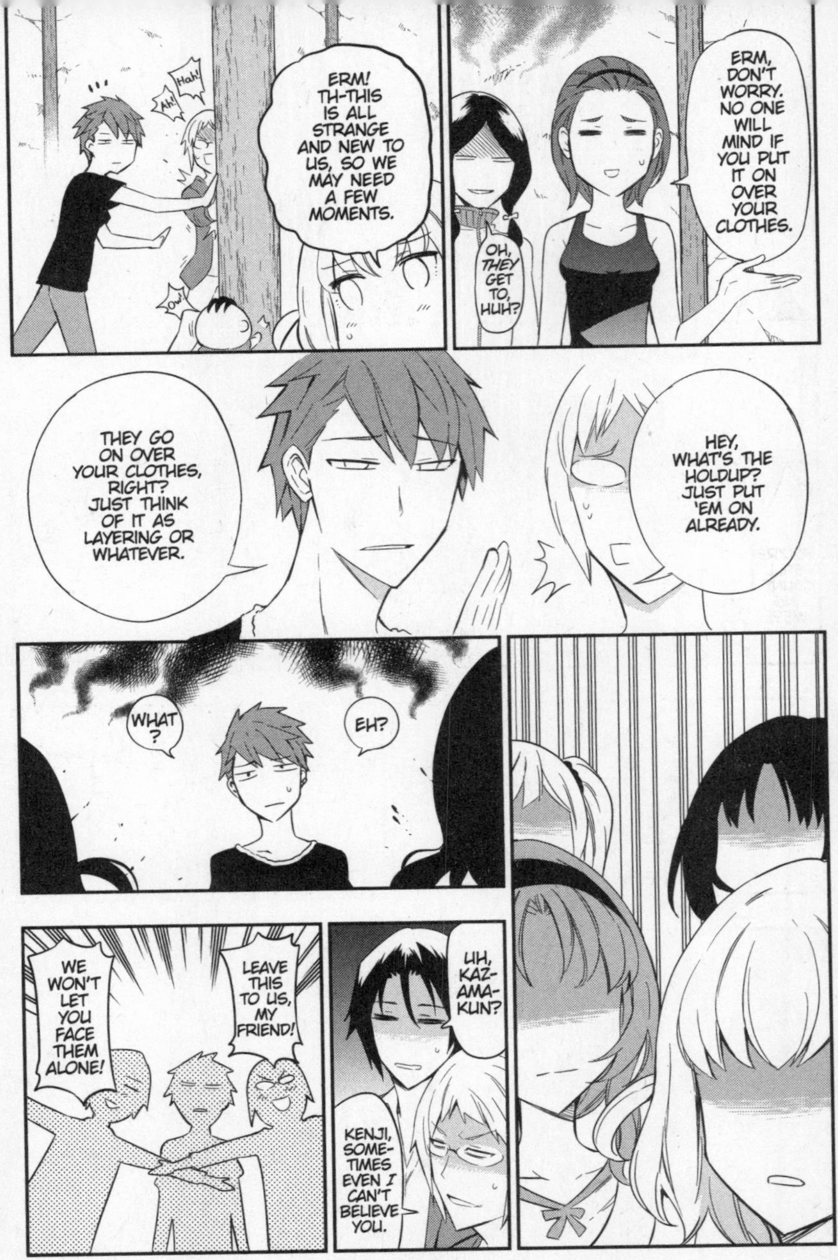
ERM, DON'T WORRY. NO ONE WILL MIND IF YOU PUT IT ON OVER YOUR CLOTHES.
OH, THEY GET TO, HUH?
ERM! TH-THIS IS ALL STRANGE AND NEW TO US, SO WE MAY NEED A FEW MOMENTS.
Hah!
Ah!
Ow!
HEY, WHAT'S THE HOLDUP? JUST PUT 'EM ON ALREADY.
THEY GO ON OVER YOUR CLOTHES, RIGHT? JUST THINK OF IT AS LAYERING OR WHATEVER.
EH?
WHAT?
UH, KAZAMA-KUN?
KENJI, SOMETIMES EVEN I CAN'T BELIEVE YOU.
LEAVE THIS TO US, MY FRIEND!
WE WON'T LET YOU FACE THEM ALONE!

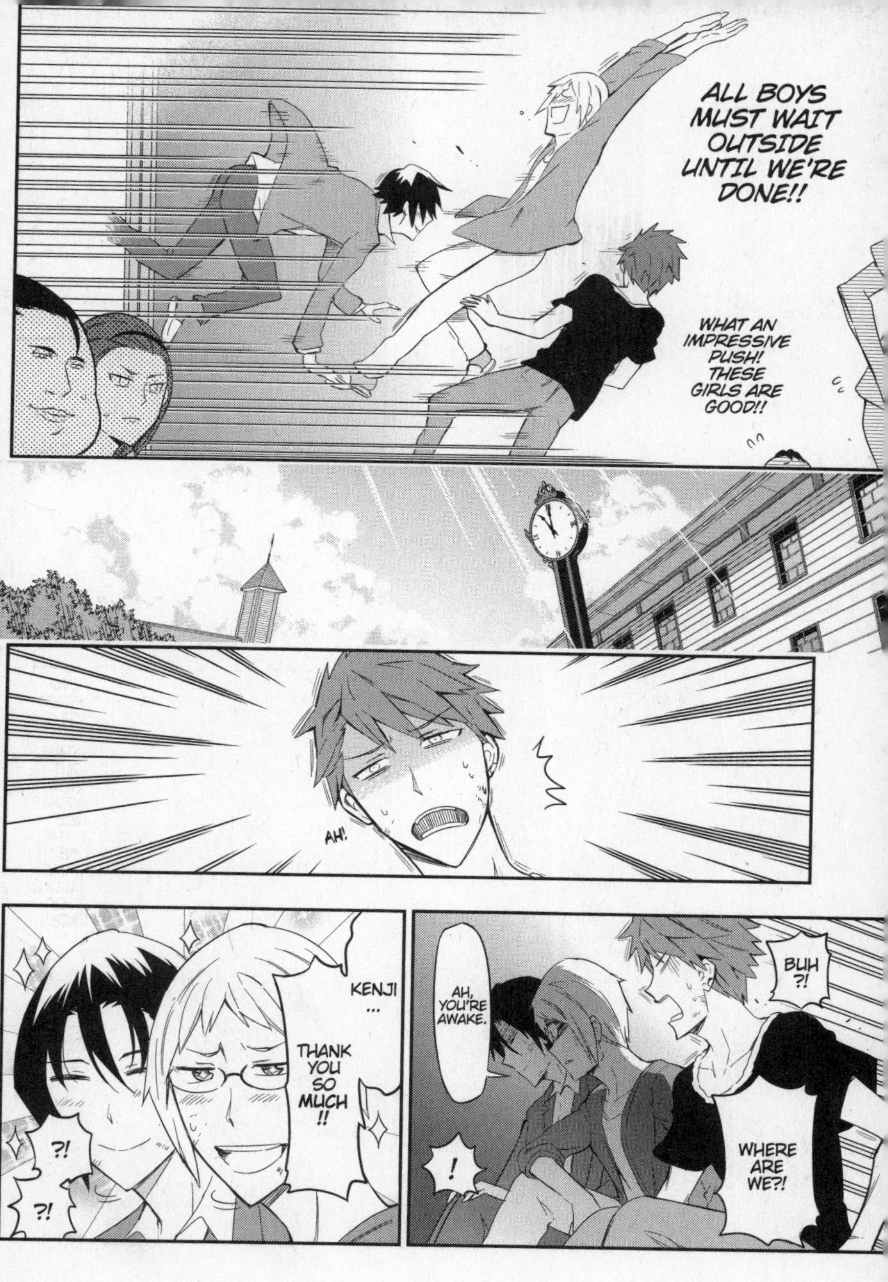
ALL BOYS MUST WAIT OUTSIDE UNTIL WE'RE DONE!!
WHAT AN IMPRESSIVE PUSH! THESE GIRLS ARE GOOD!!
AH!
BUH ?!
WHERE ARE WE?!
AH, YOU'RE AWAKE.
!
KENJI ...
THANK YOU SO MUCH !!
?!
?!

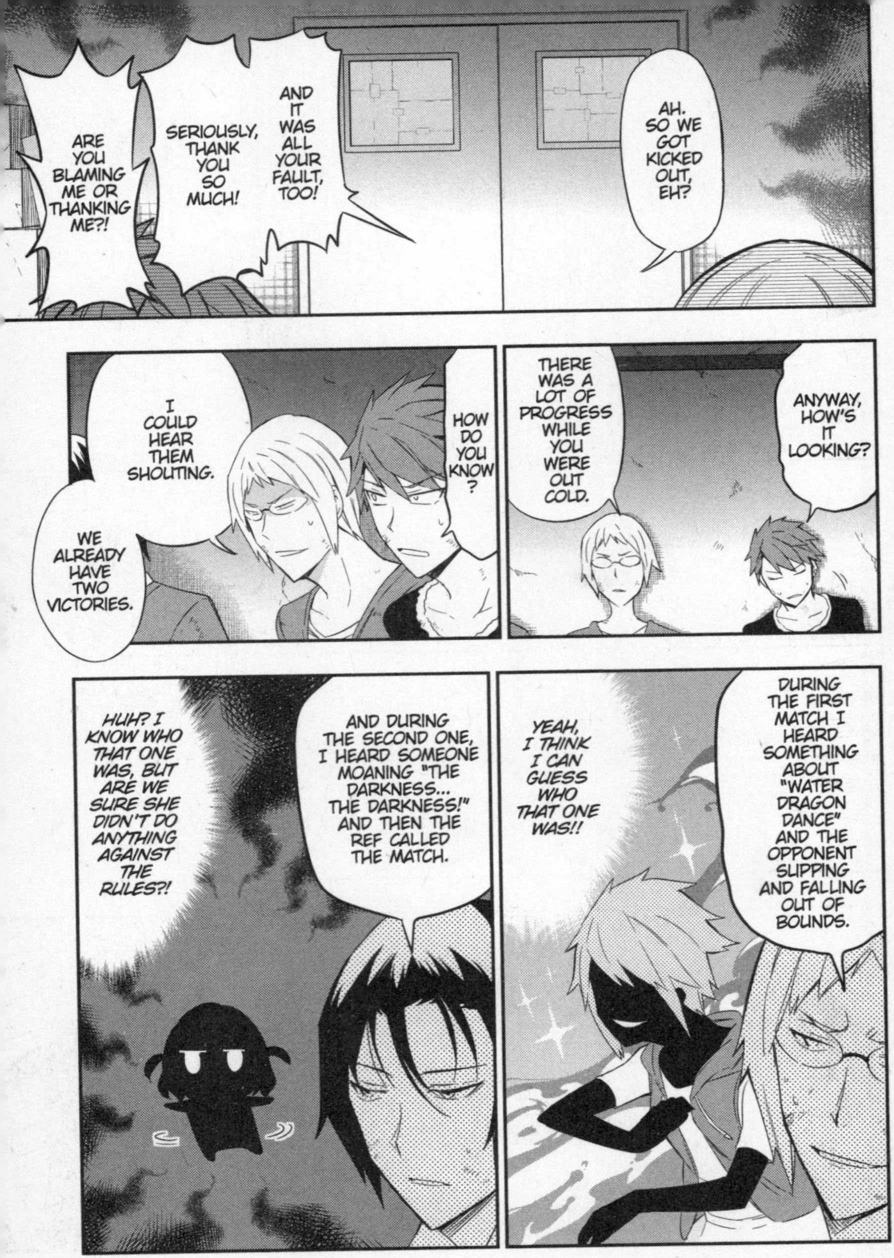
AH. SO WE GOT KICKED OUT, EH?
AND IT WAS ALL YOUR FAULT, TOO!
SERIOUSLY, THANK YOU SO MUCH!
ARE YOU BLAMING ME OR THANKING ME?!
ANYWAY, HOW'S IT LOOKING?
THERE WAS A LOT OF PROGRESS WHILE YOU WERE OUT COLD.
HOW DO YOU KNOW?
I COULD HEAR THEM SHOUTING.
WE ALREADY HAVE TWO VICTORIES.
DURING THE FIRST MATCH I HEARD SOMETHING ABOUT "WATER DRAGON DANCE" AND THE OPPONENT SLIPPING AND FALLING OUT OF BOUNDS.
YEAH, I THINK I CAN GUESS WHO THAT ONE WAS!!
AND DURING THE SECOND ONE, I HEARD SOMEONE MOANING "THE DARKNESS... THE DARKNESS!" AND THEN THE REF CALLED THE MATCH.
HUH? I KNOW WHO THAT ONE WAS, BUT ARE WE SURE SHE DIDN'T DO ANYTHING AGAINST THE RULES?!

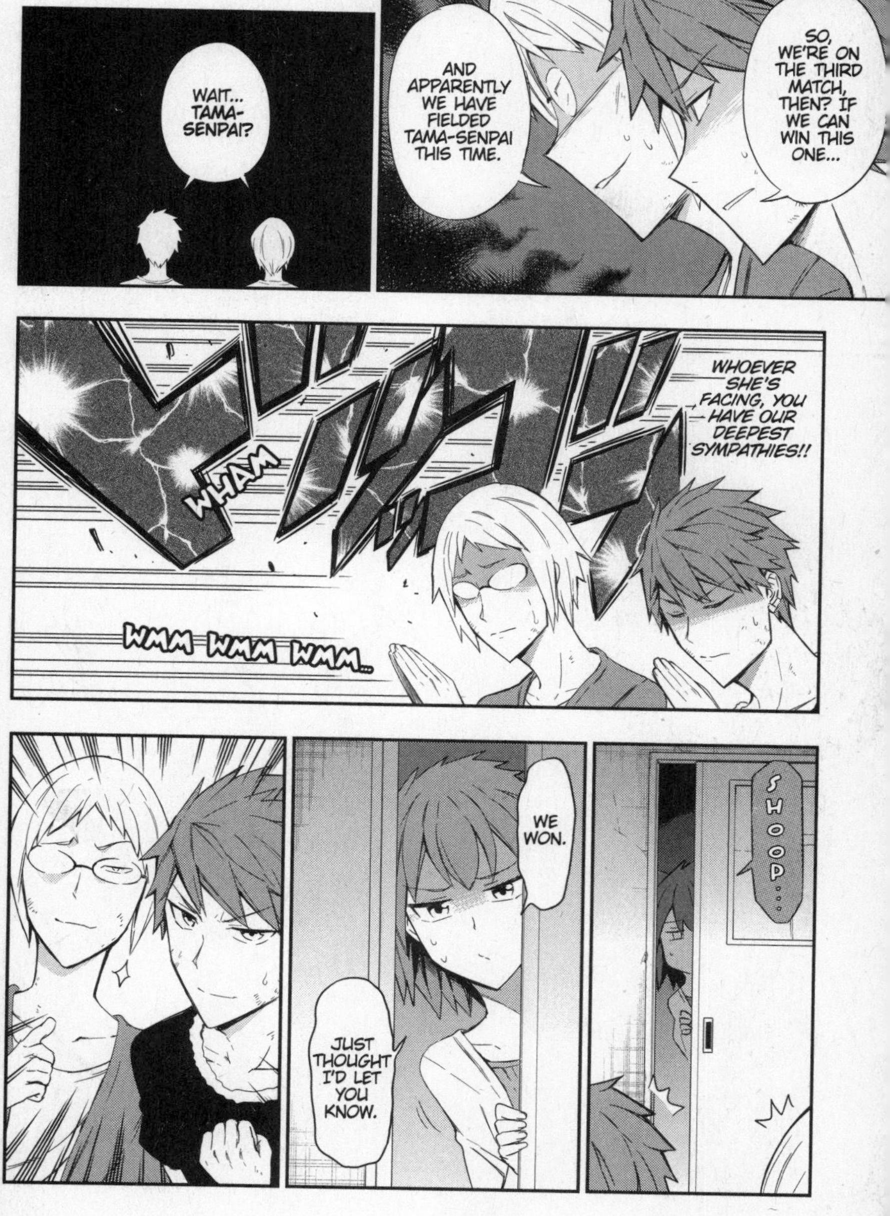
SO, WE'RE ON THE THIRD MATCH, THEN? IF WE CAN WIN THIS ONE...
AND APPARENTLY WE HAVE FIELDED TAMA-SENPAI THIS TIME.
WAIT... TAMA-SENPAI?
WHOEVER SHE'S FACING, YOU HAVE OUR DEEPEST SYMPATHIES!!
WHAM
WMM WMM WMM...
SHOOP...
WE WON.
JUST THOUGHT I'D LET YOU KNOW.

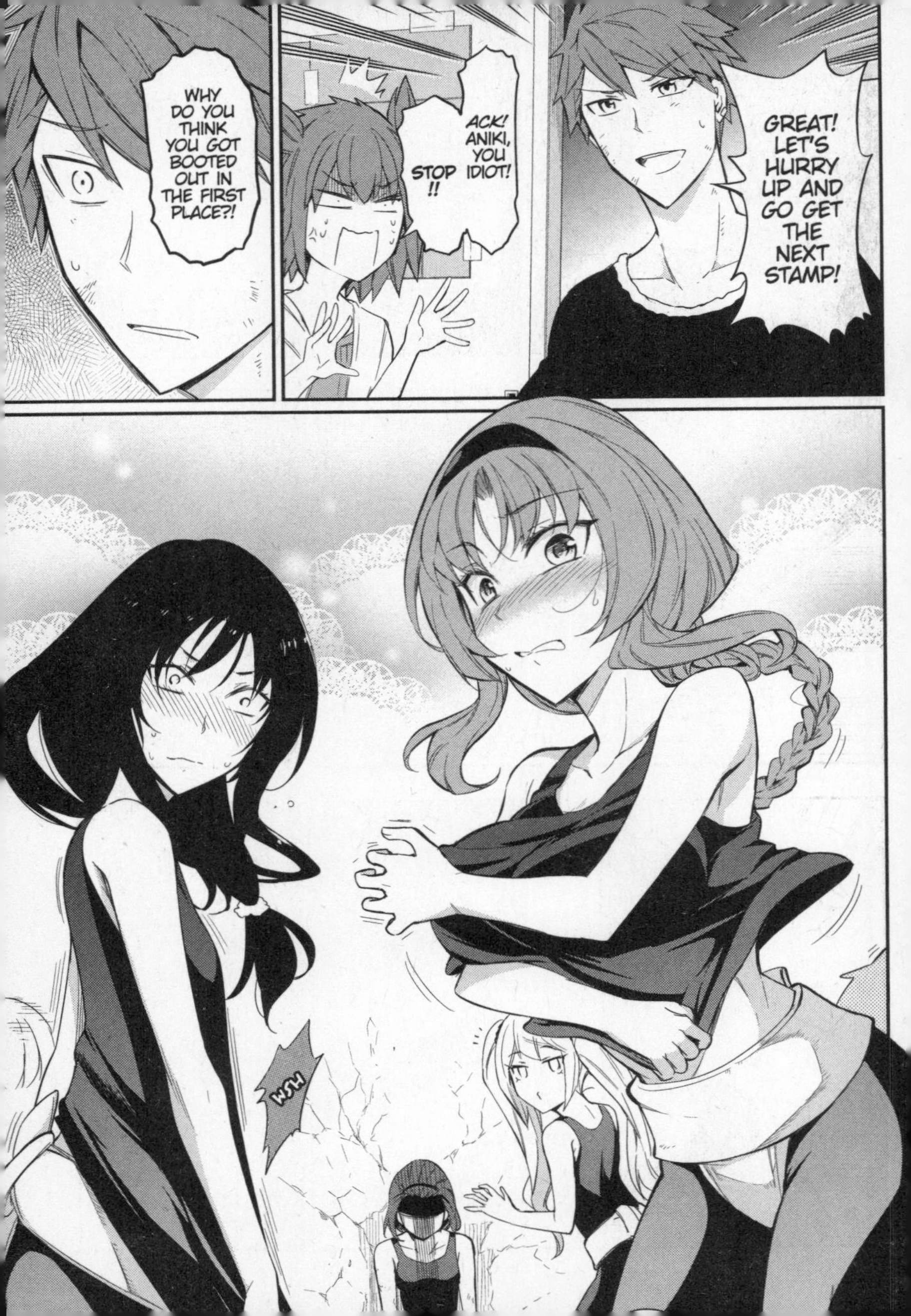
GREAT! LET'S HURRY UP AND GO GET THE NEXT STAMP!
ACK! ANIKI, YOU IDIOT!
STOP !!
WHY DO YOU THINK YOU GOT BOOTED OUT IN THE FIRST PLACE?!
WSH

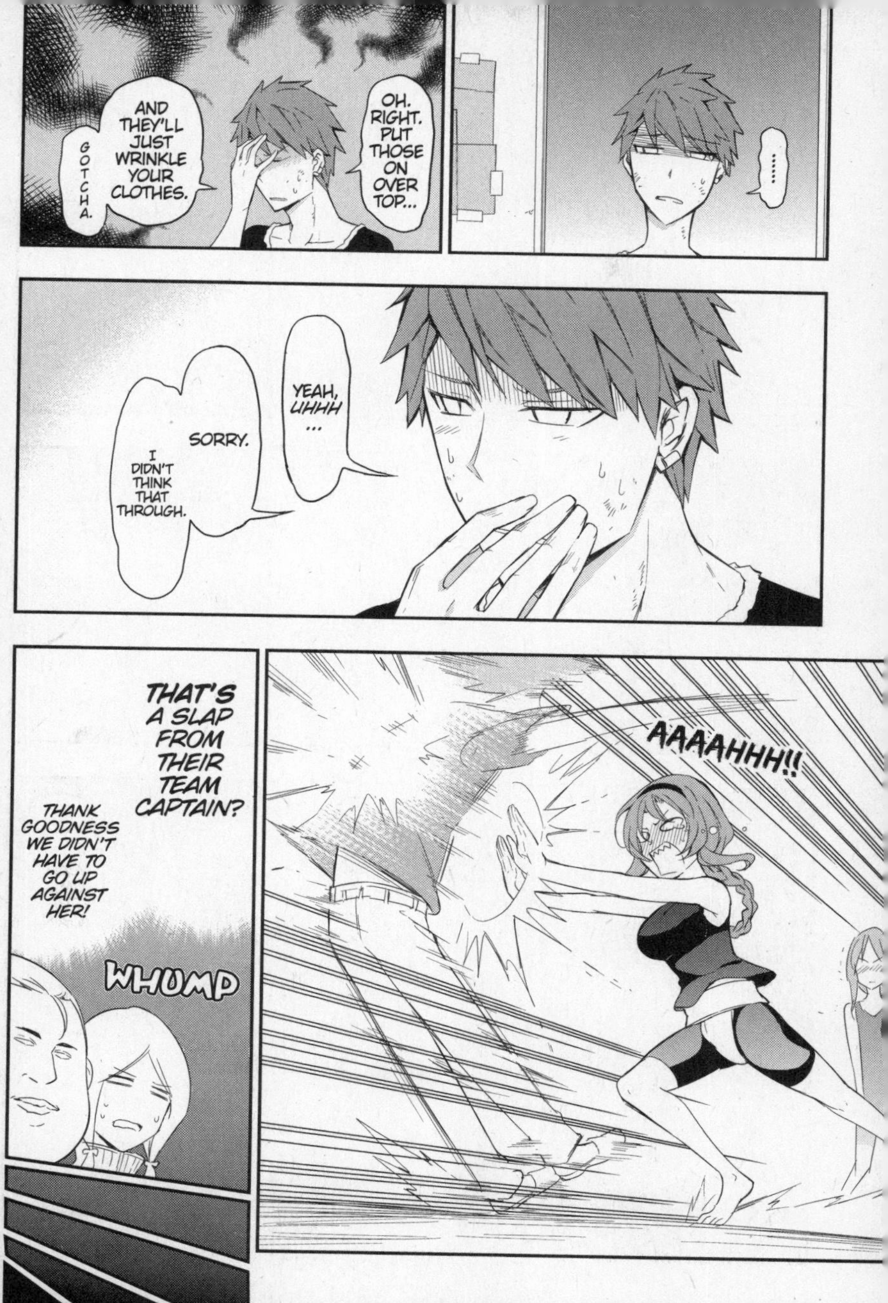
......
OH. RIGHT. PUT THOSE ON OVER TOP...
AND THEY'LL JUST WRINKLE YOUR CLOTHES.
GOTCHA.
YEAH, UHHH ...
SORRY. I DIDN'T THINK THAT THROUGH.
AAAAHHH!!
THAT'S A SLAP FROM THEIR TEAM CAPTAIN?
THANK GOODNESS WE DIDN'T HAVE TO GO UP AGAINST HER!
WHUMP

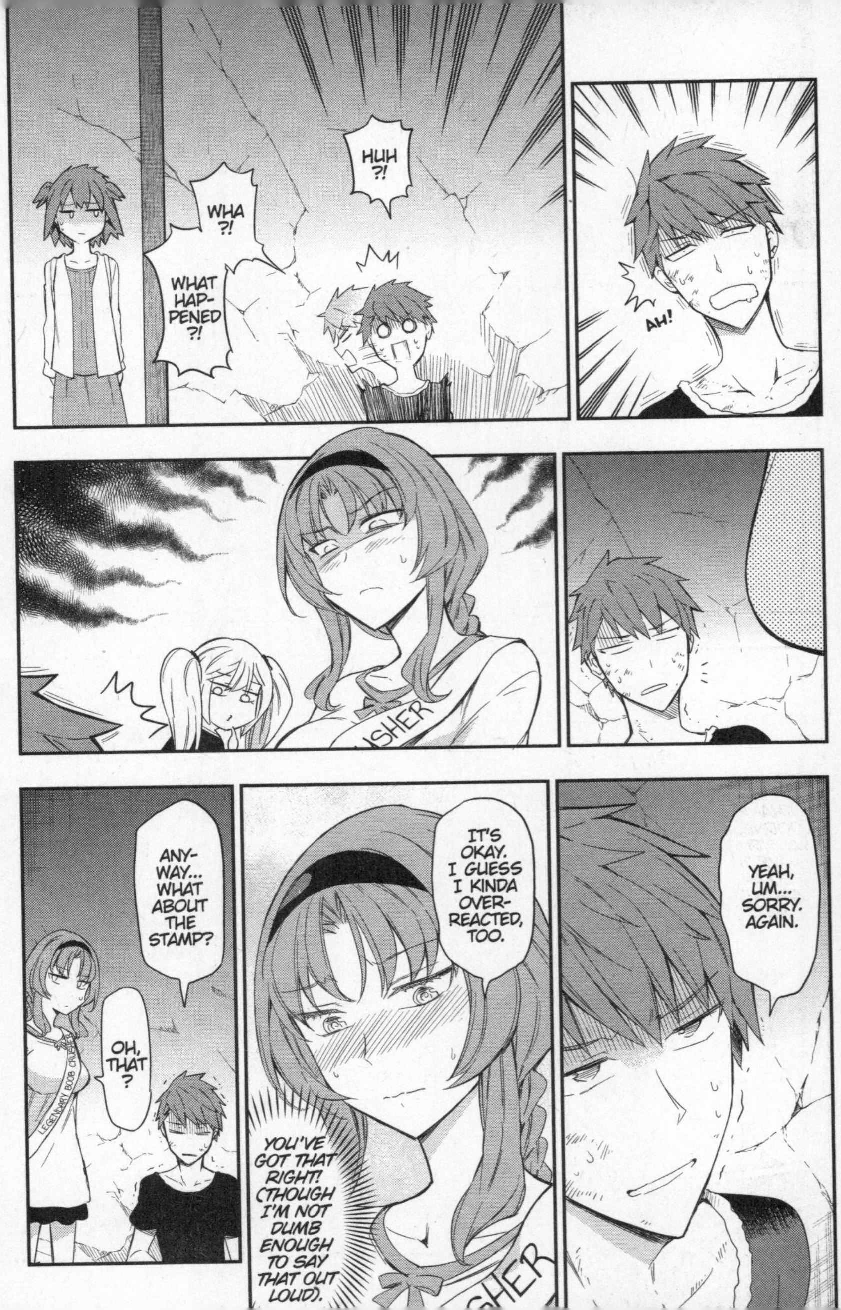
AH!
HUH ?!
WHA ?!
WHAT HAP-PENED ?!
YEAH, UM... SORRY. AGAIN.
IT'S OKAY. I GUESS I KINDA OVER-REACTED, TOO.
YOU'VE GOT THAT RIGHT! (THOUGH I'M NOT DUMB ENOUGH TO SAY THAT OUT LOUD).
ANY-WAY... WHAT ABOUT THE STAMP?
OH, THAT?
LEGENDARY BOOB CRUSHER

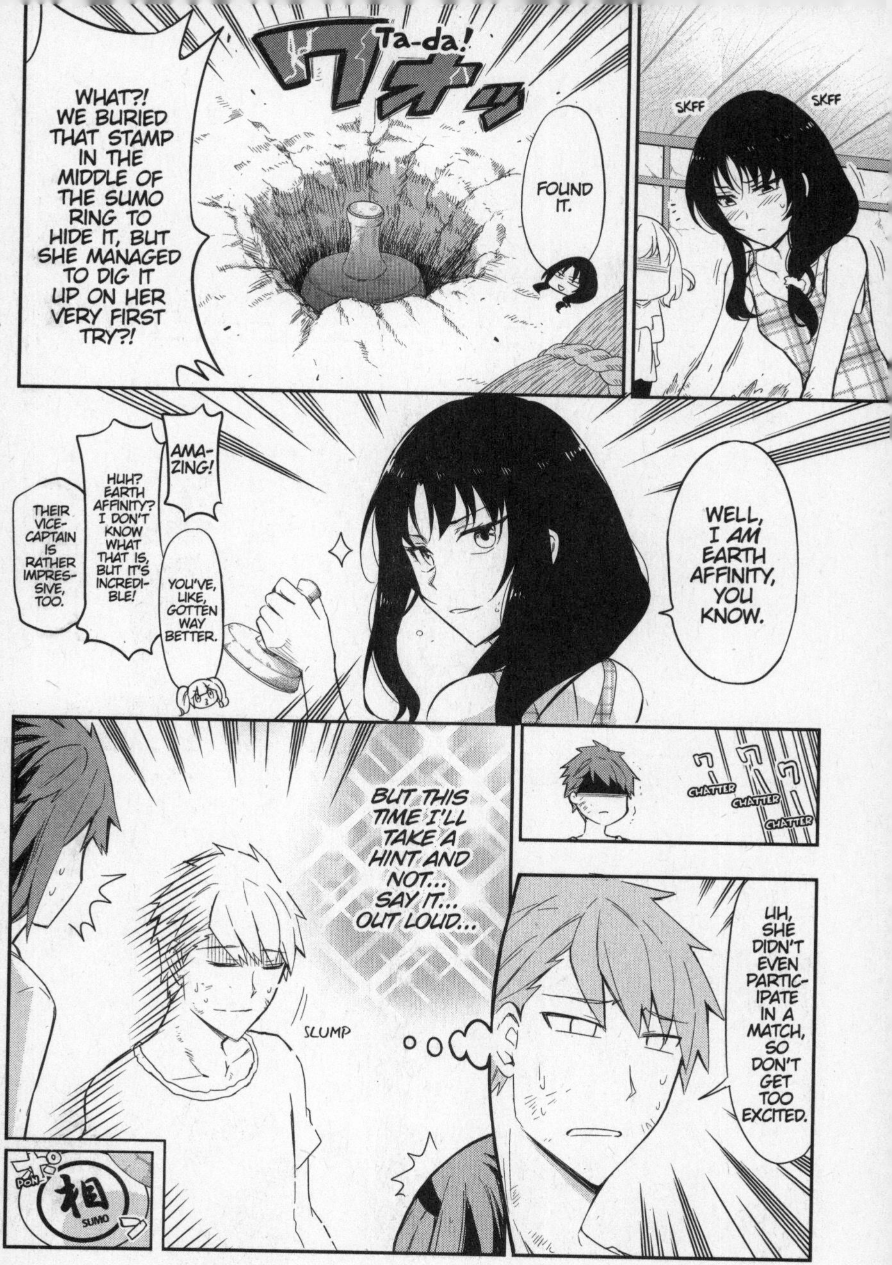
SKFF
SKFF
Ta-da!
FOUND IT.
WHAT?! WE BURIED THAT STAMP IN THE MIDDLE OF THE SUMO RING TO HIDE IT, BUT SHE MANAGED TO DIG IT UP ON HER VERY FIRST TRY?!
WELL, I *AM* EARTH AFFINITY, YOU KNOW.
AMA-ZING!
HUH? EARTH AFFINITY? I DON'T KNOW WHAT THAT IS, BUT IT'S INCREDIBLE!
YOU'VE, LIKE, GOTTEN WAY BETTER.
THEIR VICE-CAPTAIN IS RATHER IMPRESSIVE, TOO.
CHATTER
CHATTER
CHATTER
UH, SHE DIDN'T EVEN PARTICIPATE IN A MATCH, SO DON'T GET TOO EXCITED.
BUT THIS TIME I'LL TAKE A HINT AND NOT... SAY IT... OUT LOUD...
SLUMP
PON
相
SUMO

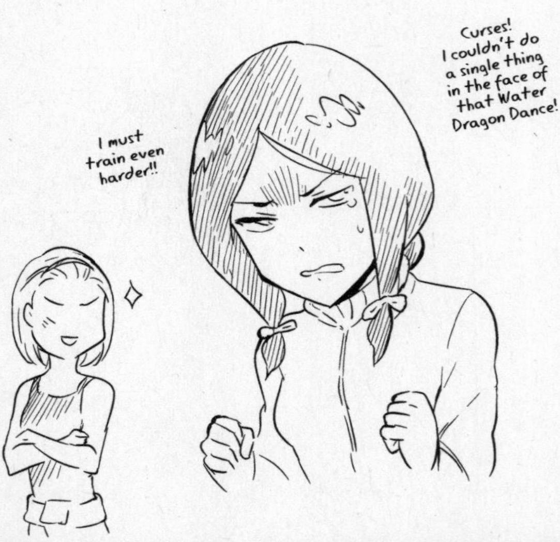
Curses! I couldn't do a single thing in the face of that Water Dragon Dance!
I must train even harder!!

D-FRAGMENTS ディーフラグメンツ!

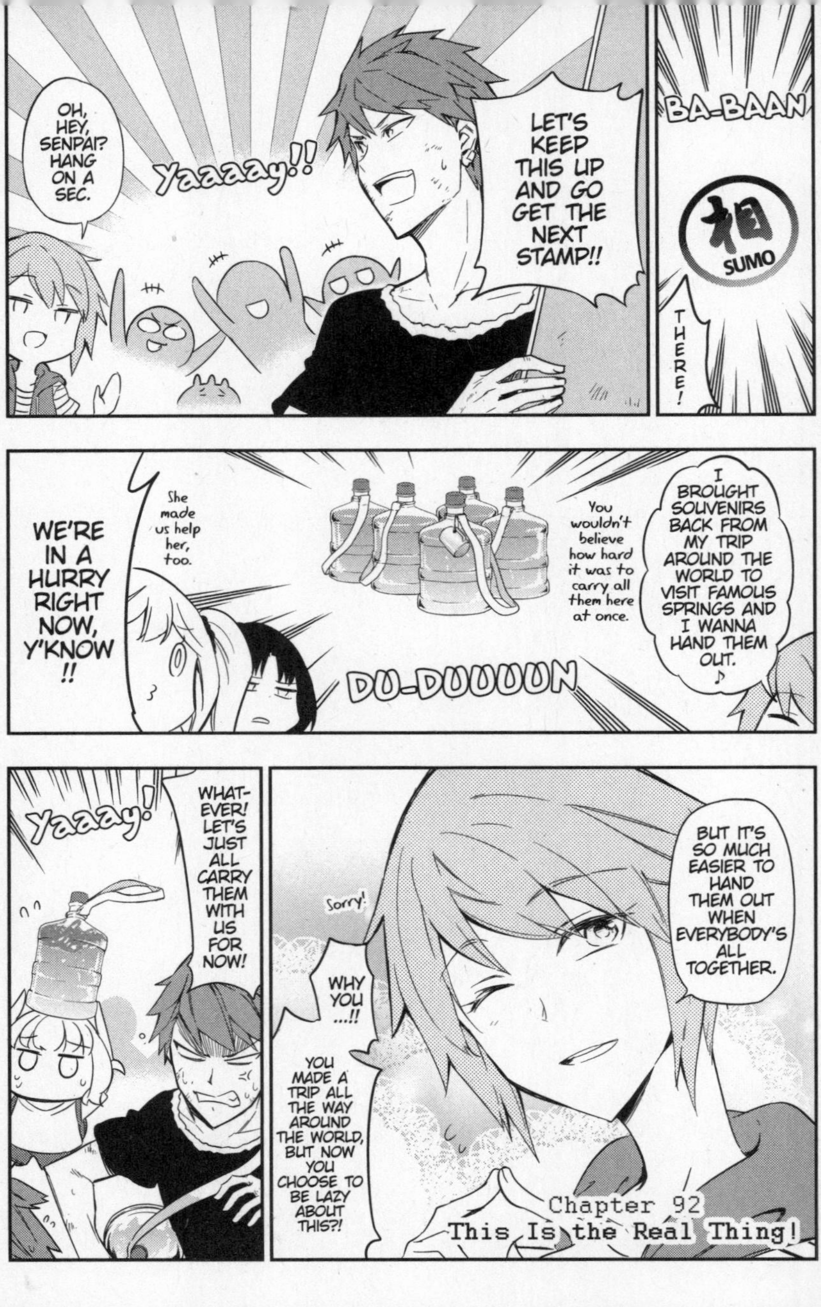
BA-BAAN
SUMO
THERE!
LET'S KEEP THIS UP AND GO GET THE NEXT STAMP!!
Yaaaay!!
OH, HEY, SENPAI? HANG ON A SEC.
I BROUGHT SOUVENIRS BACK FROM MY TRIP AROUND THE WORLD TO VISIT FAMOUS SPRINGS AND I WANNA HAND THEM OUT. ♪
You wouldn't believe how hard it was to carry all them here at once.
DU-DUUUUN
She made us help her, too.
WE'RE IN A HURRY RIGHT NOW, Y'KNOW!!
BUT IT'S SO MUCH EASIER TO HAND THEM OUT WHEN EVERYBODY'S ALL TOGETHER.
Sorry!
WHY YOU ...!!
YOU MADE A TRIP ALL THE WAY AROUND THE WORLD, BUT NOW YOU CHOOSE TO BE LAZY ABOUT THIS?!
Chapter 92
This Is the Real Thing!
WHATEVER! LET'S JUST ALL CARRY THEM WITH US FOR NOW!
Yaaay!

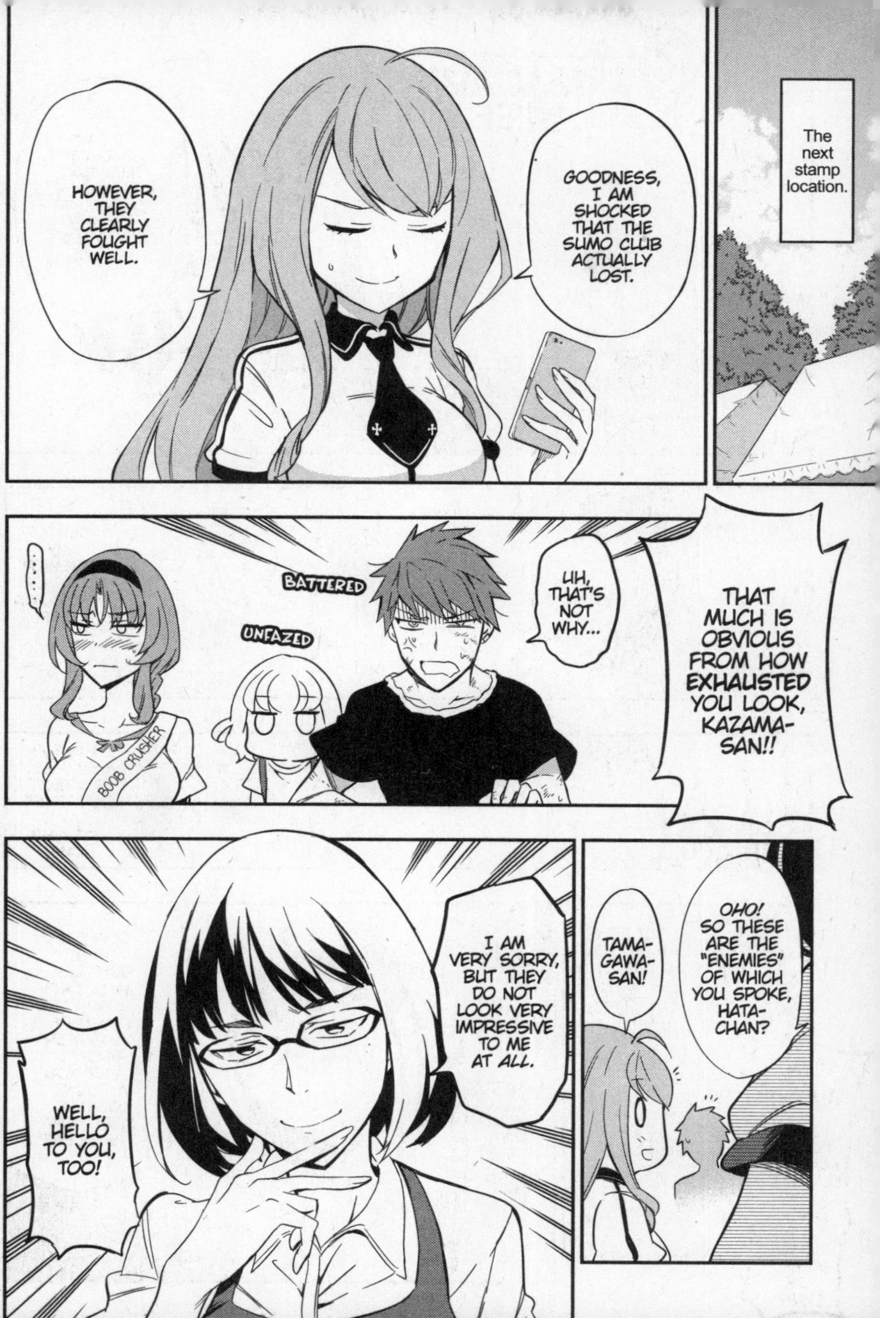
The next stamp location.
GOODNESS, I AM SHOCKED THAT THE SUMO CLUB ACTUALLY LOST.
HOWEVER, THEY CLEARLY FOUGHT WELL.
THAT MUCH IS OBVIOUS FROM HOW EXHAUSTED YOU LOOK, KAZAMA-SAN!!
UH, THAT'S NOT WHY...
BATTERED
UNFAZED
...
BOOB CRUSHER
OHO! SO THESE ARE THE "ENEMIES" OF WHICH YOU SPOKE, HATA-CHAN?
TAMA-GAWA-SAN!
I AM VERY SORRY, BUT THEY DO NOT LOOK VERY IMPRESSIVE TO ME AT ALL.
WELL, HELLO TO YOU, TOO!

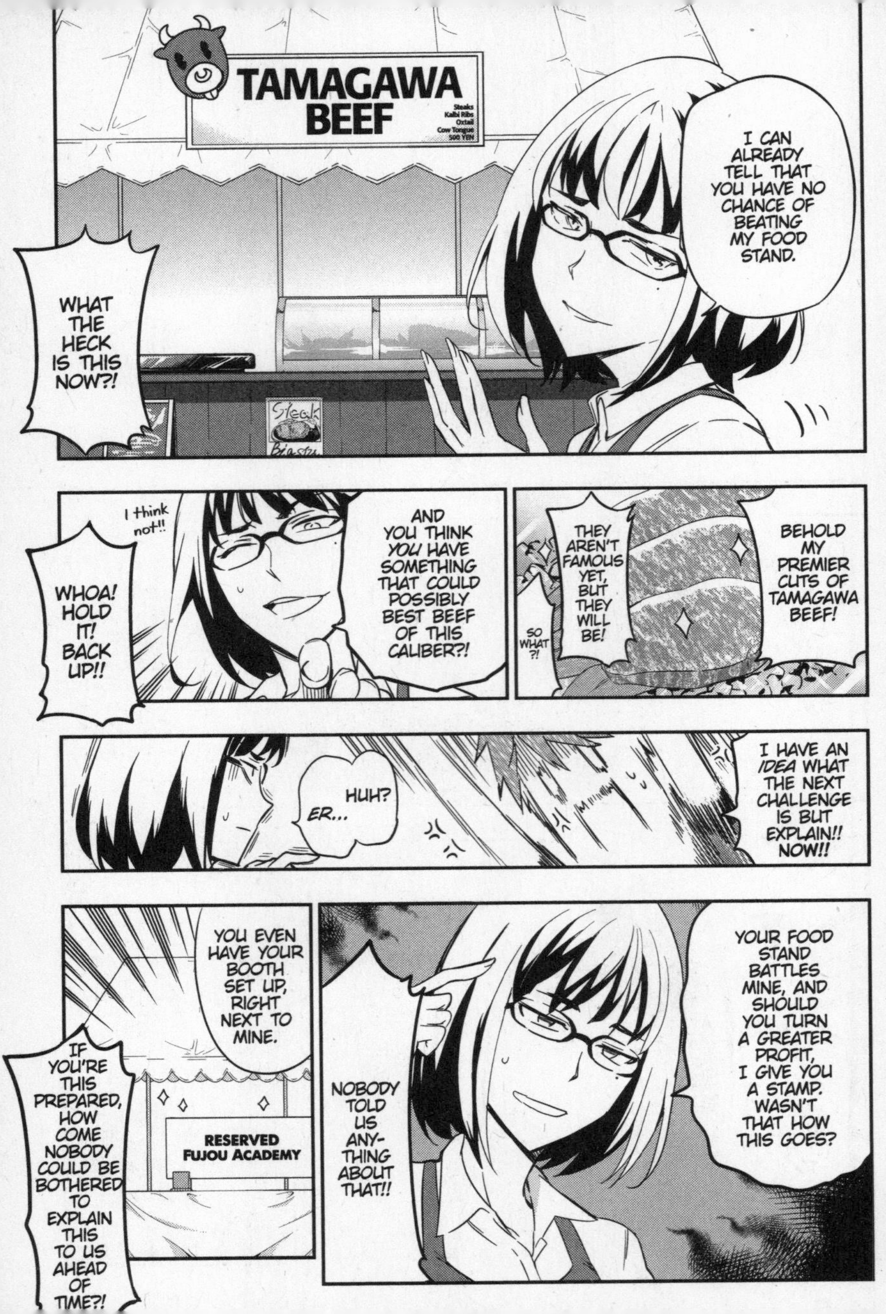
TAMAGAWA BEEF
Steaks Kalbi Ribs Oxtail Cow Tongue 500 YEN
I CAN ALREADY TELL THAT YOU HAVE NO CHANCE OF BEATING MY FOOD STAND.
WHAT THE HECK IS THIS NOW?!
BEHOLD MY PREMIER CUTS OF TAMAGAWA BEEF!
THEY AREN'T FAMOUS YET, BUT THEY WILL BE!
SO WHAT?!
AND YOU THINK *YOU* HAVE SOMETHING THAT COULD POSSIBLY BEST BEEF OF THIS CALIBER?!
I think not!!
WHOA! HOLD IT! BACK UP!!
I HAVE AN *IDEA* WHAT THE NEXT CHALLENGE IS BUT EXPLAIN!! NOW!!
HUH?
ER...
YOUR FOOD STAND BATTLES MINE, AND SHOULD YOU TURN A GREATER PROFIT, I GIVE YOU A STAMP. WASN'T THAT HOW THIS GOES?
NOBODY TOLD US ANYTHING ABOUT THAT!!
YOU EVEN HAVE YOUR BOOTH SET UP, RIGHT NEXT TO MINE.
RESERVED FUJOU ACADEMY
IF YOU'RE THIS PREPARED, HOW COME NOBODY COULD BE BOTHERED TO EXPLAIN THIS TO US AHEAD OF TIME?!

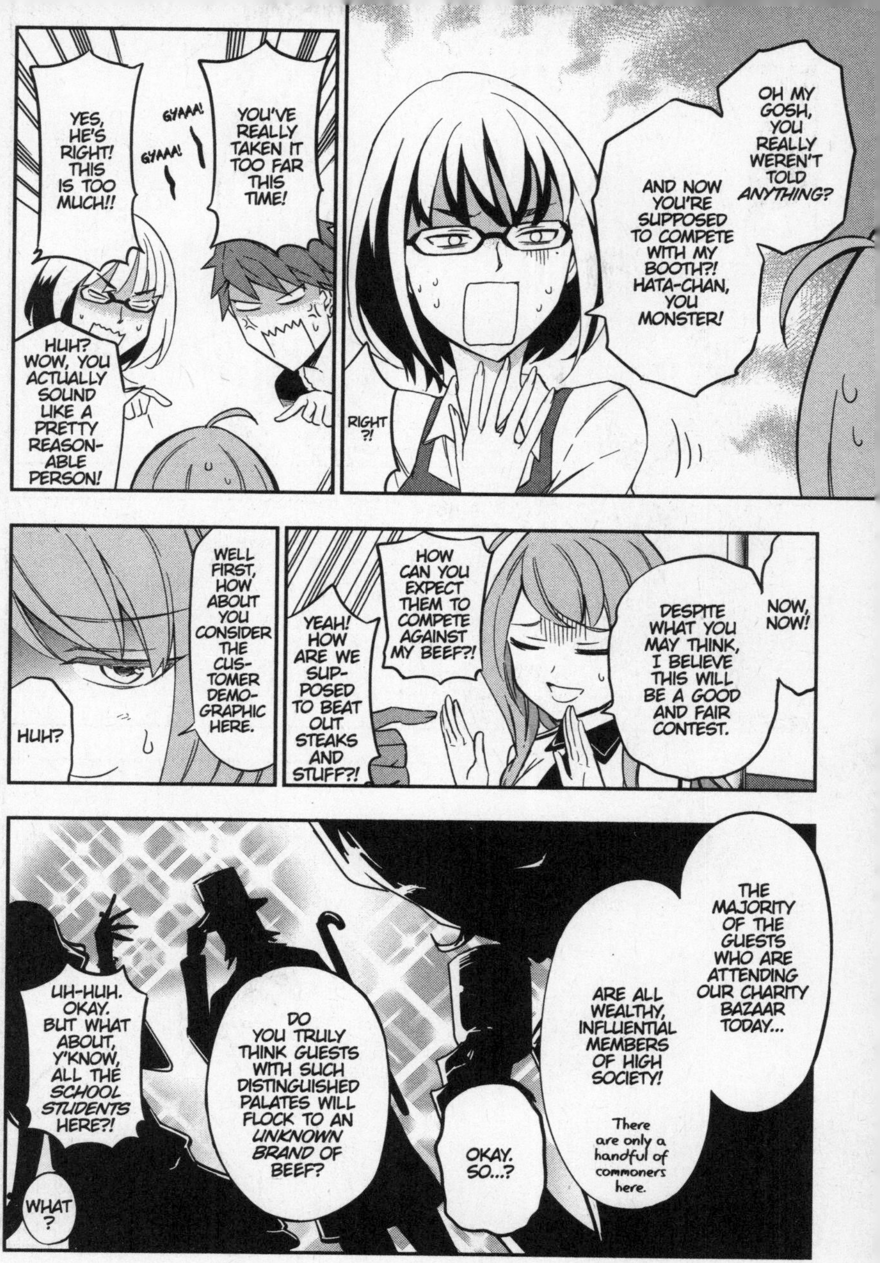
OH MY GOSH, YOU REALLY WEREN'T TOLD *ANYTHING*?
AND NOW YOU'RE SUPPOSED TO COMPETE WITH MY BOOTH?! HATA-CHAN, YOU MONSTER!
RIGHT?!
YOU'VE REALLY TAKEN IT TOO FAR THIS TIME!
GYAAA!
GYAAA!
YES, HE'S RIGHT! THIS IS TOO MUCH!!
HUH? WOW, YOU ACTUALLY SOUND LIKE A PRETTY REASONABLE PERSON!
NOW, NOW!
DESPITE WHAT YOU MAY THINK, I BELIEVE THIS WILL BE A GOOD AND FAIR CONTEST.
HOW CAN YOU EXPECT THEM TO COMPETE AGAINST MY BEEF?!
YEAH! HOW ARE WE SUPPOSED TO BEAT OUT STEAKS AND STUFF?!
WELL FIRST, HOW ABOUT YOU CONSIDER THE CUSTOMER DEMOGRAPHIC HERE.
HUH?
THE MAJORITY OF THE GUESTS WHO ARE ATTENDING OUR CHARITY BAZAAR TODAY...
ARE ALL WEALTHY, INFLUENTIAL MEMBERS OF HIGH SOCIETY!
There are only a handful of commoners here.
OKAY. SO...?
DO YOU TRULY THINK GUESTS WITH SUCH DISTINGUISHED PALATES WILL FLOCK TO AN *UNKNOWN BRAND* OF BEEF?
UH-HUH. OKAY. BUT WHAT ABOUT, Y'KNOW, ALL THE *SCHOOL STUDENTS* HERE?!
WHAT?

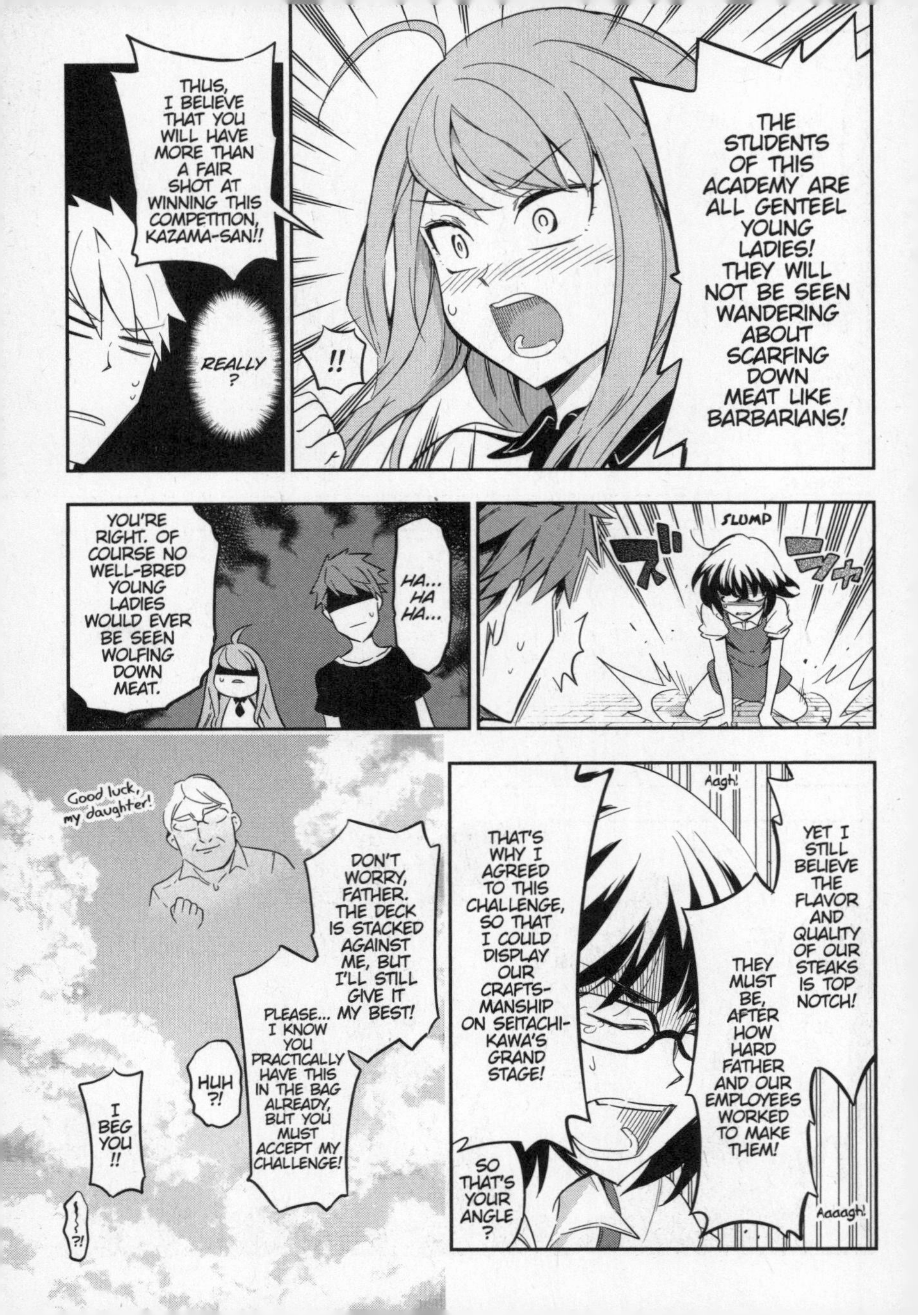
THE STUDENTS OF THIS ACADEMY ARE ALL GENTEEL YOUNG LADIES! THEY WILL NOT BE SEEN WANDERING ABOUT SCARFING DOWN MEAT LIKE BARBARIANS!
!!
THUS, I BELIEVE THAT YOU WILL HAVE MORE THAN A FAIR SHOT AT WINNING THIS COMPETITION, KAZAMA-SAN!!
REALLY?
SLUMP
YOU'RE RIGHT. OF COURSE NO WELL-BRED YOUNG LADIES WOULD EVER BE SEEN WOLFING DOWN MEAT.
HA... HA HA...
Aagh!
YET I STILL BELIEVE THE FLAVOR AND QUALITY OF OUR STEAKS IS TOP NOTCH!
THEY MUST BE, AFTER HOW HARD FATHER AND OUR EMPLOYEES WORKED TO MAKE THEM!
THAT'S WHY I AGREED TO THIS CHALLENGE, SO THAT I COULD DISPLAY OUR CRAFTSMANSHIP ON SEITACHIKAWA'S GRAND STAGE!
Aaaagh!
SO THAT'S YOUR ANGLE?
Good luck, my daughter!
DON'T WORRY, FATHER. THE DECK IS STACKED AGAINST ME, BUT I'LL STILL GIVE IT MY BEST!
PLEASE... I KNOW YOU PRACTICALLY HAVE THIS IN THE BAG ALREADY, BUT YOU MUST ACCEPT MY CHALLENGE!
HUH?!
I BEG YOU!!
......?!

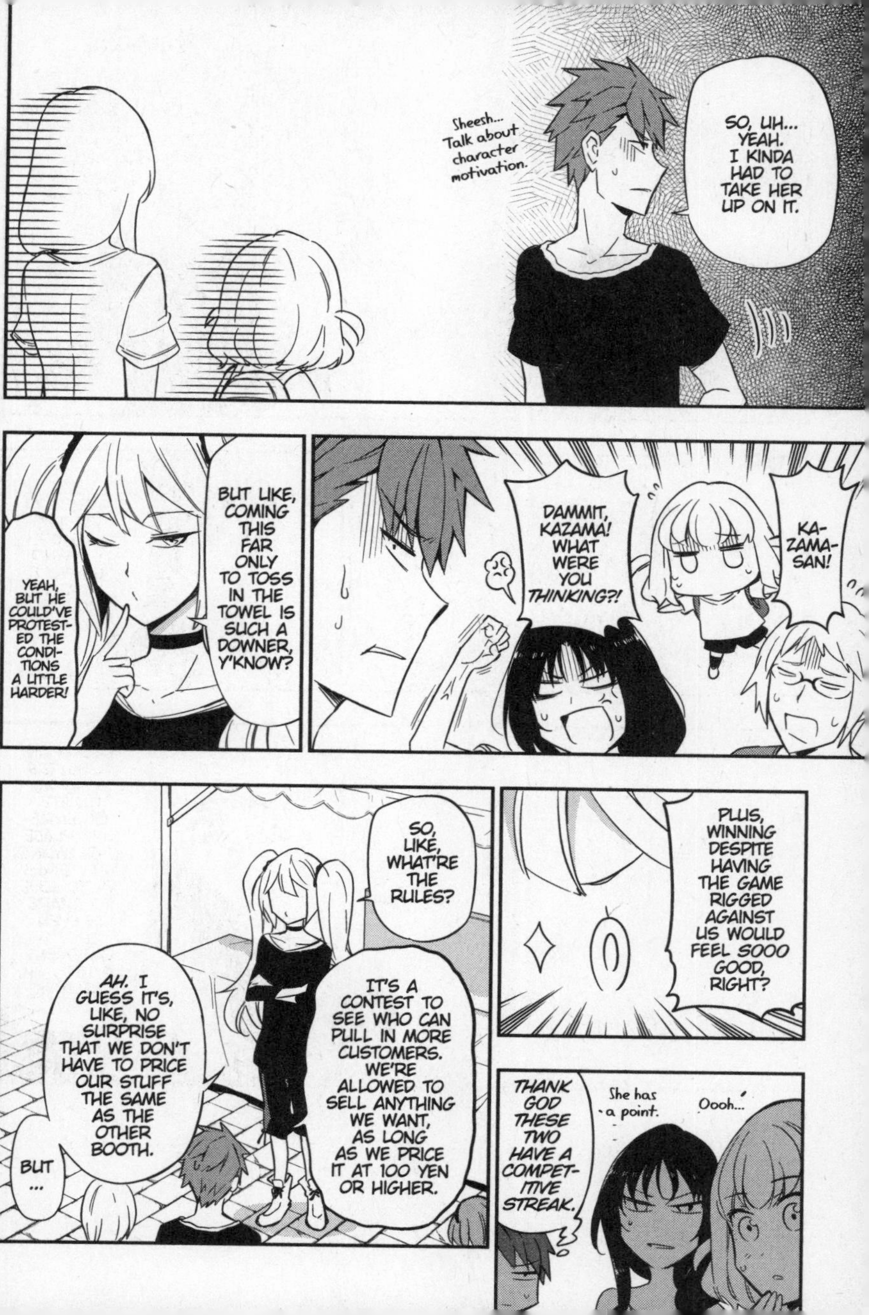
SO, UH... YEAH. I KINDA HAD TO TAKE HER UP ON IT.
Sheesh... Talk about character motivation.
KA-ZAMA-SAN!
DAMMIT, KAZAMA! WHAT WERE YOU *THINKING?!*
BUT LIKE, COMING THIS FAR ONLY TO TOSS IN THE TOWEL IS SUCH A DOWNER, Y'KNOW?
YEAH, BUT HE COULD'VE PROTEST-ED THE CONDI-TIONS A LITTLE HARDER!
PLUS, WINNING DESPITE HAVING THE GAME RIGGED AGAINST US WOULD FEEL SOOO GOOD, RIGHT?
Oooh...
She has a point.
THANK GOD THESE TWO HAVE A COMPET-ITIVE STREAK.
SO, LIKE, WHAT'RE THE RULES?
IT'S A CONTEST TO SEE WHO CAN PULL IN MORE CUSTOMERS. WE'RE ALLOWED TO SELL ANYTHING WE WANT, AS LONG AS WE PRICE IT AT 100 YEN OR HIGHER.
AH. I GUESS IT'S, LIKE, NO SURPRISE THAT WE DON'T HAVE TO PRICE OUR STUFF THE SAME AS THE OTHER BOOTH.
BUT ...

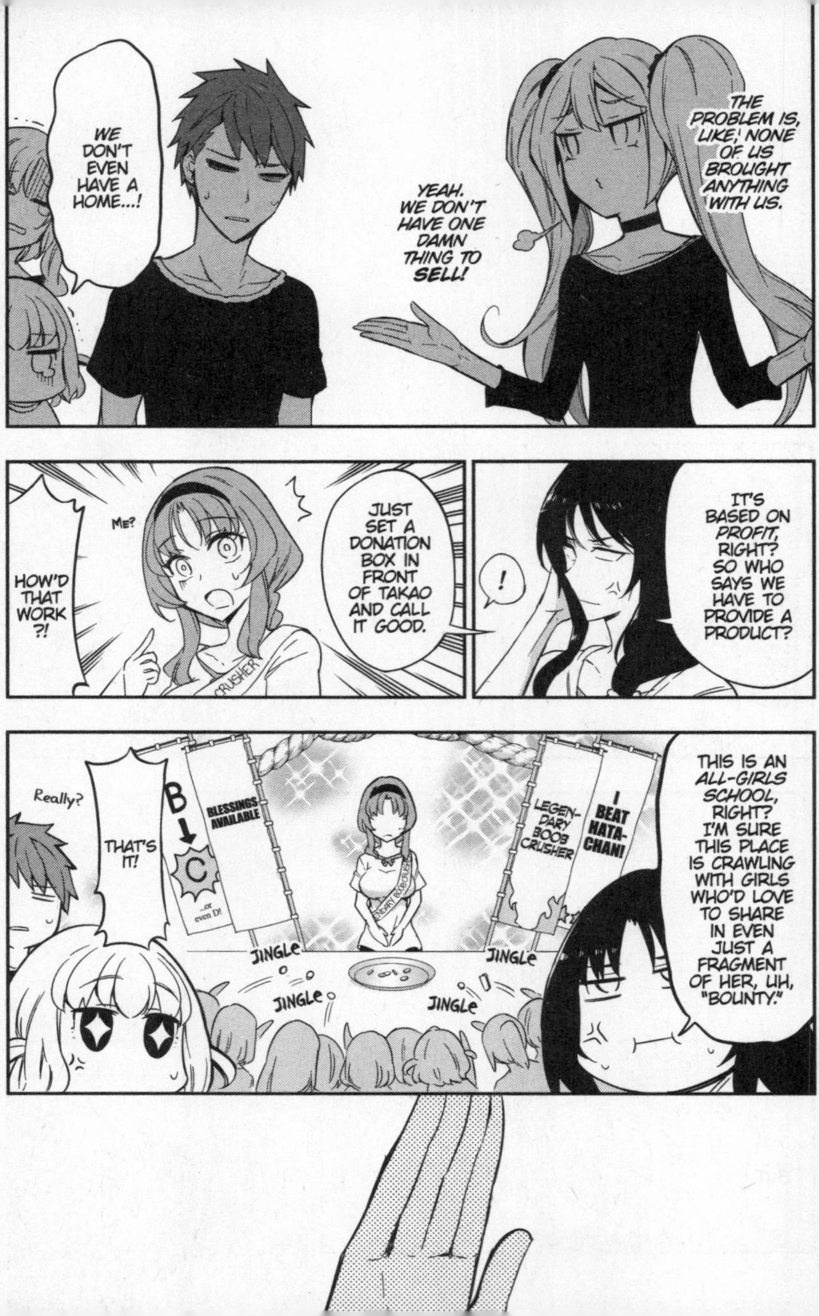
THE PROBLEM IS, LIKE, NONE OF US BROUGHT ANYTHING WITH US.
YEAH. WE DON'T HAVE ONE DAMN THING TO SELL!
WE DON'T EVEN HAVE A HOME...!
IT'S BASED ON PROFIT, RIGHT? SO WHO SAYS WE HAVE TO PROVIDE A PRODUCT?
!
JUST SET A DONATION BOX IN FRONT OF TAKAO AND CALL IT GOOD.
Me?
HOW'D THAT WORK?!
CRUSHER
THIS IS AN ALL-GIRLS SCHOOL, RIGHT? I'M SURE THIS PLACE IS CRAWLING WITH GIRLS WHO'D LOVE TO SHARE IN EVEN JUST A FRAGMENT OF HER, UH, "BOUNTY."
I BEAT HATA-CHAN!
LEGENDARY BOOB CRUSHER
BLESSINGS AVAILABLE
B
C
...or even D!
THAT'S IT!
Really?
JINGLE
JINGLE
JINGLE
JINGLE

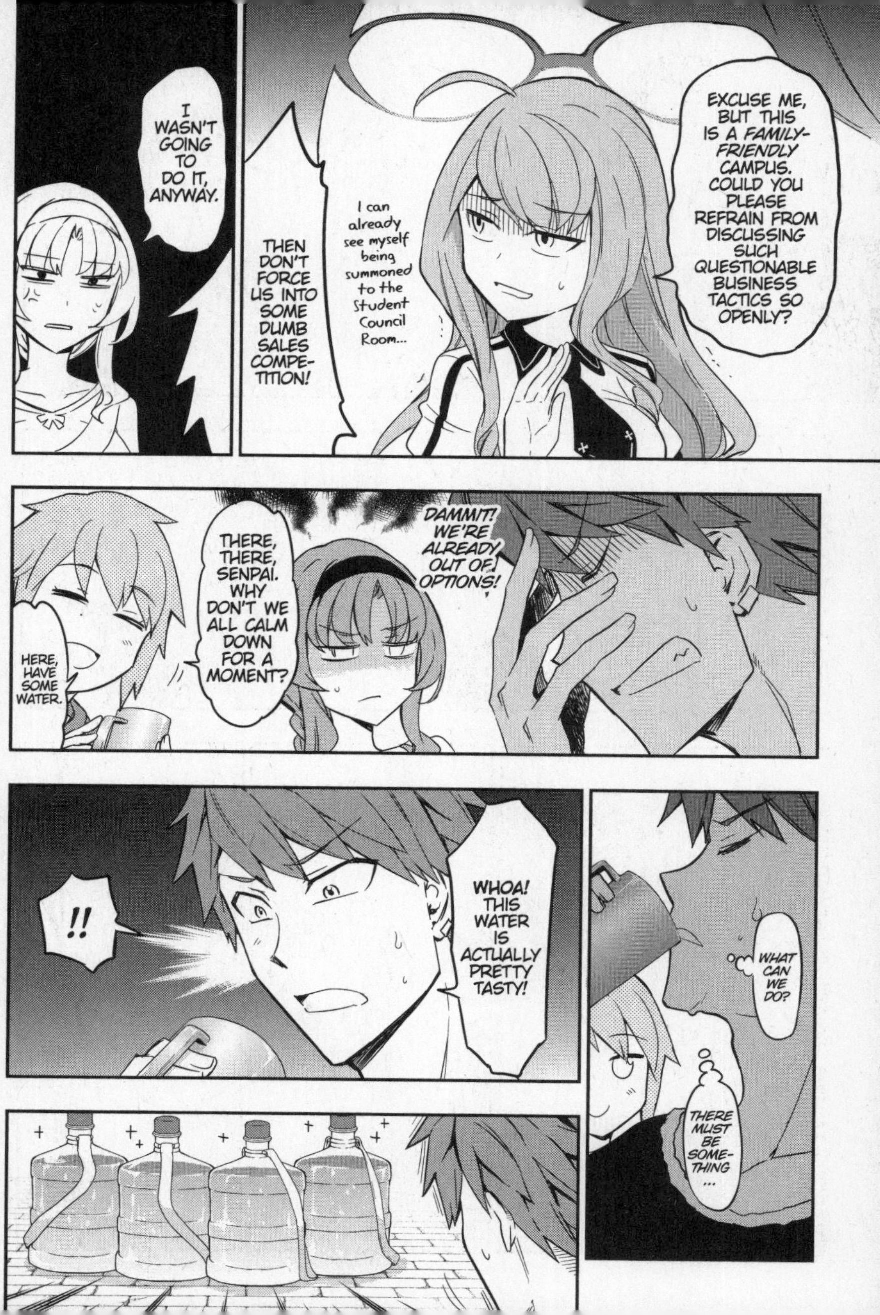
EXCUSE ME, BUT THIS IS A *FAMILY-FRIENDLY* CAMPUS. COULD YOU PLEASE REFRAIN FROM DISCUSSING SUCH QUESTIONABLE BUSINESS TACTICS SO OPENLY?
I can already see myself being summoned to the Student Council Room...
THEN DON'T FORCE US INTO SOME DUMB SALES COMPETITION!
I WASN'T GOING TO DO IT, ANYWAY.
DAMMIT! WE'RE ALREADY OUT OF OPTIONS!
THERE, THERE, SENPAI. WHY DON'T WE ALL CALM DOWN FOR A MOMENT?
HERE, HAVE SOME WATER.
WHAT CAN WE DO?
THERE MUST BE SOME-THING...
WHOA! THIS WATER IS ACTUALLY PRETTY TASTY!
!!

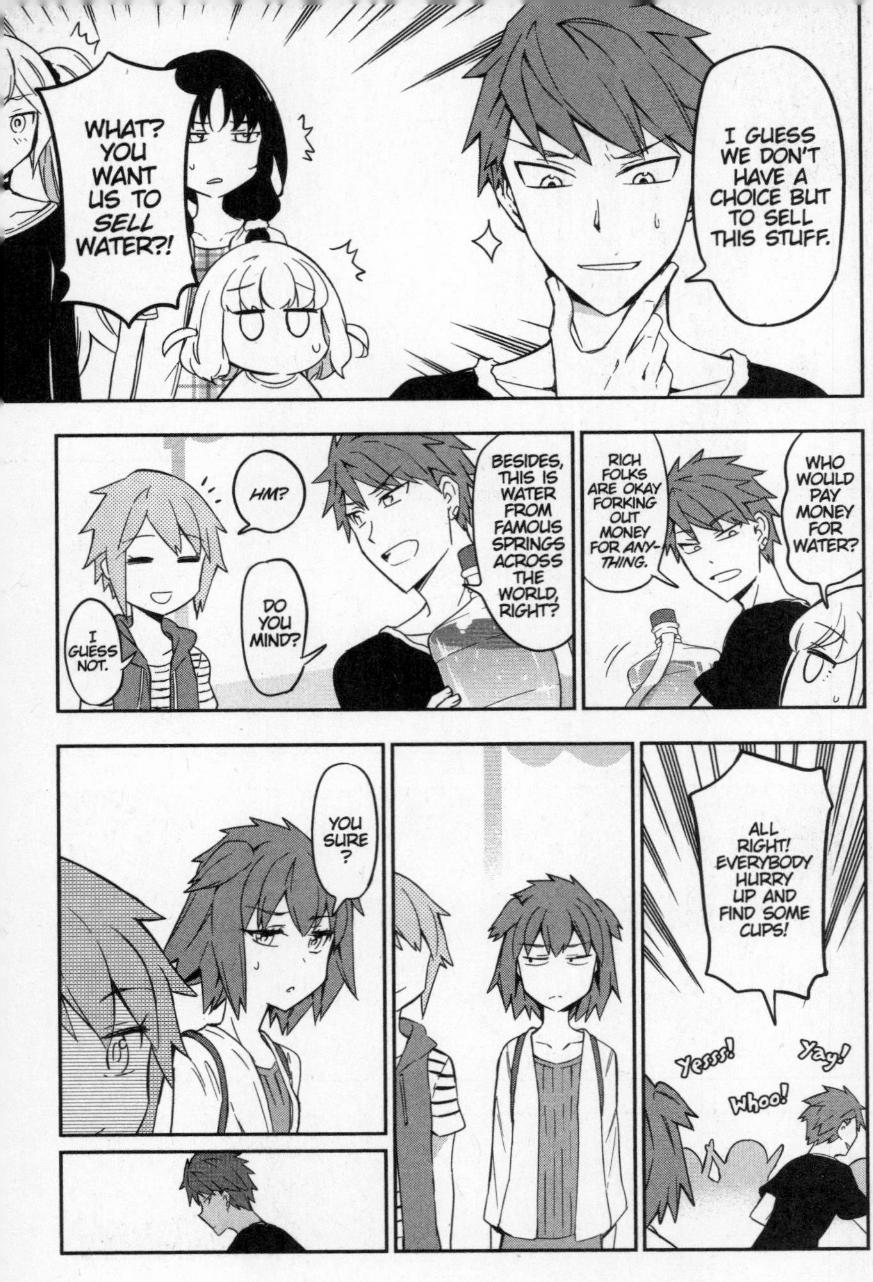
I GUESS WE DON'T HAVE A CHOICE BUT TO SELL THIS STUFF.
WHAT? YOU WANT US TO SELL WATER?!
WHO WOULD PAY MONEY FOR WATER?
RICH FOLKS ARE OKAY FORKING OUT MONEY FOR ANY-THING.
BESIDES, THIS IS WATER FROM FAMOUS SPRINGS ACROSS THE WORLD, RIGHT?
HM?
DO YOU MIND?
I GUESS NOT.
ALL RIGHT! EVERYBODY HURRY UP AND FIND SOME CUPS!
Yay!
Yesss!
Whoo!
YOU SURE?

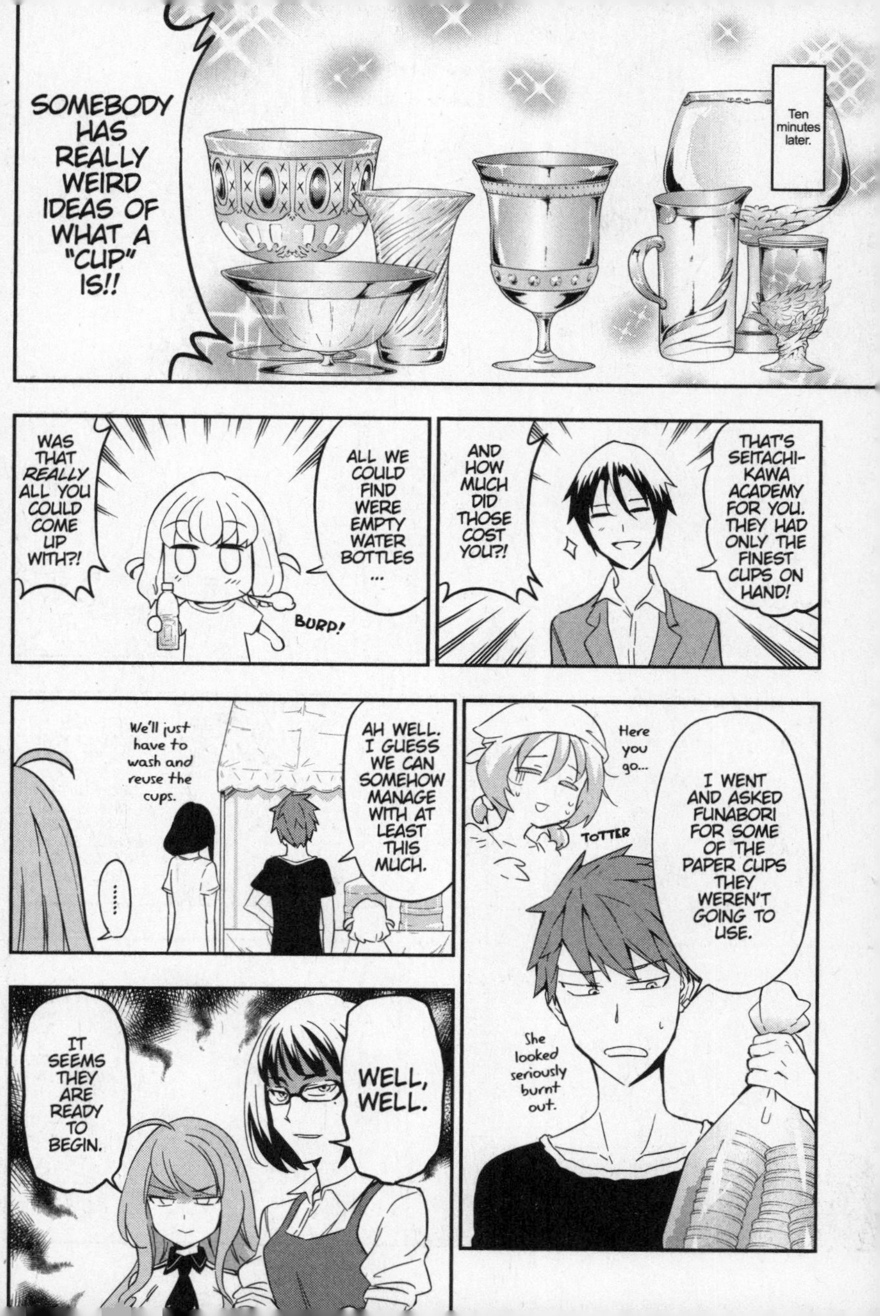
Ten minutes later.
SOMEBODY HAS REALLY WEIRD IDEAS OF WHAT A "CUP" IS!!
THAT'S SEITACHIKAWA ACADEMY FOR YOU. THEY HAD ONLY THE FINEST CUPS ON HAND!
AND HOW MUCH DID THOSE COST YOU?!
ALL WE COULD FIND WERE EMPTY WATER BOTTLES...
BURP!
WAS THAT REALLY ALL YOU COULD COME UP WITH?!
Here you go...
I WENT AND ASKED FUNABORI FOR SOME OF THE PAPER CUPS THEY WEREN'T GOING TO USE.
TOTTER
She looked seriously burnt out.
AH WELL. I GUESS WE CAN SOMEHOW MANAGE WITH AT LEAST THIS MUCH.
We'll just have to wash and reuse the cups.
......
WELL, WELL.
IT SEEMS THEY ARE READY TO BEGIN.

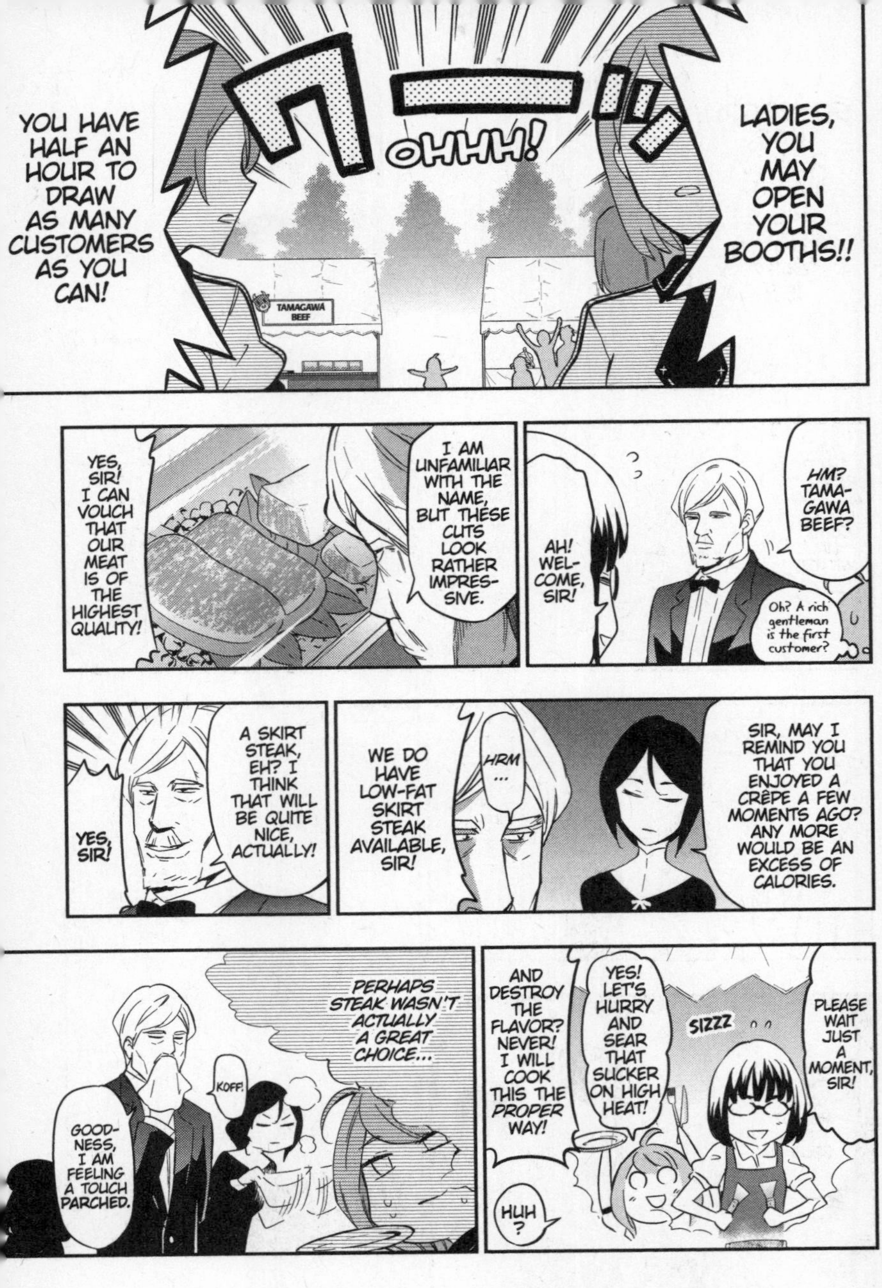
LADIES, YOU MAY OPEN YOUR BOOTHS!!
OHHHH!
YOU HAVE HALF AN HOUR TO DRAW AS MANY CUSTOMERS AS YOU CAN!
TAMAGAWA BEEF
HM? TAMAGAWA BEEF?
Oh? A rich gentleman is the first customer?
AH! WELCOME, SIR!
I AM UNFAMILIAR WITH THE NAME, BUT THESE CUTS LOOK RATHER IMPRESSIVE.
YES, SIR! I CAN VOUCH THAT OUR MEAT IS OF THE HIGHEST QUALITY!
SIR, MAY I REMIND YOU THAT YOU ENJOYED A CRÊPE A FEW MOMENTS AGO? ANY MORE WOULD BE AN EXCESS OF CALORIES.
HRM...
WE DO HAVE LOW-FAT SKIRT STEAK AVAILABLE, SIR!
A SKIRT STEAK, EH? I THINK THAT WILL BE QUITE NICE, ACTUALLY!
YES, SIR!
PLEASE WAIT JUST A MOMENT, SIR!
SIZZZ
YES! LET'S HURRY AND SEAR THAT SUCKER ON HIGH HEAT!
AND DESTROY THE FLAVOR? NEVER! I WILL COOK THIS THE PROPER WAY!
HUH?
PERHAPS STEAK WASN'T ACTUALLY A GREAT CHOICE...
KOFF!
GOODNESS, I AM FEELING A TOUCH PARCHED.

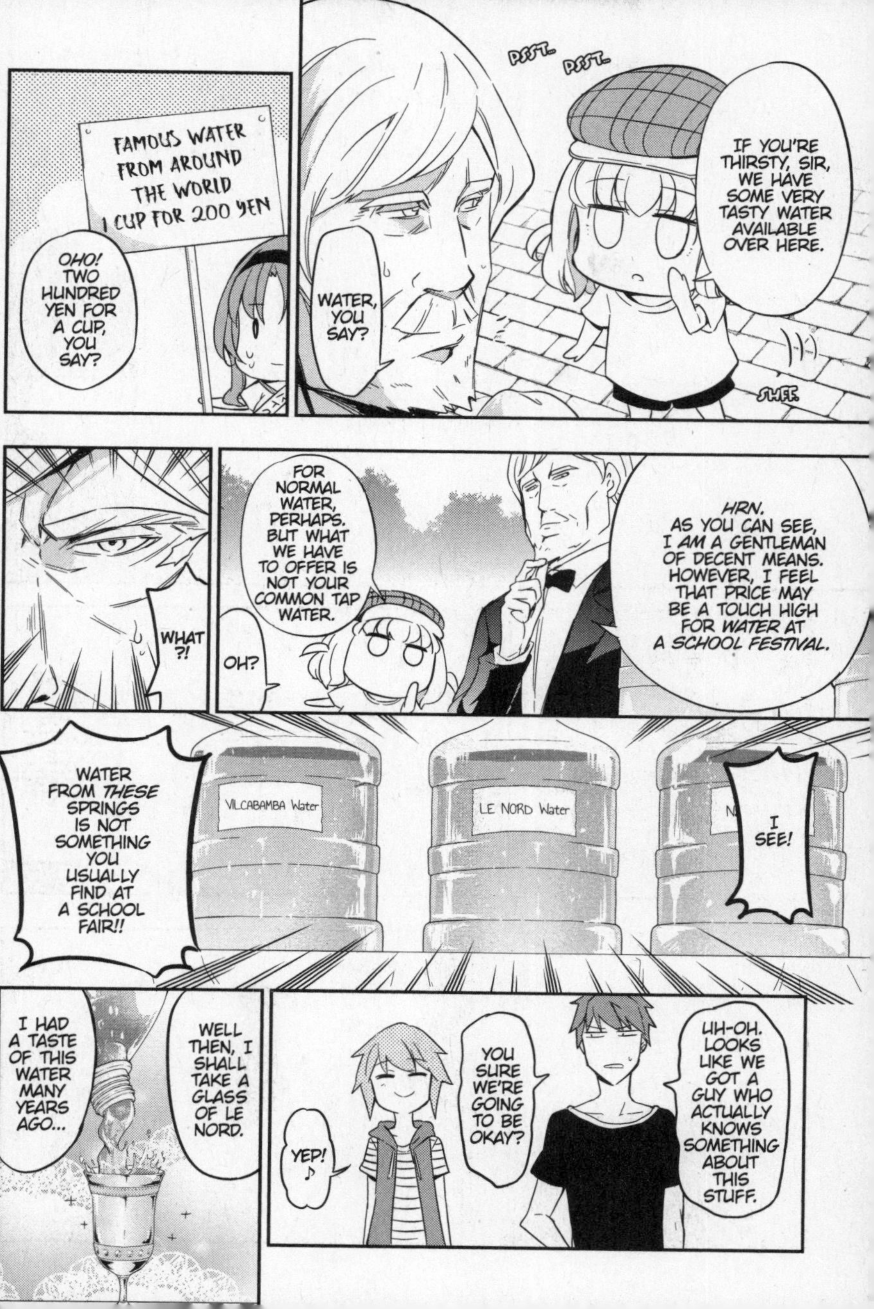
PSST... PSST...
IF YOU'RE THIRSTY, SIR, WE HAVE SOME VERY TASTY WATER AVAILABLE OVER HERE.
WATER, YOU SAY?
SHUFF.
FAMOUS WATER FROM AROUND THE WORLD 1 CUP FOR 200 YEN
OHO! TWO HUNDRED YEN FOR A CUP, YOU SAY?
HRN. AS YOU CAN SEE, I AM A GENTLEMAN OF DECENT MEANS. HOWEVER, I FEEL THAT PRICE MAY BE A TOUCH HIGH FOR WATER AT A SCHOOL FESTIVAL.
FOR NORMAL WATER, PERHAPS. BUT WHAT WE HAVE TO OFFER IS NOT YOUR COMMON TAP WATER.
OH?
WHAT?!
I SEE!
LE NORD Water
VILCABAMBA Water
WATER FROM THESE SPRINGS IS NOT SOMETHING YOU USUALLY FIND AT A SCHOOL FAIR!!
UH-OH. LOOKS LIKE WE GOT A GUY WHO ACTUALLY KNOWS SOMETHING ABOUT THIS STUFF.
YOU SURE WE'RE GOING TO BE OKAY?
YEP! ♪
WELL THEN, I SHALL TAKE A GLASS OF LE NORD.
I HAD A TASTE OF THIS WATER MANY YEARS AGO...

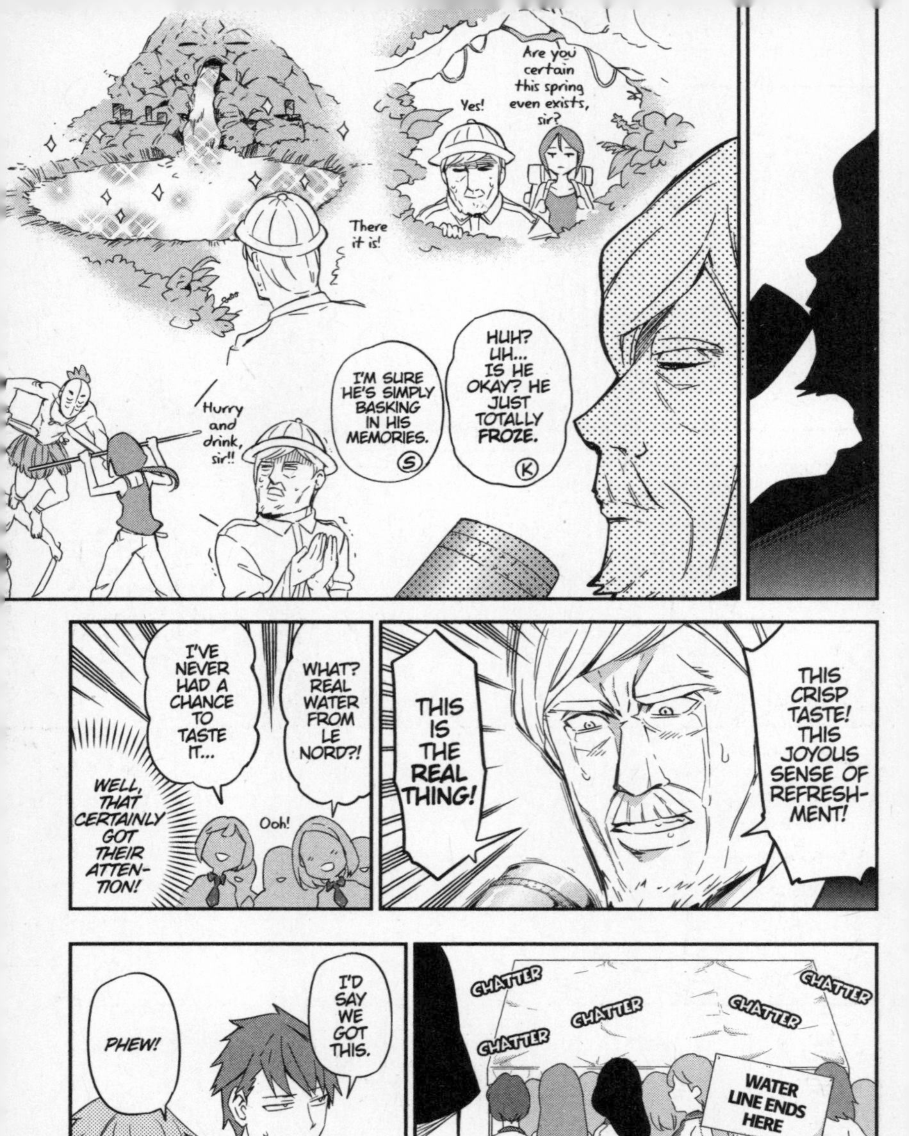

Are you certain this spring even exists, sir?
Yes!
There it is!
HUH? UH... IS HE OKAY? HE JUST TOTALLY FROZE. (K)
I'M SURE HE'S SIMPLY BASKING IN HIS MEMORIES. (S)
Hurry and drink, sir!!
THIS CRISP TASTE! THIS JOYOUS SENSE OF REFRESHMENT!
THIS IS THE REAL THING!
WHAT? REAL WATER FROM LE NORD?!
I'VE NEVER HAD A CHANCE TO TASTE IT...
Ooh!
WELL, THAT CERTAINLY GOT THEIR ATTENTION!
CHATTER
CHATTER
CHATTER
CHATTER
WATER LINE ENDS HERE
I'D SAY WE GOT THIS.
PHEW!

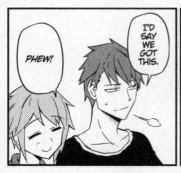

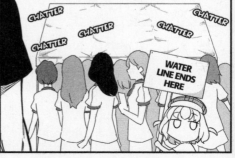

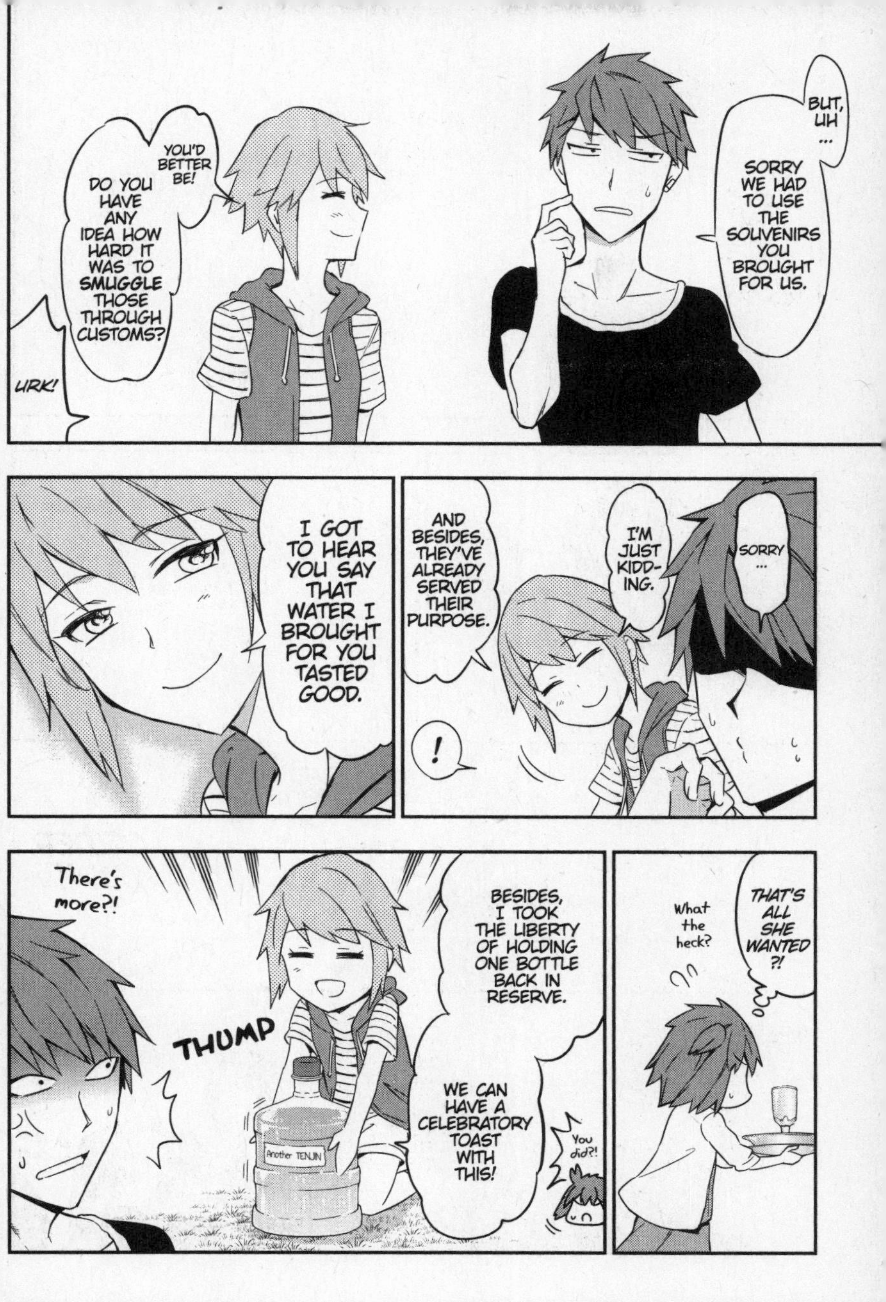
BUT, UH ...
SORRY WE HAD TO USE THE SOUVENIRS YOU BROUGHT FOR US.
YOU'D BETTER BE!
DO YOU HAVE ANY IDEA HOW HARD IT WAS TO SMUGGLE THOSE THROUGH CUSTOMS?
URK!
SORRY ...
I'M JUST KIDD-ING.
AND BESIDES, THEY'VE ALREADY SERVED THEIR PURPOSE.
!
I GOT TO HEAR YOU SAY THAT WATER I BROUGHT FOR YOU TASTED GOOD.
THAT'S ALL SHE WANTED?!
What the heck?
BESIDES, I TOOK THE LIBERTY OF HOLDING ONE BOTTLE BACK IN RESERVE.
THUMP
There's more?!
Another TENJIN
WE CAN HAVE A CELEBRATORY TOAST WITH THIS!
You did?!

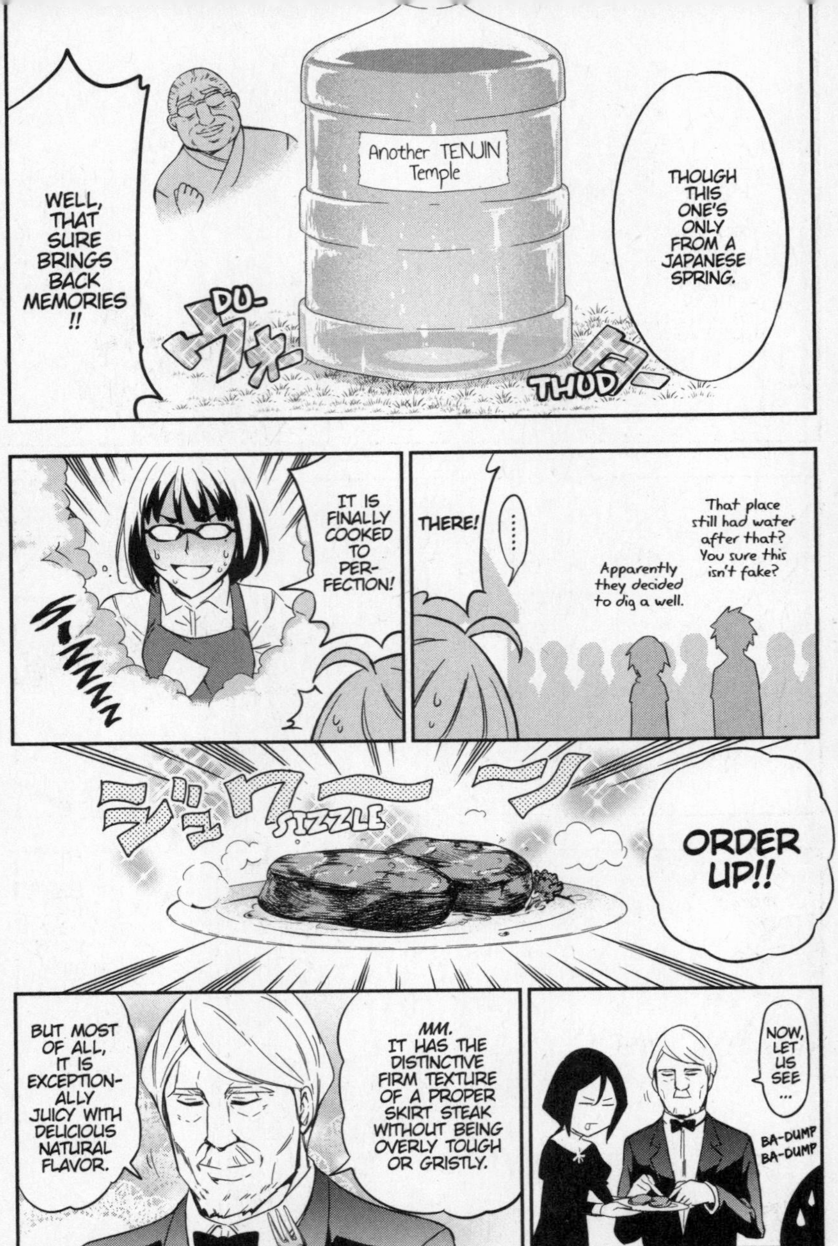
THOUGH THIS ONE'S ONLY FROM A JAPANESE SPRING.
Another TENJIN Temple
THUD
DU-
WELL, THAT SURE BRINGS BACK MEMORIES!!
That place still had water after that? You sure this isn't fake?
Apparently they decided to dig a well.
......
THERE!
IT IS FINALLY COOKED TO PERFECTION!
ORDER UP!!
SIZZLE
NOW, LET US SEE ...
BA-DUMP BA-DUMP
MM. IT HAS THE DISTINCTIVE FIRM TEXTURE OF A PROPER SKIRT STEAK WITHOUT BEING OVERLY TOUGH OR GRISTLY.
BUT MOST OF ALL, IT IS EXCEPTIONALLY JUICY WITH DELICIOUS NATURAL FLAVOR.

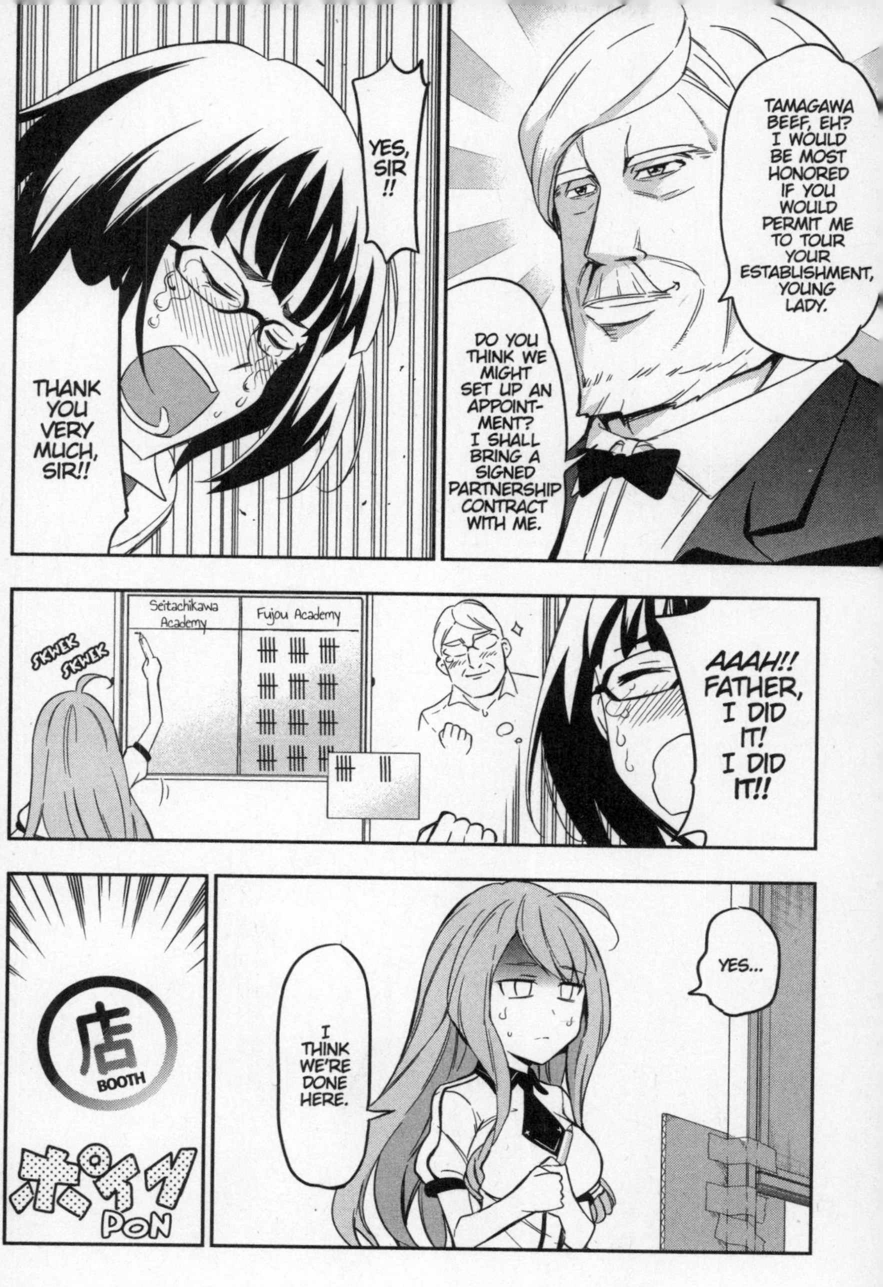
TAMAGAWA BEEF, EH? I WOULD BE MOST HONORED IF YOU WOULD PERMIT ME TO TOUR YOUR ESTABLISHMENT, YOUNG LADY.
DO YOU THINK WE MIGHT SET UP AN APPOINT-MENT? I SHALL BRING A SIGNED PARTNERSHIP CONTRACT WITH ME.
YES, SIR!!
THANK YOU VERY MUCH, SIR!!
AAAH!! FATHER, I DID IT! I DID IT!!
Seitachikawa Academy
Fujou Academy
SKWEK SKWEK
YES...
I THINK WE'RE DONE HERE.
店
BOOTH
ポイッ
PON

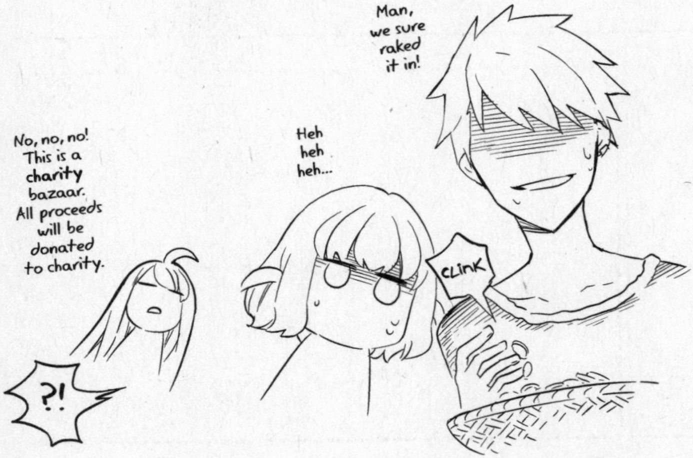
Man, we sure raked it in!
CLINK
Heh heh heh...
No, no, no! This is a charity bazaar. All proceeds will be donated to charity.
?!

D-FRAGMENTS ディーふらぐメンツ!

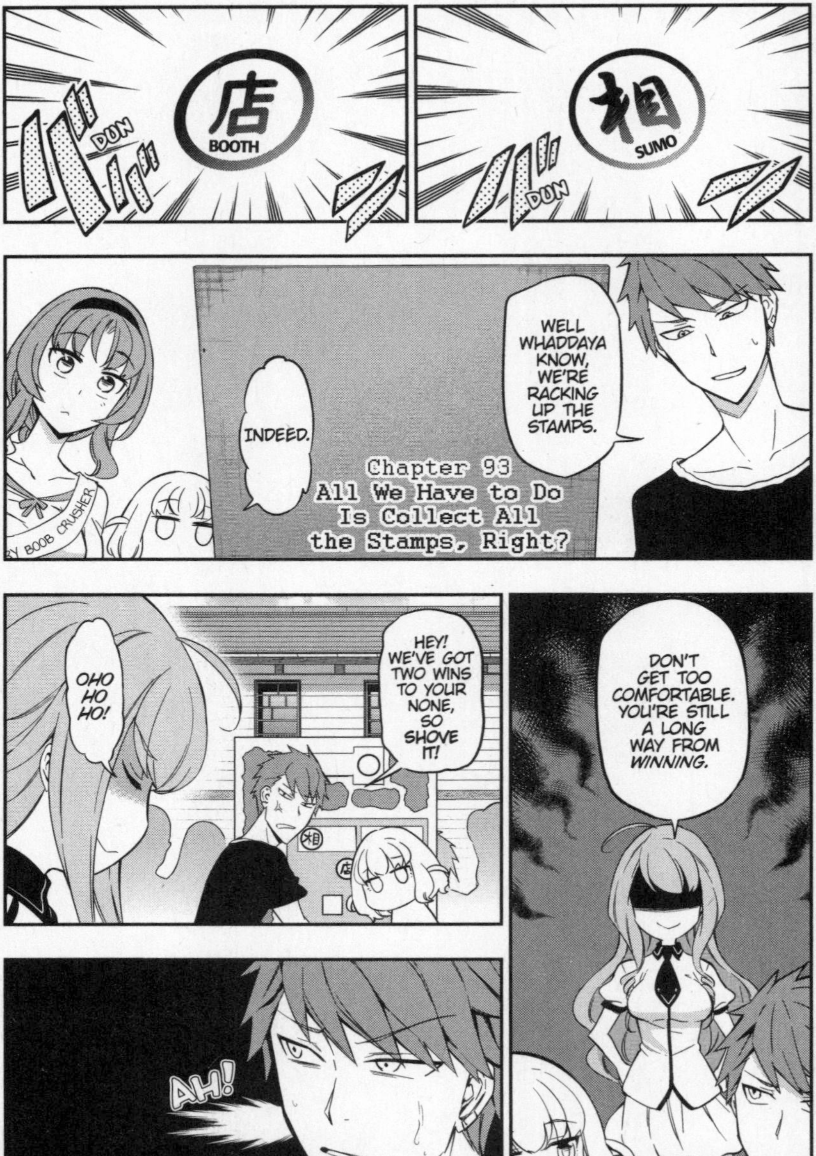
相
SUMO
DUN
店
BOOTH
DUN
WELL WHADDAYA KNOW, WE'RE RACKING UP THE STAMPS.
Chapter 93 All We Have to Do Is Collect All the Stamps, Right?
INDEED.
RY BOOB CRUSHER
DON'T GET TOO COMFORTABLE. YOU'RE STILL A LONG WAY FROM WINNING.
HEY! WE'VE GOT TWO WINS TO YOUR NONE, SO SHOVE IT!
OHO HO HO!
AH!

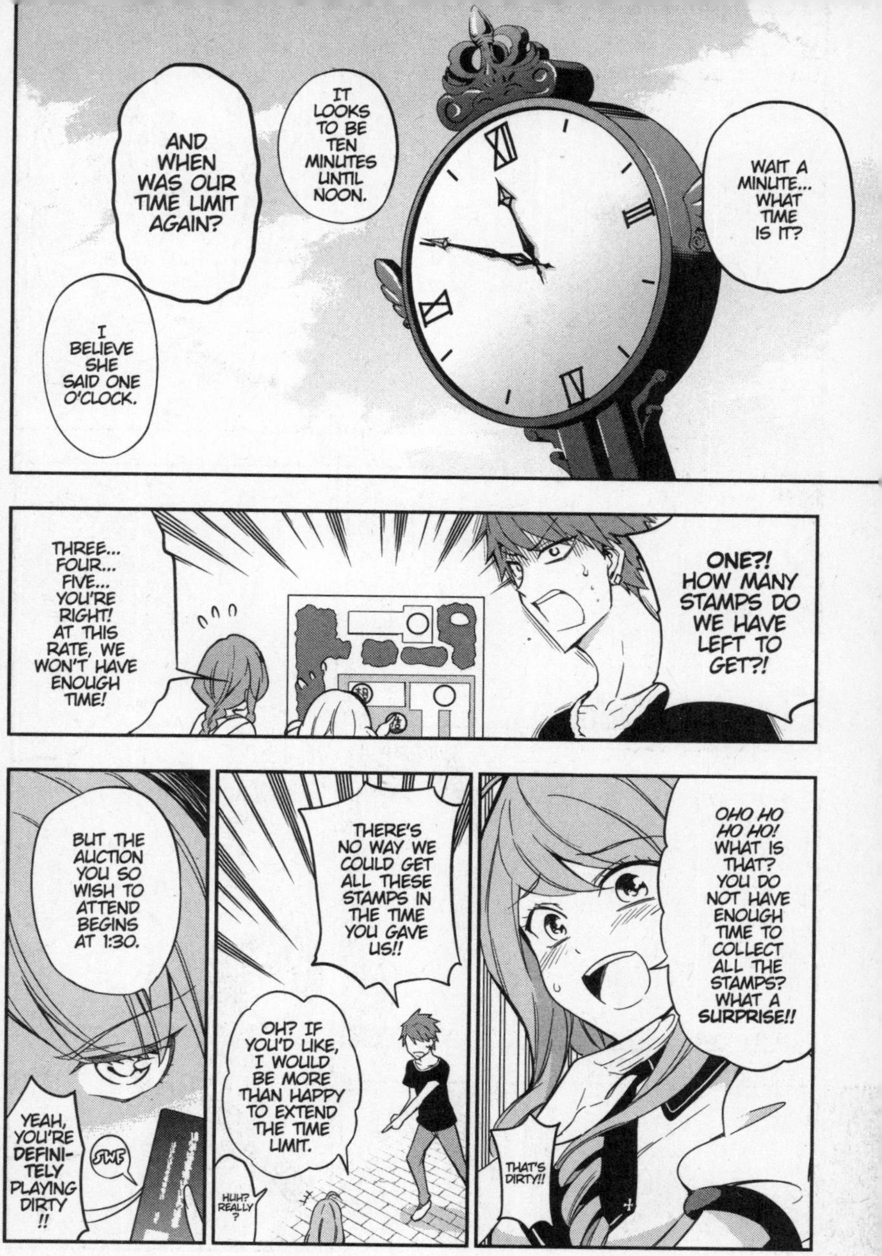
WAIT A MINUTE... WHAT TIME IS IT?
IT LOOKS TO BE TEN MINUTES UNTIL NOON.
AND WHEN WAS OUR TIME LIMIT AGAIN?
I BELIEVE SHE SAID ONE O'CLOCK.
ONE?! HOW MANY STAMPS DO WE HAVE LEFT TO GET?!
THREE... FOUR... FIVE... YOU'RE RIGHT! AT THIS RATE, WE WON'T HAVE ENOUGH TIME!
OHO HO HO HO! WHAT IS THAT? YOU DO NOT HAVE ENOUGH TIME TO COLLECT ALL THE STAMPS? WHAT A SURPRISE!!
THAT'S DIRTY!!
THERE'S NO WAY WE COULD GET ALL THESE STAMPS IN THE TIME YOU GAVE US!!
OH? IF YOU'D LIKE, I WOULD BE MORE THAN HAPPY TO EXTEND THE TIME LIMIT.
HUH? REALLY?
BUT THE AUCTION YOU SO WISH TO ATTEND BEGINS AT 1:30.
SWF
YEAH, YOU'RE DEFINITELY PLAYING DIRTY!!

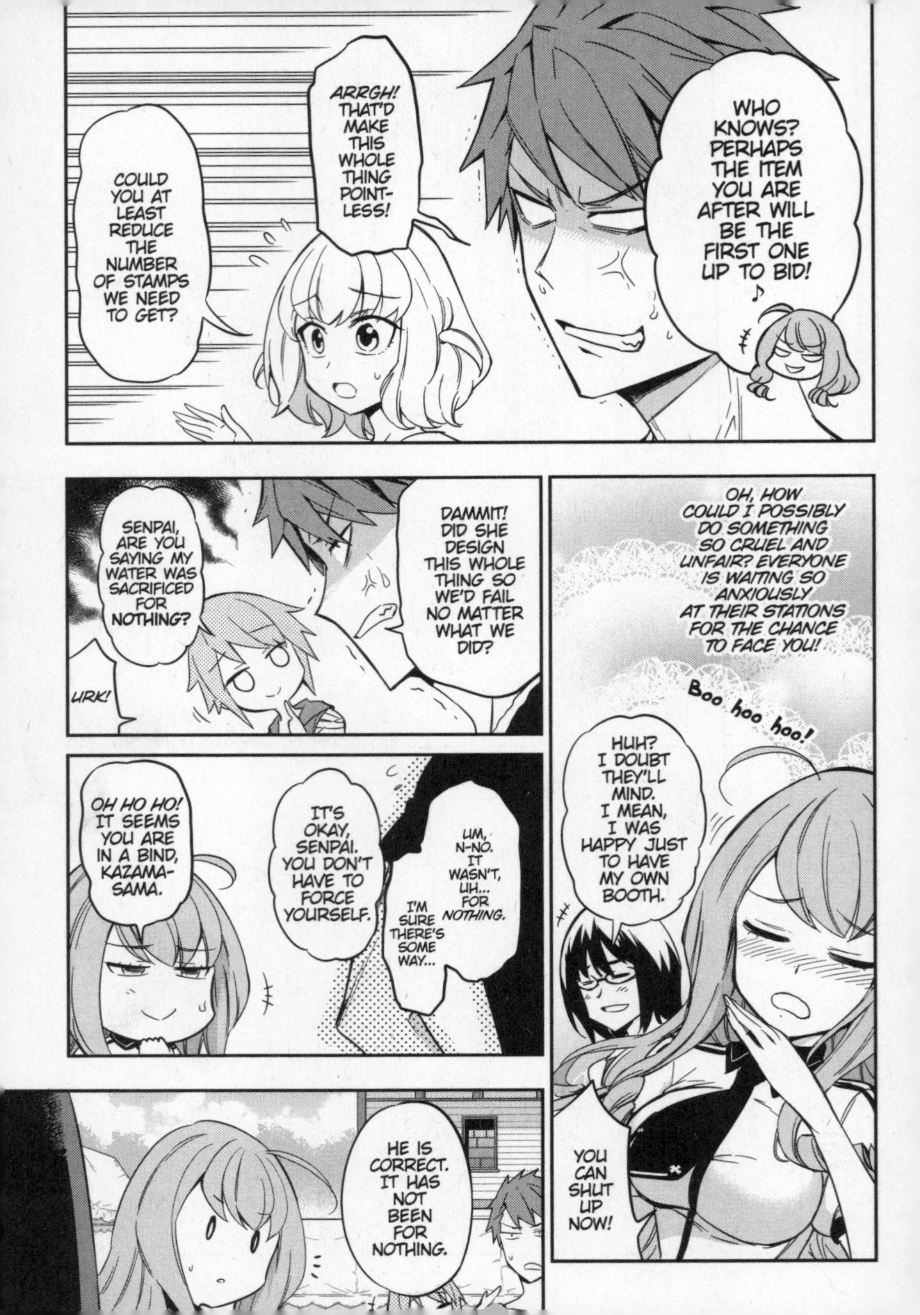
WHO KNOWS? PERHAPS THE ITEM YOU ARE AFTER WILL BE THE FIRST ONE UP TO BID! ♪
ARRGH! THAT'D MAKE THIS WHOLE THING POINT-LESS!
COULD YOU AT LEAST REDUCE THE NUMBER OF STAMPS WE NEED TO GET?
OH, HOW COULD I POSSIBLY DO SOMETHING SO CRUEL AND UNFAIR? EVERYONE IS WAITING SO ANXIOUSLY AT THEIR STATIONS FOR THE CHANCE TO FACE YOU!
Boo hoo hoo!
HUH? I DOUBT THEY'LL MIND. I MEAN, I WAS HAPPY JUST TO HAVE MY OWN BOOTH.
YOU CAN SHUT UP NOW!
DAMMIT! DID SHE DESIGN THIS WHOLE THING SO WE'D FAIL NO MATTER WHAT WE DID?
SENPAI, ARE YOU SAYING MY WATER WAS SACRIFICED FOR NOTHING?
URK!
UM, N-NO. IT WASN'T, UH... FOR NOTHING.
I'M SURE THERE'S SOME WAY...
IT'S OKAY, SENPAI. YOU DON'T HAVE TO FORCE YOURSELF.
OH HO HO! IT SEEMS YOU ARE IN A BIND, KAZAMA-SAMA.
HE IS CORRECT. IT HAS NOT BEEN FOR NOTHING.

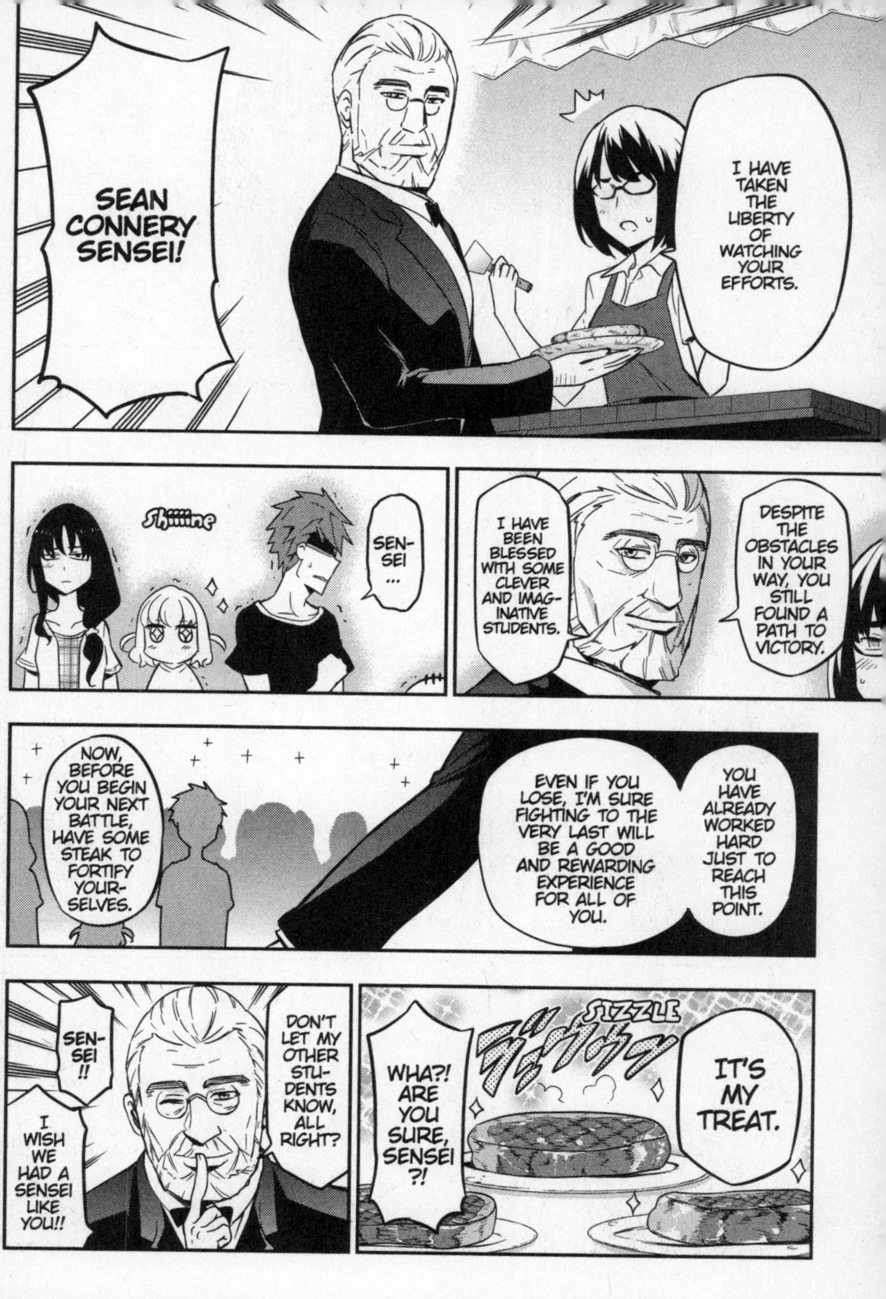
I HAVE TAKEN THE LIBERTY OF WATCHING YOUR EFFORTS.
SEAN CONNERY SENSEI!
DESPITE THE OBSTACLES IN YOUR WAY, YOU STILL FOUND A PATH TO VICTORY.
I HAVE BEEN BLESSED WITH SOME CLEVER AND IMAG-INATIVE STUDENTS.
SEN-SEI ...
Shiiiine
YOU HAVE ALREADY WORKED HARD JUST TO REACH THIS POINT.
EVEN IF YOU LOSE, I'M SURE FIGHTING TO THE VERY LAST WILL BE A GOOD AND REWARDING EXPERIENCE FOR ALL OF YOU.
NOW, BEFORE YOU BEGIN YOUR NEXT BATTLE, HAVE SOME STEAK TO FORTIFY YOUR-SELVES.
IT'S MY TREAT.
SIZZLE
WHA?! ARE YOU SURE, SENSEI?!
DON'T LET MY OTHER STU-DENTS KNOW, ALL RIGHT?
SEN-SEI!!
I WISH WE HAD A SENSEI LIKE YOU!!

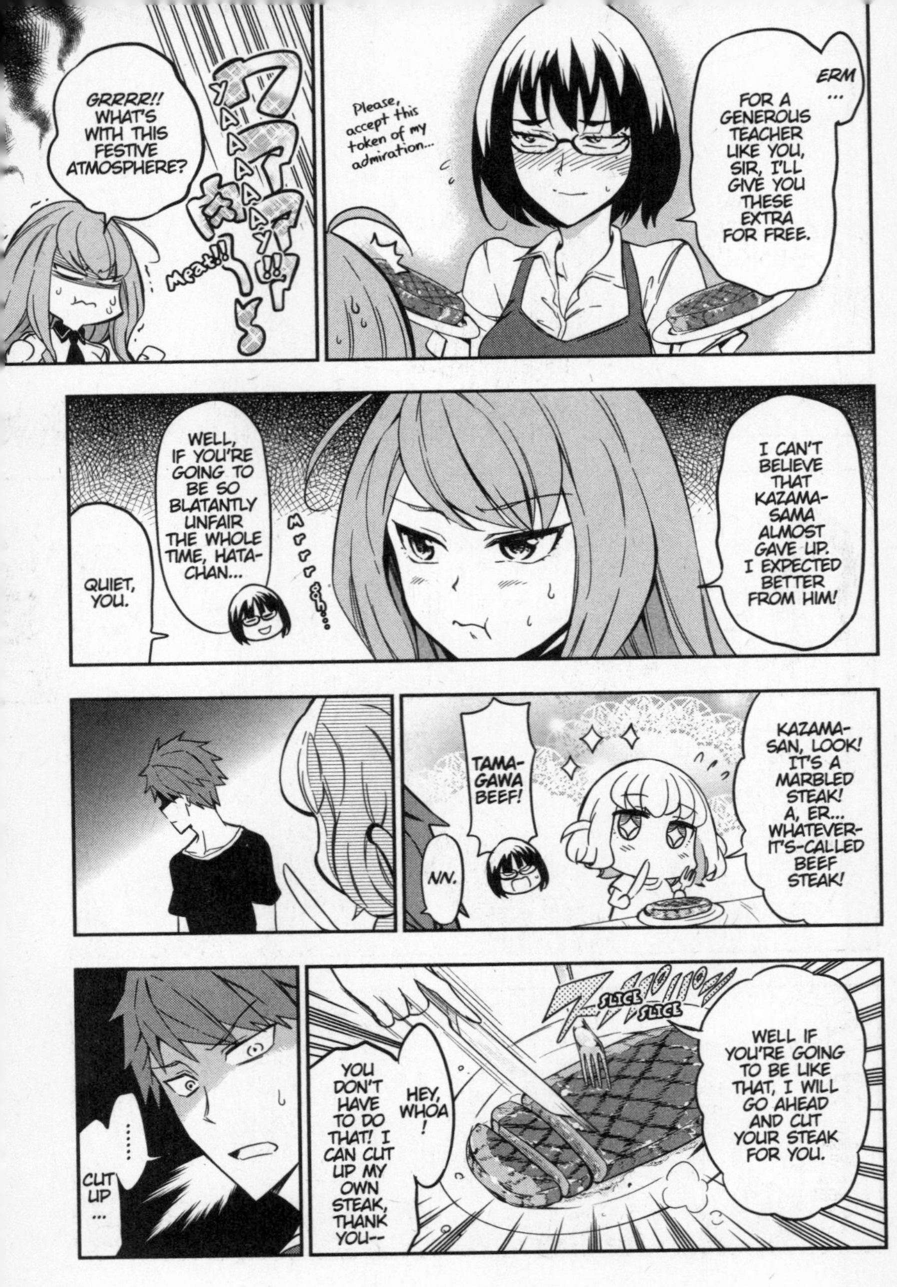
ERM ...
FOR A GENEROUS TEACHER LIKE YOU, SIR, I'LL GIVE YOU THESE EXTRA FOR FREE.
Please, accept this token of my admiration...
YAAAAAAY!!
Meat!!
GRRRR!! WHAT'S WITH THIS FESTIVE ATMOSPHERE?
I CAN'T BELIEVE THAT KAZAMA-SAMA ALMOST GAVE UP. I EXPECTED BETTER FROM HIM!
Mrrrrgh...
WELL, IF YOU'RE GOING TO BE SO BLATANTLY UNFAIR THE WHOLE TIME, HATA-CHAN...
QUIET, YOU.
KAZAMA-SAN, LOOK! IT'S A MARBLED STEAK! A, ER... WHATEVER-IT'S-CALLED BEEF STEAK!
TAMA-GAWA BEEF!
NN.
WELL IF YOU'RE GOING TO BE LIKE THAT, I WILL GO AHEAD AND CUT YOUR STEAK FOR YOU.
SLICE SLICE
HEY, WHOA!
YOU DON'T HAVE TO DO THAT! I CAN CUT UP MY OWN STEAK, THANK YOU--
......
CUT UP ...

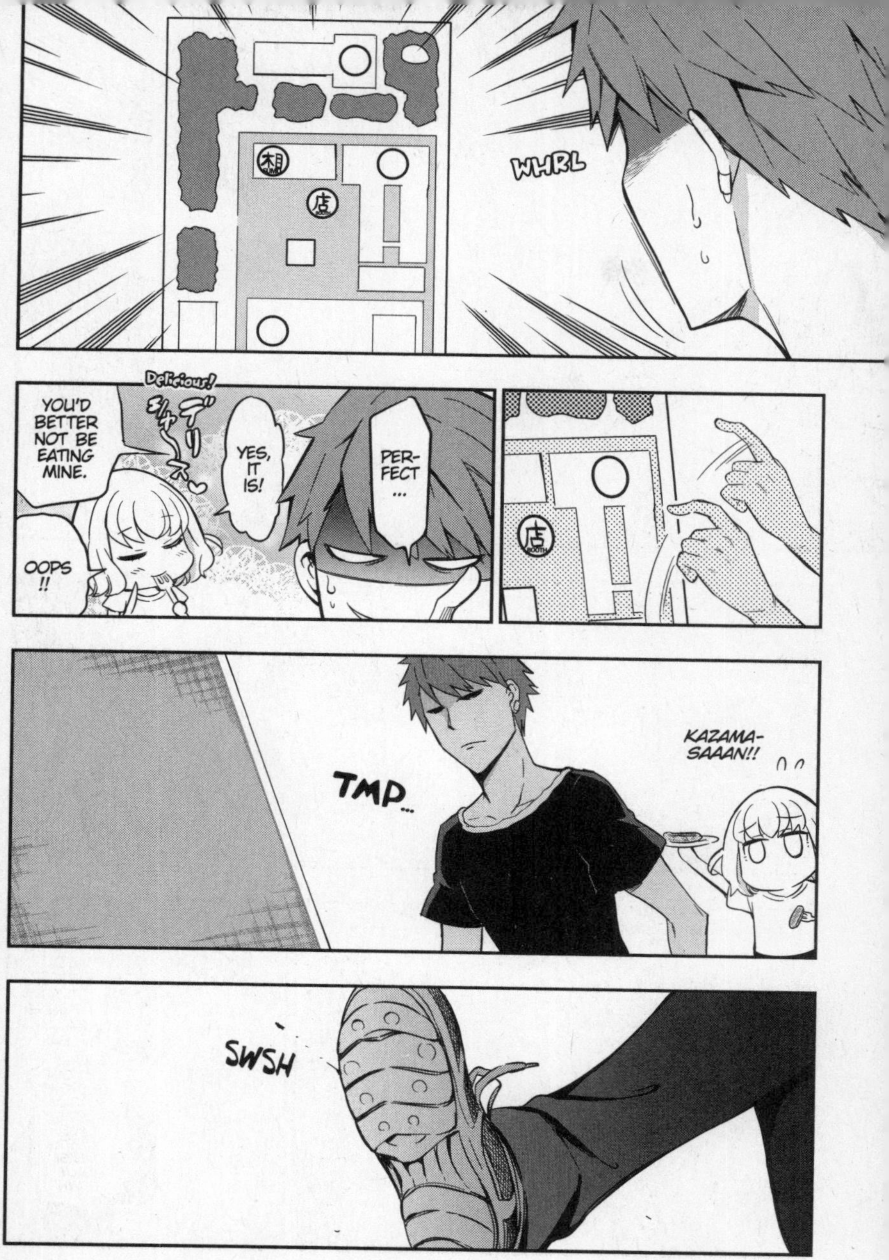
WHRL
店
BOOTH
PER-
FECT
...
YES,
IT
IS!
Delicious!
デリシャス
YOU'D
BETTER
NOT BE
EATING
MINE.
OOPS
!!
KAZAMA-
SAAAN!!
TMP...
SWSH

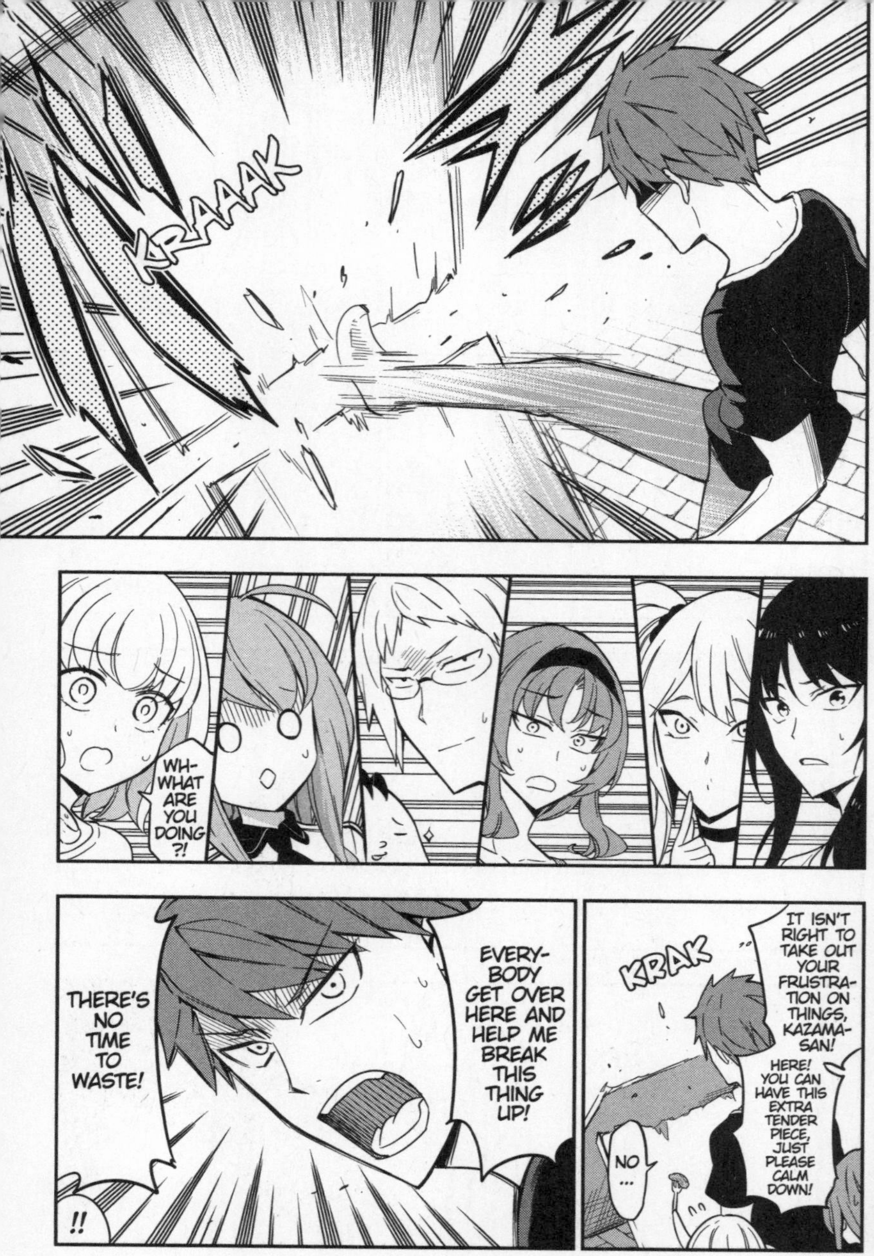
KRAAAK
WH-WHAT ARE YOU DOING?!
IT ISN'T RIGHT TO TAKE OUT YOUR FRUSTRATION ON THINGS, KAZAMA-SAN!
KRAK
HERE! YOU CAN HAVE THIS EXTRA TENDER PIECE, JUST PLEASE CALM DOWN!
NO ...
EVERYBODY GET OVER HERE AND HELP ME BREAK THIS THING UP!
THERE'S NO TIME TO WASTE!
!!

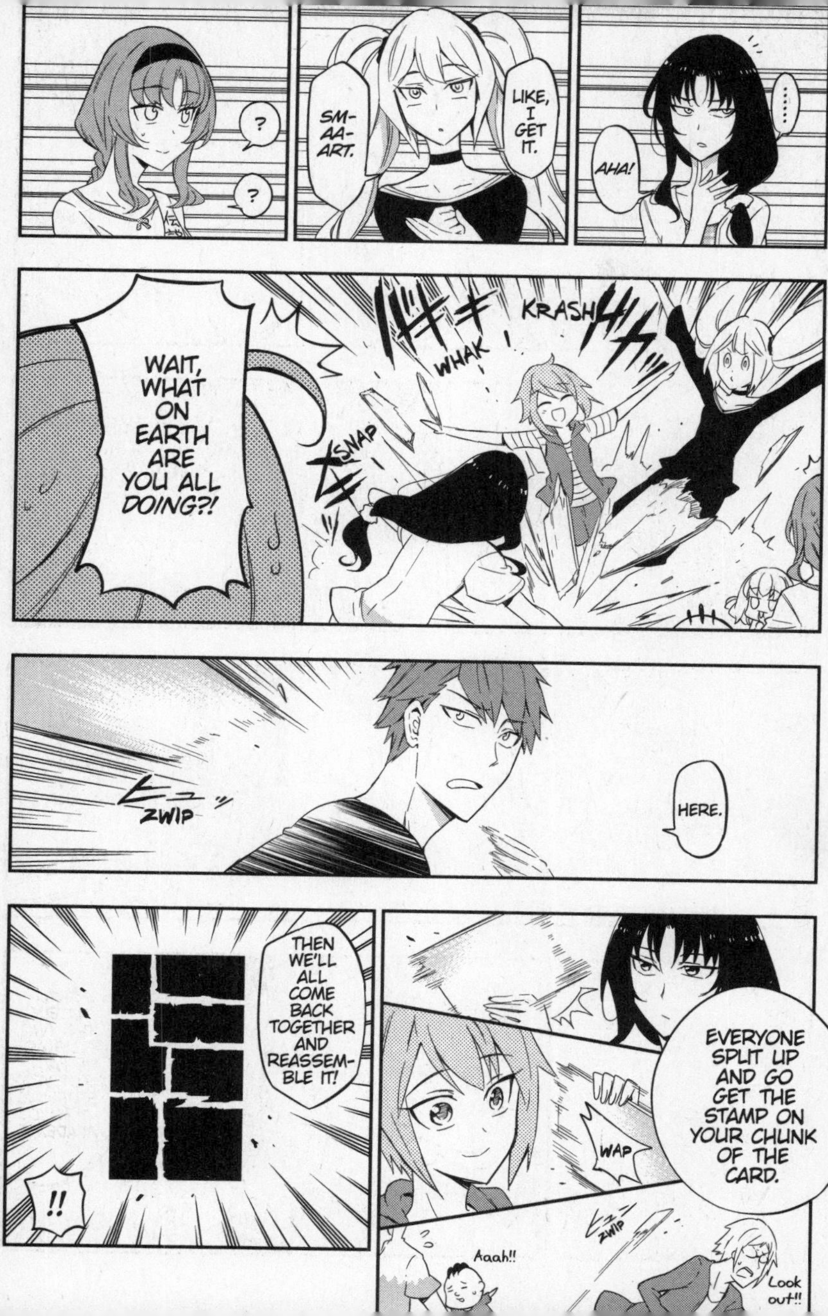
……
AHA!
LIKE, I GET IT.
SM-AA-ART.
?
?
KRASH
WHAK
SNAP
WAIT, WHAT ON EARTH ARE YOU ALL DOING?!
HERE.
ZWIP
EVERYONE SPLIT UP AND GO GET THE STAMP ON YOUR CHUNK OF THE CARD.
WAP
ZWIP
Look out!!
Aaah!!
THEN WE'LL ALL COME BACK TOGETHER AND REASSEMBLE IT!
!!

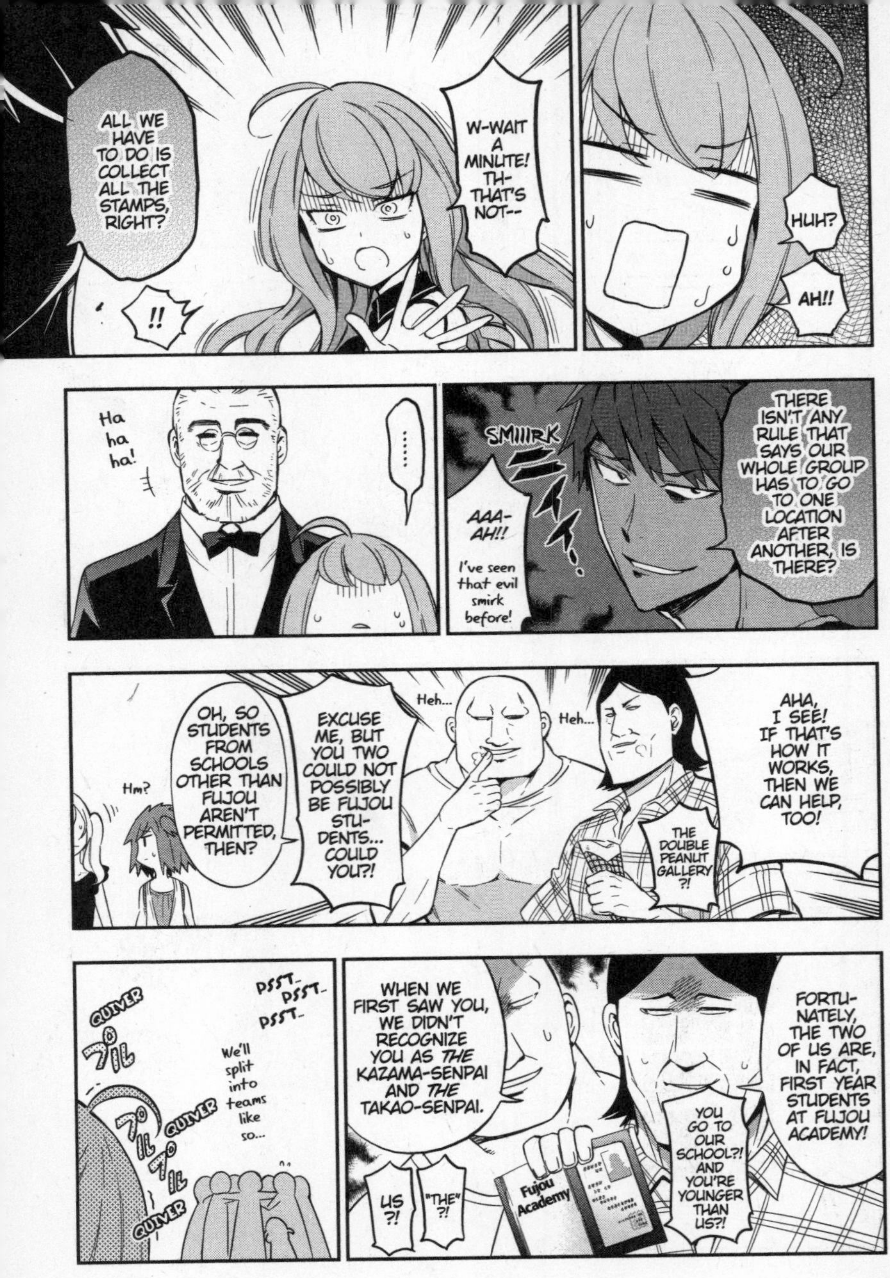
HUH?
AH!!
W-WAIT A MINUTE! TH-THAT'S NOT--
ALL WE HAVE TO DO IS COLLECT ALL THE STAMPS, RIGHT?
!!
THERE ISN'T ANY RULE THAT SAYS OUR WHOLE GROUP HAS TO GO TO ONE LOCATION AFTER ANOTHER, IS THERE?
SMIIIRK
AAA-AH!!
I've seen that evil smirk before!
......
Ha ha ha!
AHA, I SEE! IF THAT'S HOW IT WORKS, THEN WE CAN HELP, TOO!
THE DOUBLE PEANUT GALLERY?!
Heh...
Heh...
EXCUSE ME, BUT YOU TWO COULD NOT POSSIBLY BE FUJOU STU-DENTS... COULD YOU?!
OH, SO STUDENTS FROM SCHOOLS OTHER THAN FUJOU AREN'T PERMITTED, THEN?
Hm?
FORTU-NATELY, THE TWO OF US ARE, IN FACT, FIRST YEAR STUDENTS AT FUJOU ACADEMY!
YOU GO TO OUR SCHOOL?! AND YOU'RE YOUNGER THAN US?!
WHEN WE FIRST SAW YOU, WE DIDN'T RECOGNIZE YOU AS THE KAZAMA-SENPAI AND THE TAKAO-SENPAI.
Fujou Academy
"THE"?!
US?!
PSST.. PSST.. PSST..
We'll split into teams like so...
QUIVER
QUIVER
QUIVER

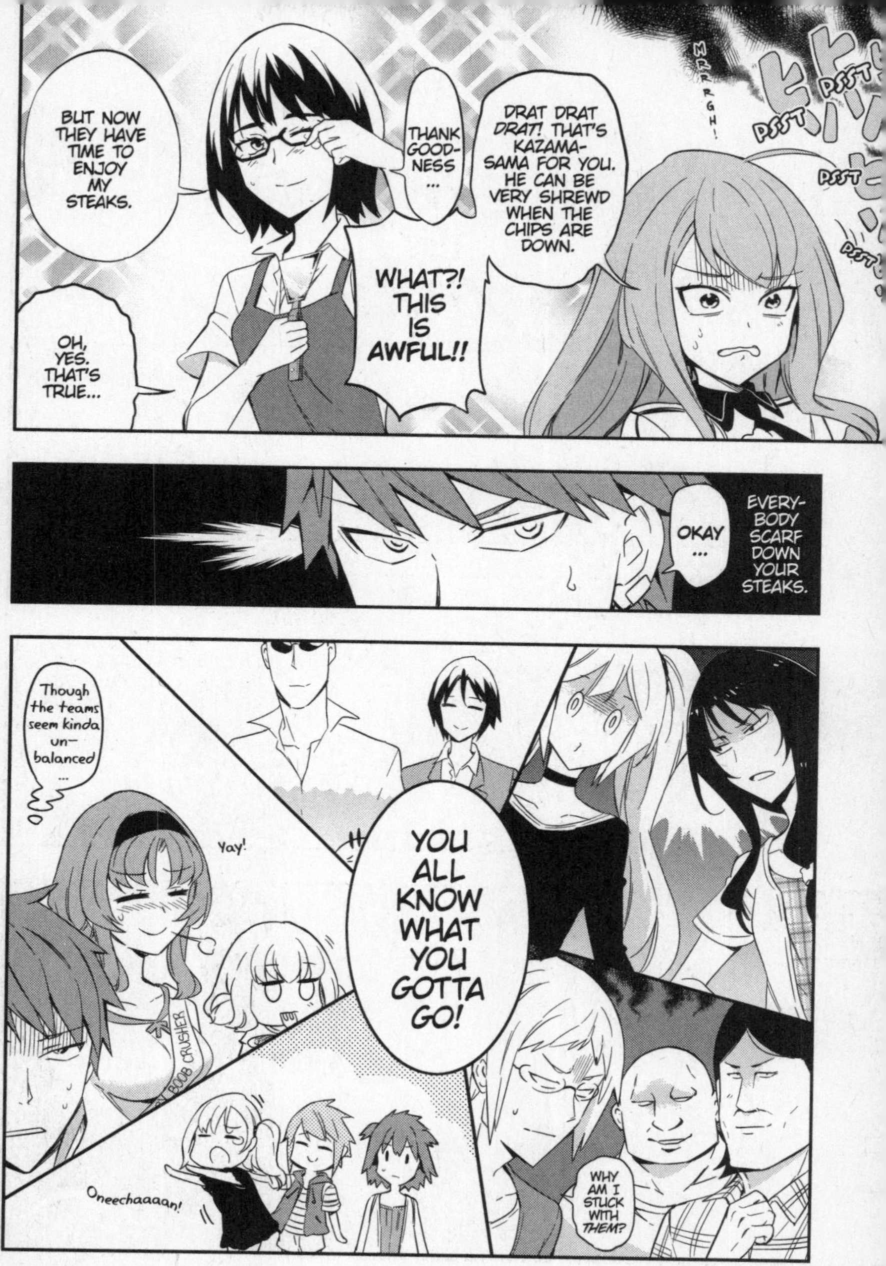
MRRRGH!
PSST PSST PSST PSST PSST
DRAT DRAT DRAT! THAT'S KAZAMA-SAMA FOR YOU. HE CAN BE VERY SHREWD WHEN THE CHIPS ARE DOWN.
THANK GOODNESS ...
BUT NOW THEY HAVE TIME TO ENJOY MY STEAKS.
WHAT?! THIS IS AWFUL!!
OH, YES. THAT'S TRUE...
EVERYBODY SCARF DOWN YOUR STEAKS.
OKAY ...
YOU ALL KNOW WHAT YOU GOTTA GO!
WHY AM I STUCK WITH THEM?
Though the teams seem kinda un-balanced ...
Yay!
BOOB CRUSHER
Oneechaaaan!

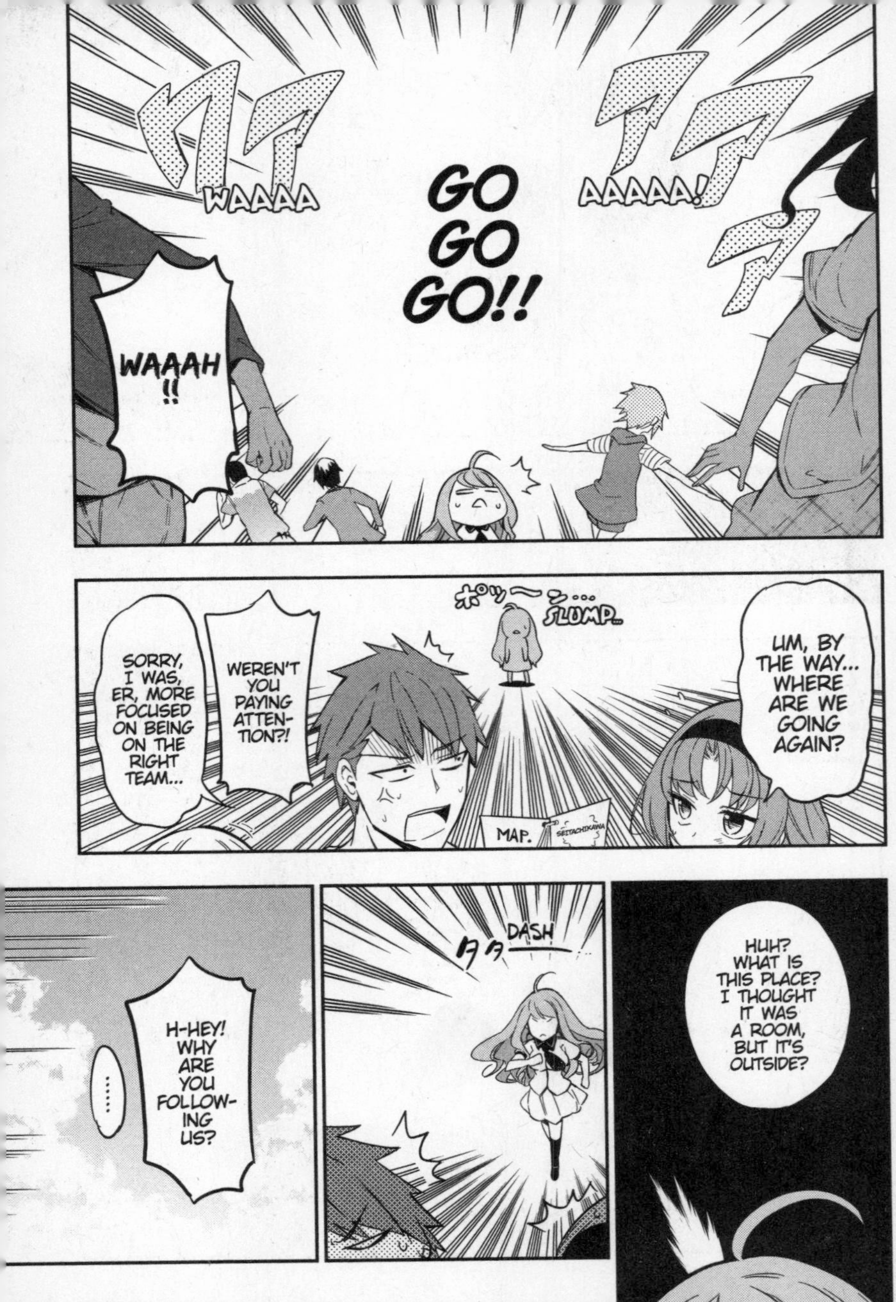
AAAAA!
GO GO GO!!
WAAAA
WAAAH!!
ポッ〜ン…
SLUMP...
UM, BY THE WAY... WHERE ARE WE GOING AGAIN?
WEREN'T YOU PAYING ATTENTION?!
SORRY, I WAS, ER, MORE FOCUSED ON BEING ON THE RIGHT TEAM...
SEITACHIKAWA
MAP.
HUH? WHAT IS THIS PLACE? I THOUGHT IT WAS A ROOM, BUT IT'S OUTSIDE?
タタ
DASH
H-HEY! WHY ARE YOU FOLLOWING US?
......

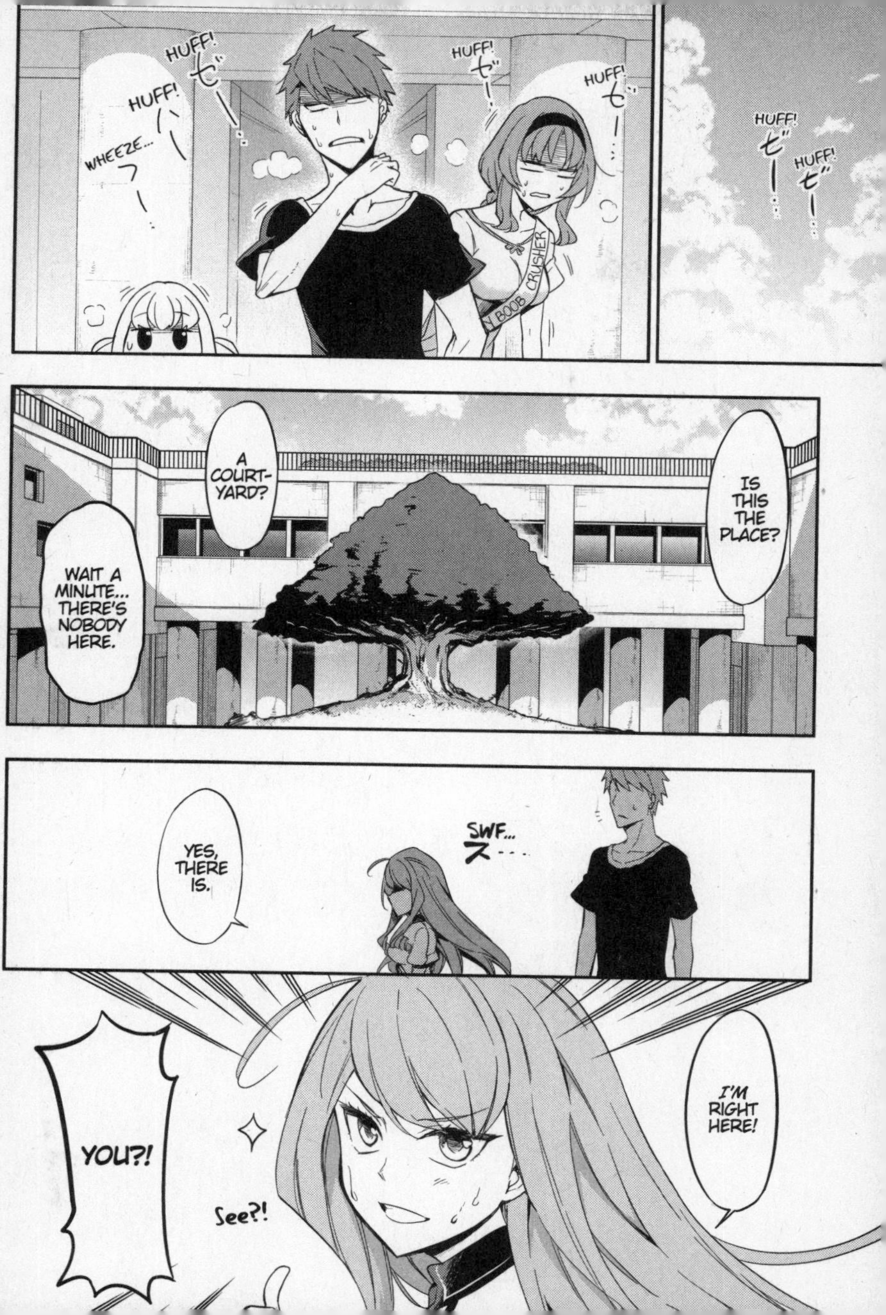
HUFF!
ゼー…
HUFF!
ゼー…
HUFF!
ゼー…
HUFF!
ゼー…
BOOB CRUSHER
HUFF!
ゼー…
HUFF!
ハー
WHEEZE...
フー…
IS THIS THE PLACE?
A COURT-YARD?
WAIT A MINUTE... THERE'S NOBODY HERE.
SWF...
ス…
YES, THERE IS.
I'M RIGHT HERE!
YOU?!
See?!

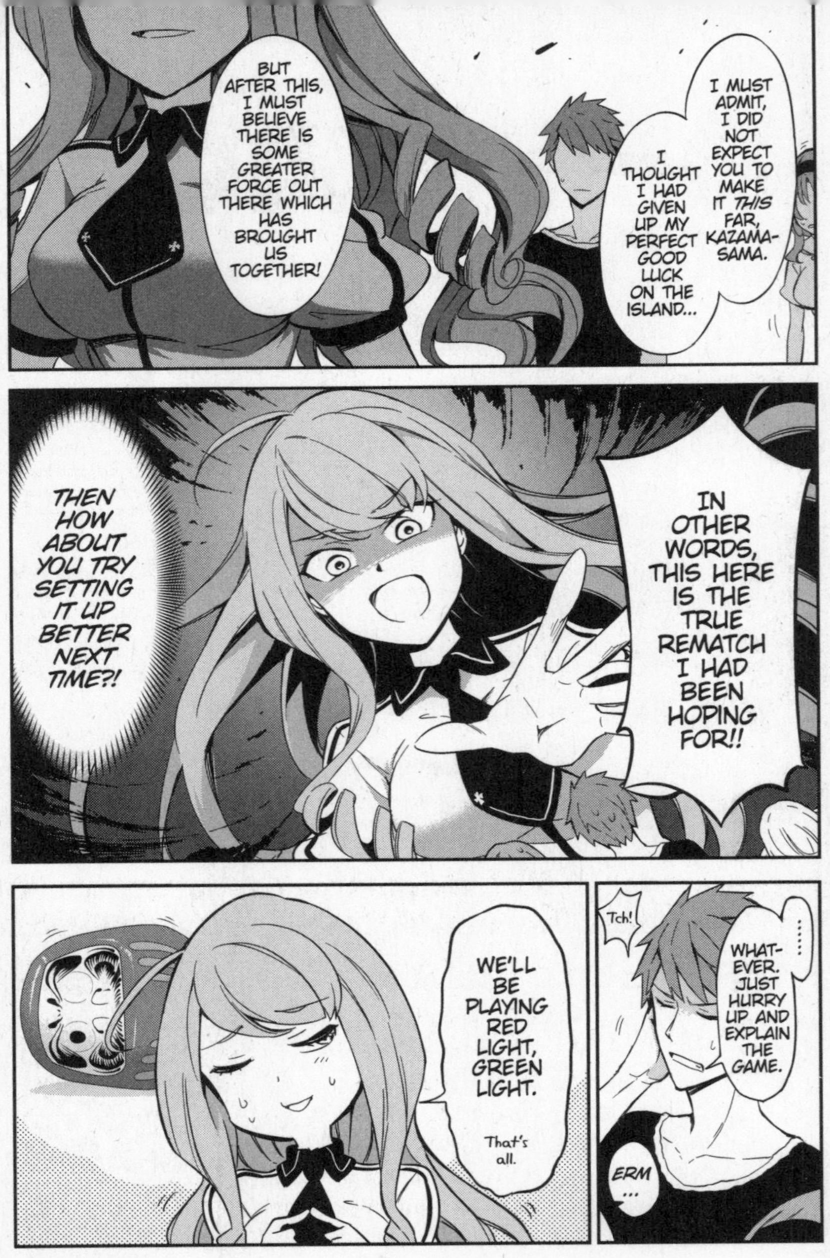
I MUST ADMIT, I DID NOT EXPECT YOU TO MAKE IT *THIS* FAR, KAZAMA-SAMA.
I THOUGHT I HAD GIVEN UP MY PERFECT GOOD LUCK ON THE ISLAND...
BUT AFTER THIS, I MUST BELIEVE THERE IS SOME GREATER FORCE OUT THERE WHICH HAS BROUGHT US TOGETHER!
IN OTHER WORDS, THIS HERE IS THE TRUE REMATCH I HAD BEEN HOPING FOR!!
THEN HOW ABOUT YOU TRY SETTING IT UP BETTER NEXT TIME?!
Tch!
......
WHAT-EVER. JUST HURRY UP AND EXPLAIN THE GAME.
ERM ...
WE'LL BE PLAYING RED LIGHT, GREEN LIGHT.
That's all.

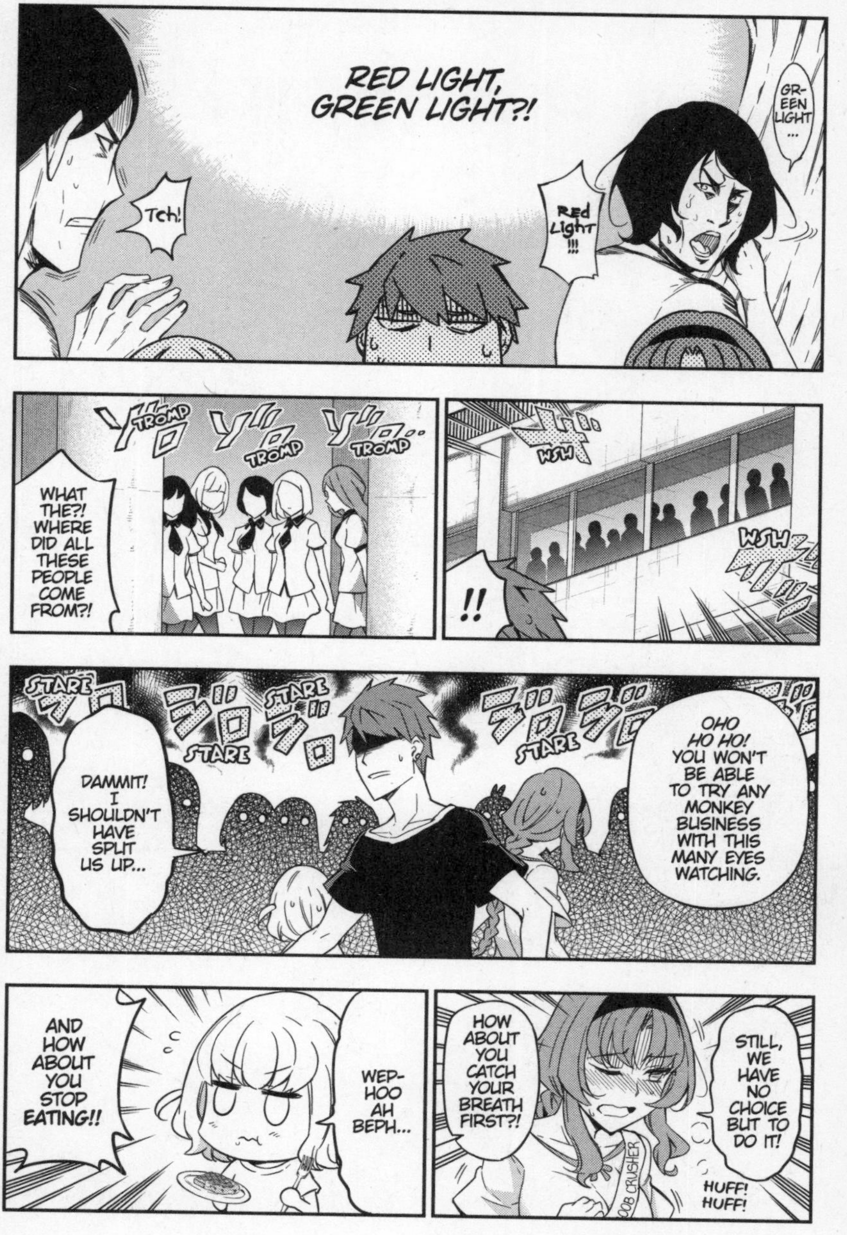
GR-EEN LIGHT...
RED LIGHT, GREEN LIGHT?!
Red Light!!!
Tch!
WSH
WSH
!!
TROMP
TROMP
TROMP
WHAT THE?! WHERE DID ALL THESE PEOPLE COME FROM?!
OHO HO HO! YOU WON'T BE ABLE TO TRY ANY MONKEY BUSINESS WITH THIS MANY EYES WATCHING.
STARE
STARE
STARE
STARE
DAMMIT! I SHOULDN'T HAVE SPLIT US UP...
STILL, WE HAVE NO CHOICE BUT TO DO IT!
HOW ABOUT YOU CATCH YOUR BREATH FIRST?!
HUFF! HUFF!
WEP-HOO AH BEPH...
AND HOW ABOUT YOU STOP EATING!!

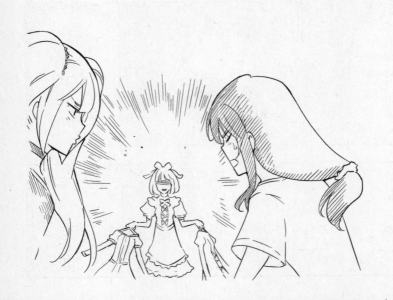

D-FRAGMENTS
ディーふらぐ!

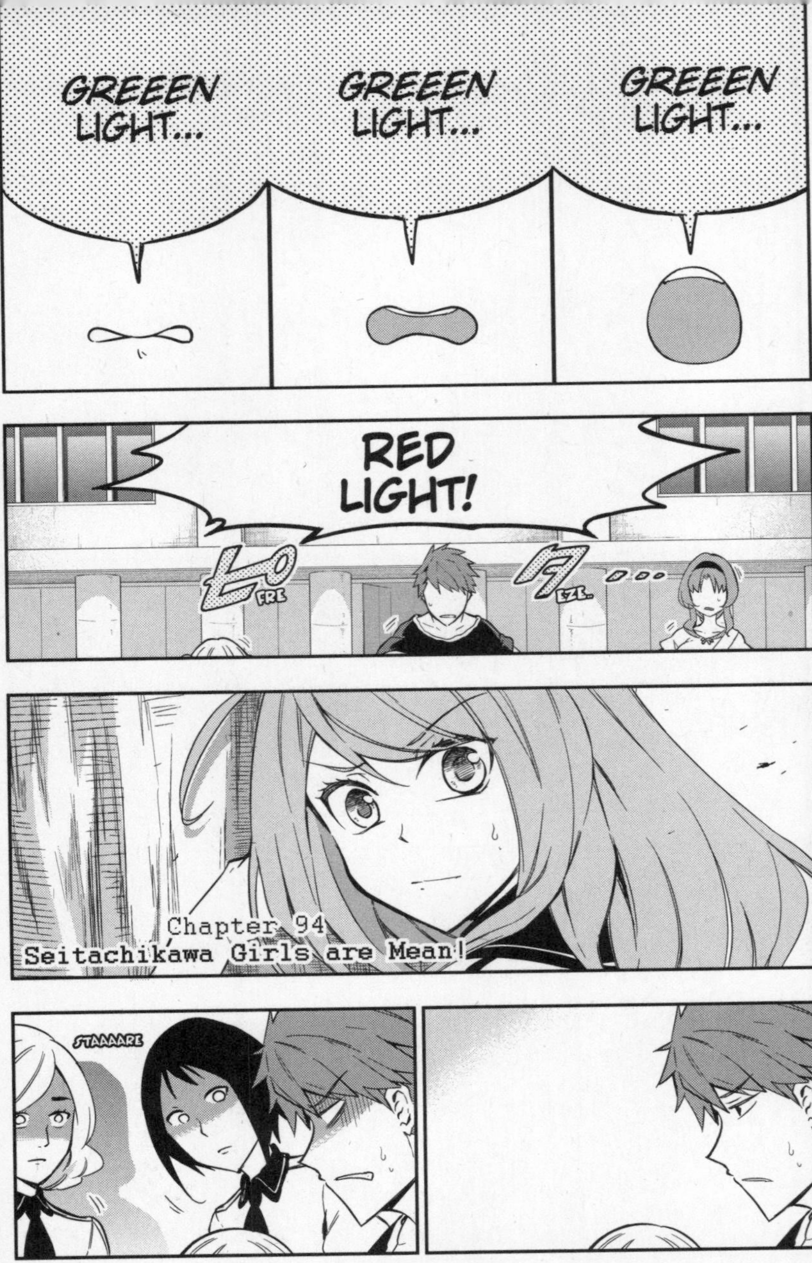
GREEEN LIGHT...
GREEEN LIGHT...
GREEEN LIGHT...
RED LIGHT!
ピ FRE
タ EZE...
Chapter 94
Seitachikawa Girls are Mean!
STAAAARE

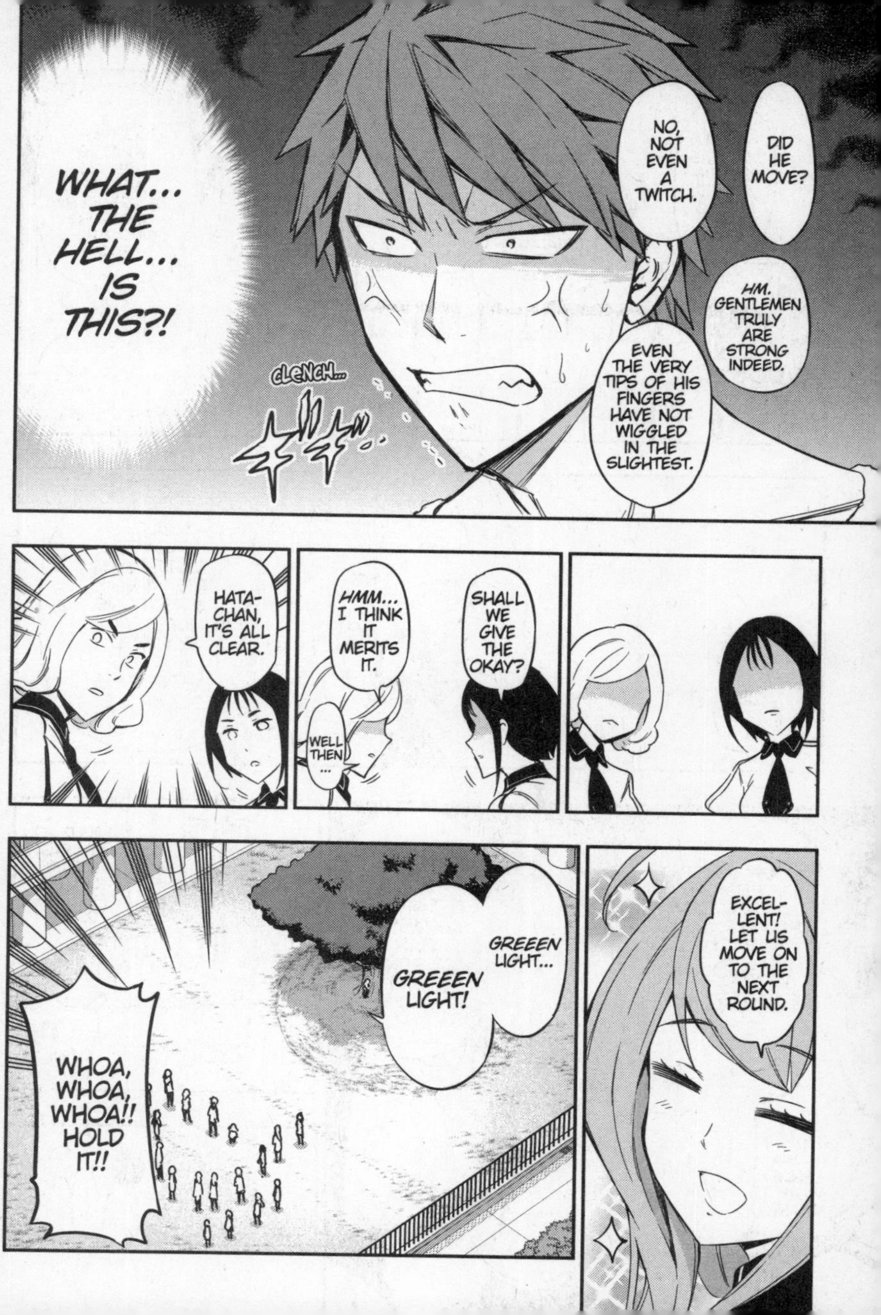
DID HE MOVE?
NO, NOT EVEN A TWITCH.
HM. GENTLEMEN TRULY ARE STRONG INDEED.
EVEN THE VERY TIPS OF HIS FINGERS HAVE NOT WIGGLED IN THE SLIGHTEST.
WHAT... THE HELL... IS THIS?!
CLENCH...
SHALL WE GIVE THE OKAY?
HMM... I THINK IT MERITS IT.
WELL THEN ...
HATA-CHAN, IT'S ALL CLEAR.
EXCEL-LENT! LET US MOVE ON TO THE NEXT ROUND.
GREEEN LIGHT...
GREEEN LIGHT!
WHOA, WHOA, WHOA!! HOLD IT!!

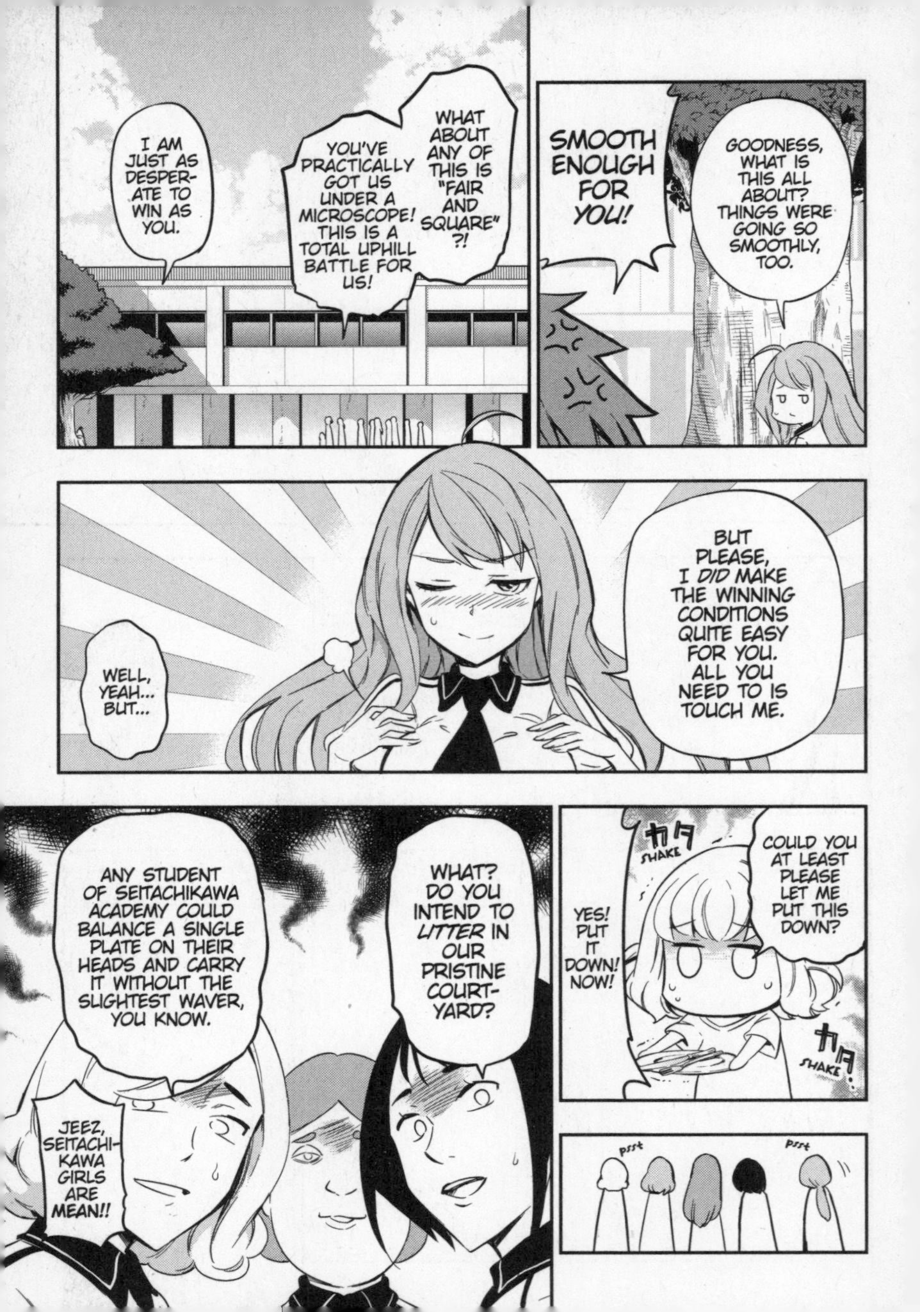
GOODNESS, WHAT IS THIS ALL ABOUT? THINGS WERE GOING SO SMOOTHLY, TOO.
SMOOTH ENOUGH FOR YOU!
WHAT ABOUT ANY OF THIS IS "FAIR AND SQUARE"?!
YOU'VE PRACTICALLY GOT US UNDER A MICROSCOPE! THIS IS A TOTAL UPHILL BATTLE FOR US!
I AM JUST AS DESPER-ATE TO WIN AS YOU.
BUT PLEASE, I DID MAKE THE WINNING CONDITIONS QUITE EASY FOR YOU. ALL YOU NEED TO IS TOUCH ME.
WELL, YEAH... BUT...
カタ SHAKE
COULD YOU AT LEAST PLEASE LET ME PUT THIS DOWN?
YES! PUT IT DOWN! NOW!
カタ SHAKE
psst
psst
WHAT? DO YOU INTEND TO LITTER IN OUR PRISTINE COURT-YARD?
ANY STUDENT OF SEITACHIKAWA ACADEMY COULD BALANCE A SINGLE PLATE ON THEIR HEADS AND CARRY IT WITHOUT THE SLIGHTEST WAVER, YOU KNOW.
JEEZ, SEITACHI-KAWA GIRLS ARE MEAN!!

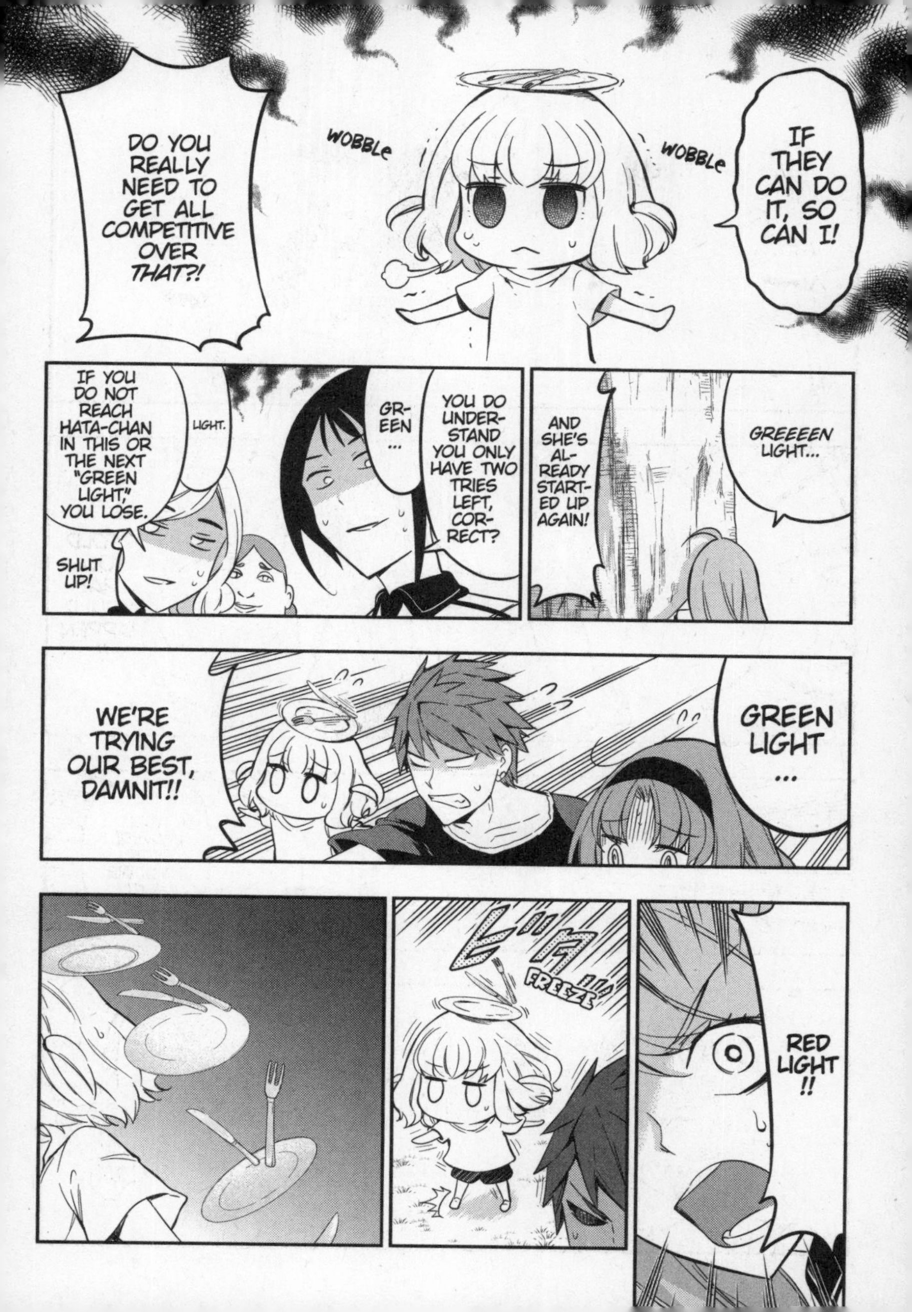
IF THEY CAN DO IT, SO CAN I!
WOBBLE
WOBBLE
DO YOU REALLY NEED TO GET ALL COMPETITIVE OVER THAT?!
GREEEEN LIGHT...
AND SHE'S ALREADY STARTED UP AGAIN!
YOU DO UNDERSTAND YOU ONLY HAVE TWO TRIES LEFT, CORRECT?
GR-EEN ...
LIGHT.
IF YOU DO NOT REACH HATA-CHAN IN THIS OR THE NEXT "GREEN LIGHT," YOU LOSE.
SHUT UP!
GREEN LIGHT ...
WE'RE TRYING OUR BEST, DAMNIT!!
RED LIGHT !!
FREEZE!!

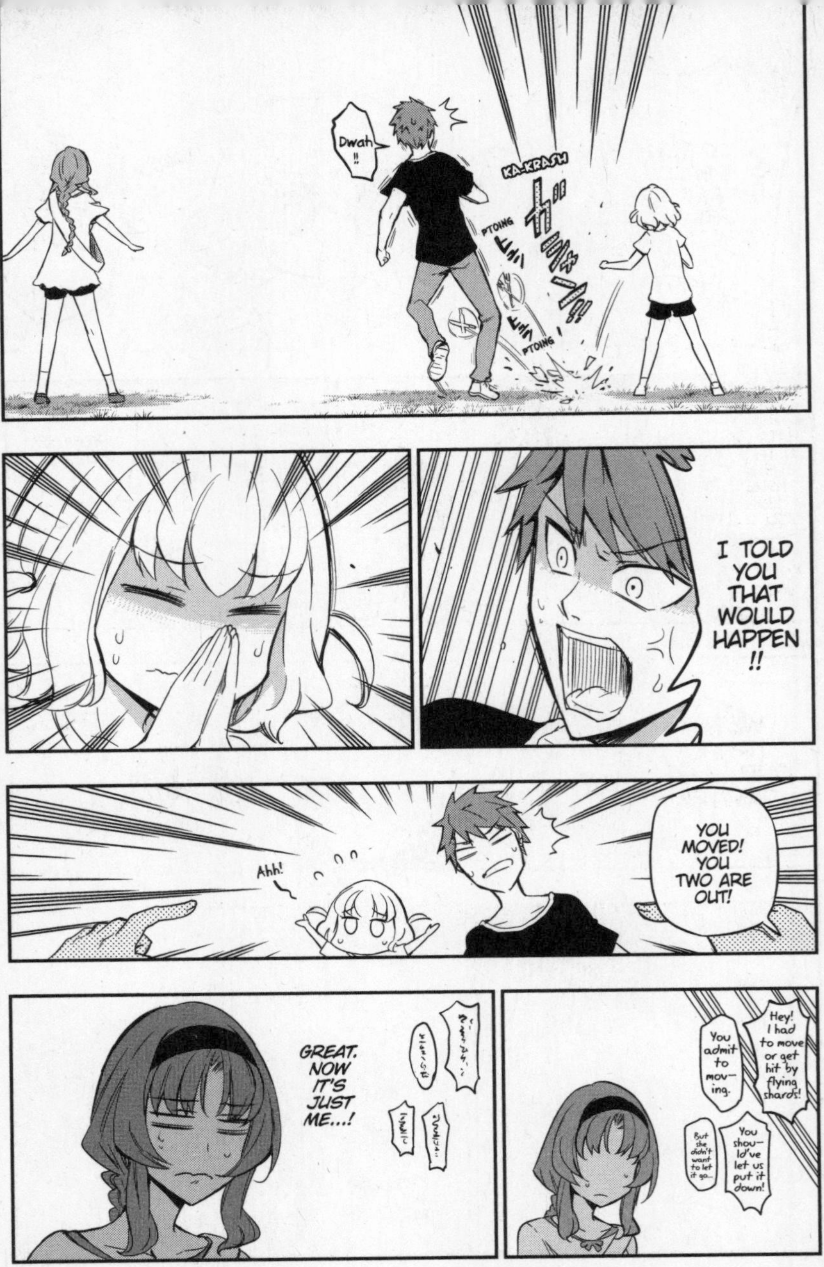
KA-KRASH
Dwah!!
PTOING
PTOING
I TOLD YOU THAT WOULD HAPPEN!!
YOU MOVED! YOU TWO ARE OUT!
Ahh!
Hey! I had to move or get hit by flying shards!
You admit to mov-ing.
You shou-ld've let us put it down!
But she didn't want to let it go...
GREAT. NOW IT'S JUST ME...!

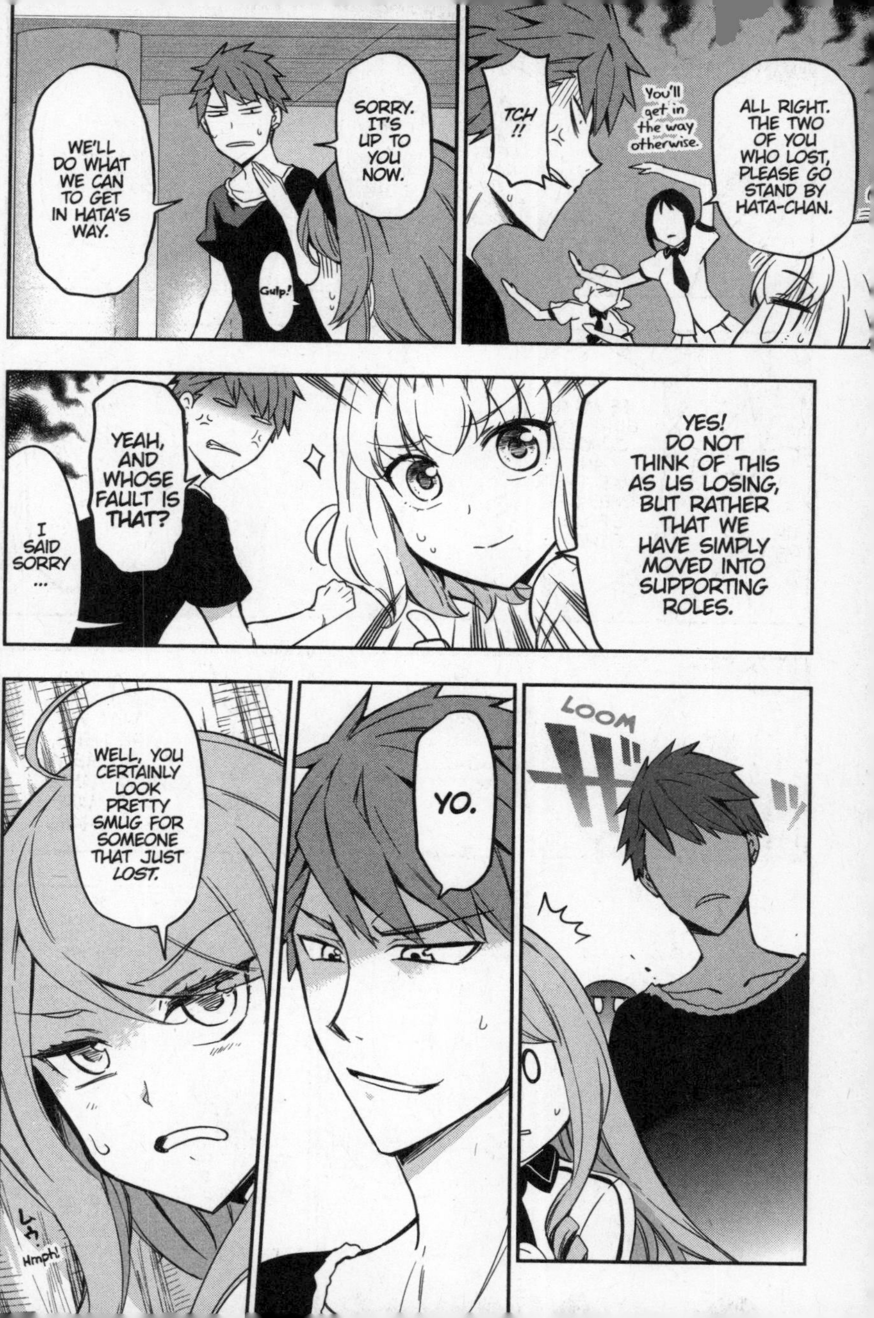
ALL RIGHT. THE TWO OF YOU WHO LOST, PLEASE GO STAND BY HATA-CHAN.
You'll get in the way otherwise.
TCH!!
SORRY. IT'S UP TO YOU NOW.
WE'LL DO WHAT WE CAN TO GET IN HATA'S WAY.
Gulp!
YES! DO NOT THINK OF THIS AS US LOSING, BUT RATHER THAT WE HAVE SIMPLY MOVED INTO SUPPORTING ROLES.
YEAH, AND WHOSE FAULT IS THAT?
I SAID SORRY ...
LOOM
YO.
WELL, YOU CERTAINLY LOOK PRETTY SMUG FOR SOMEONE THAT JUST LOST.
Hmph!

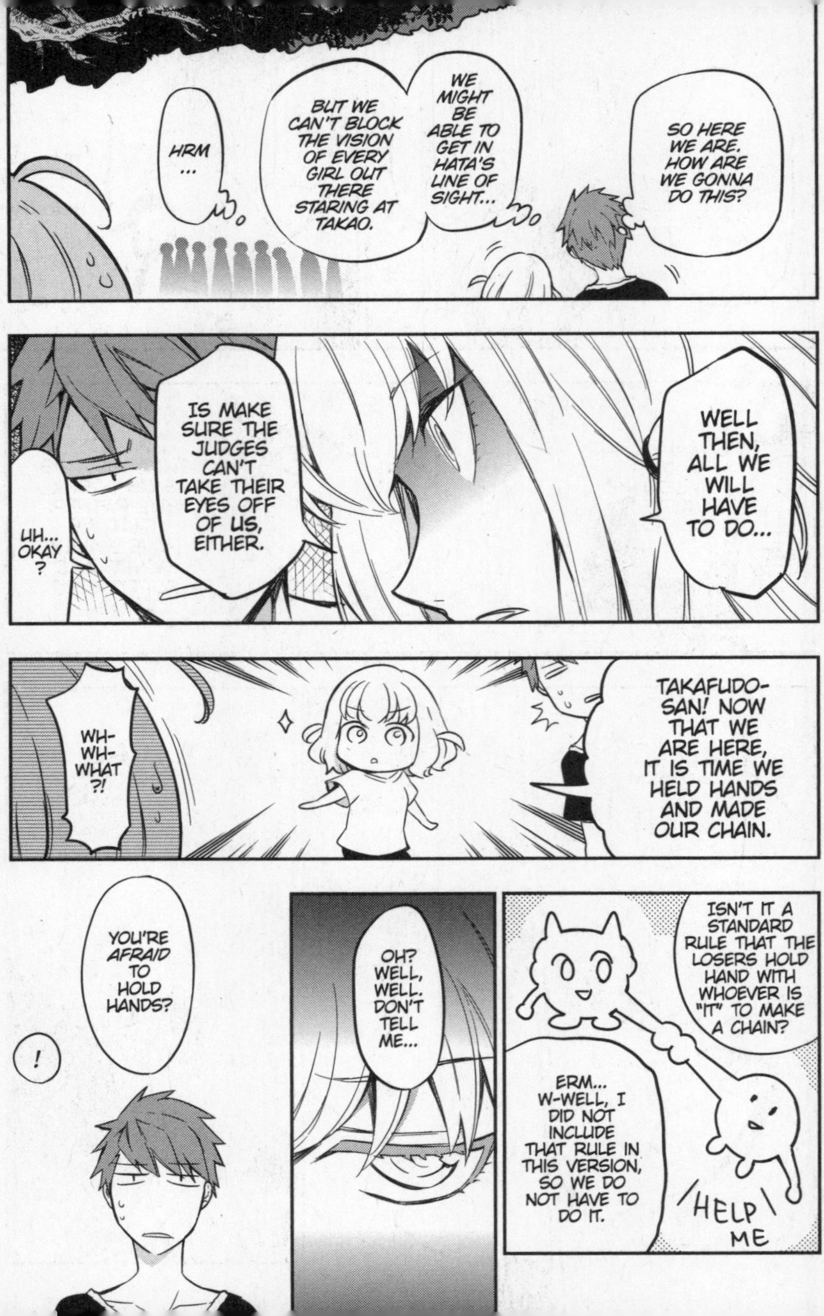
SO HERE WE ARE. HOW ARE WE GONNA DO THIS?
WE MIGHT BE ABLE TO GET IN HATA'S LINE OF SIGHT...
BUT WE CAN'T BLOCK THE VISION OF EVERY GIRL OUT THERE STARING AT TAKAO.
HRM ...
WELL THEN, ALL WE WILL HAVE TO DO...
IS MAKE SURE THE JUDGES CAN'T TAKE THEIR EYES OFF OF US, EITHER.
UH... OKAY ?
TAKAFUDO-SAN! NOW THAT WE ARE HERE, IT IS TIME WE HELD HANDS AND MADE OUR CHAIN.
WH-WH-WHAT ?!
ISN'T IT A STANDARD RULE THAT THE LOSERS HOLD HAND WITH WHOEVER IS "IT" TO MAKE A CHAIN?
ERM... W-WELL, I DID NOT INCLUDE THAT RULE IN THIS VERSION, SO WE DO NOT HAVE TO DO IT.
HELP ME
OH? WELL, WELL. DON'T TELL ME...
YOU'RE AFRAID TO HOLD HANDS?
!

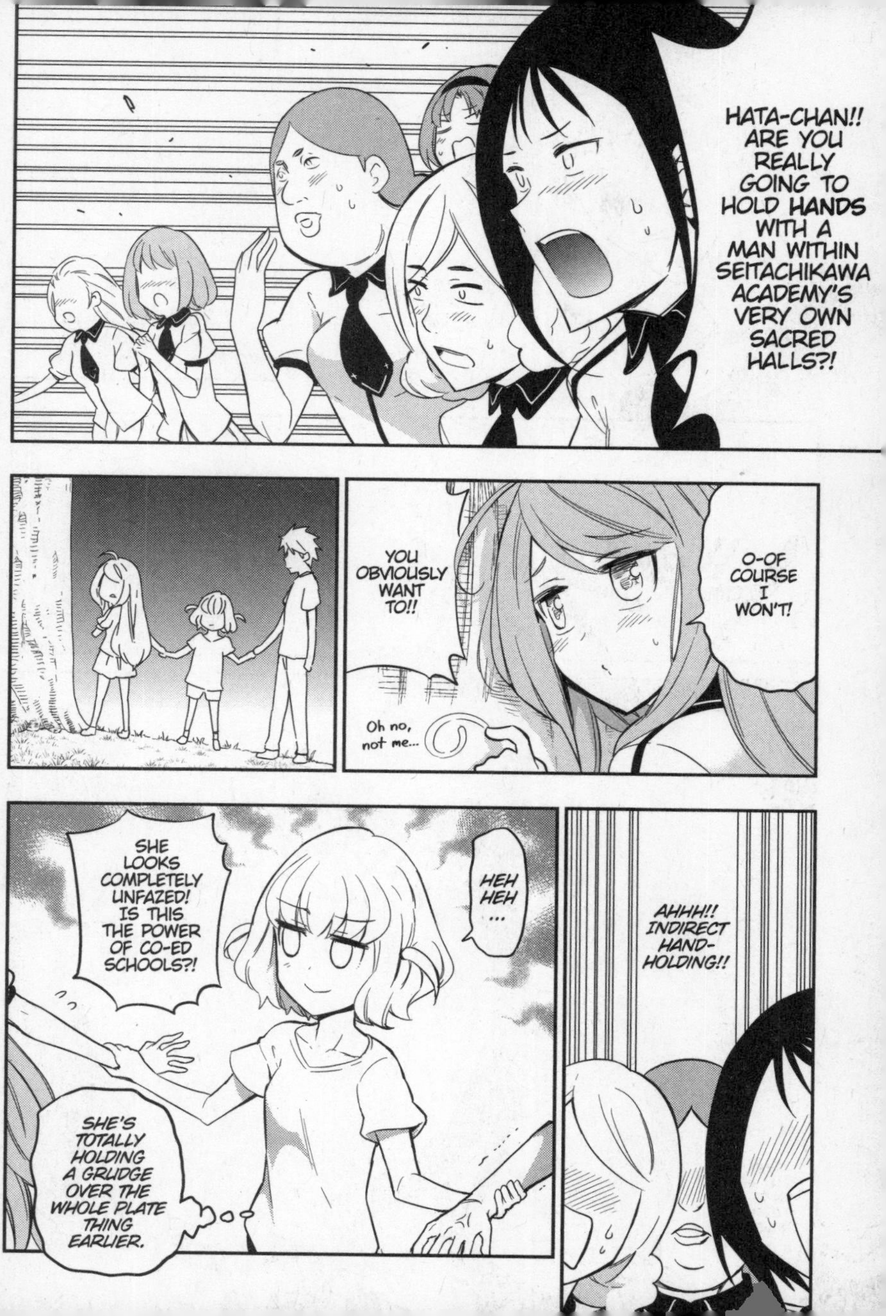
HATA-CHAN!! ARE YOU REALLY GOING TO HOLD HANDS WITH A MAN WITHIN SEITACHIKAWA ACADEMY'S VERY OWN SACRED HALLS?!
O-OF COURSE I WON'T!
YOU OBVIOUSLY WANT TO!!
Oh no, not me...
AHHH!! INDIRECT HAND-HOLDING!!
HEH HEH ...
SHE LOOKS COMPLETELY UNFAZED! IS THIS THE POWER OF CO-ED SCHOOLS?!
SHE'S TOTALLY HOLDING A GRUDGE OVER THE WHOLE PLATE THING EARLIER.

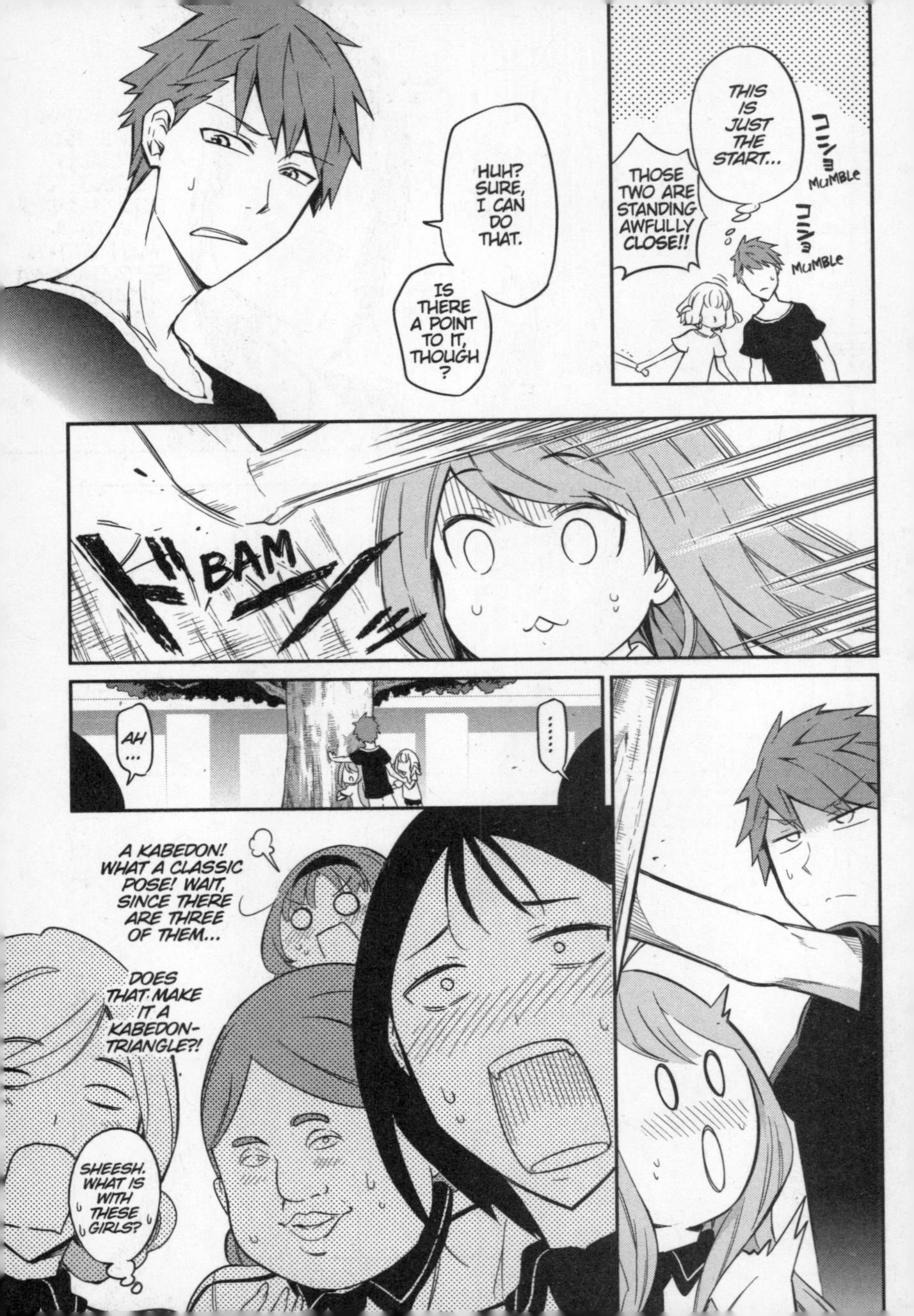

THIS IS JUST THE START...
THOSE TWO ARE STANDING AWFULLY CLOSE!!
MUMBLE
MUMBLE
HUH? SURE, I CAN DO THAT.
IS THERE A POINT TO IT, THOUGH?
BAM
......
AH...
A KABEDON! WHAT A CLASSIC POSE! WAIT, SINCE THERE ARE THREE OF THEM...
DOES THAT MAKE IT A KABEDON-TRIANGLE?!
SHEESH. WHAT IS WITH THESE GIRLS?

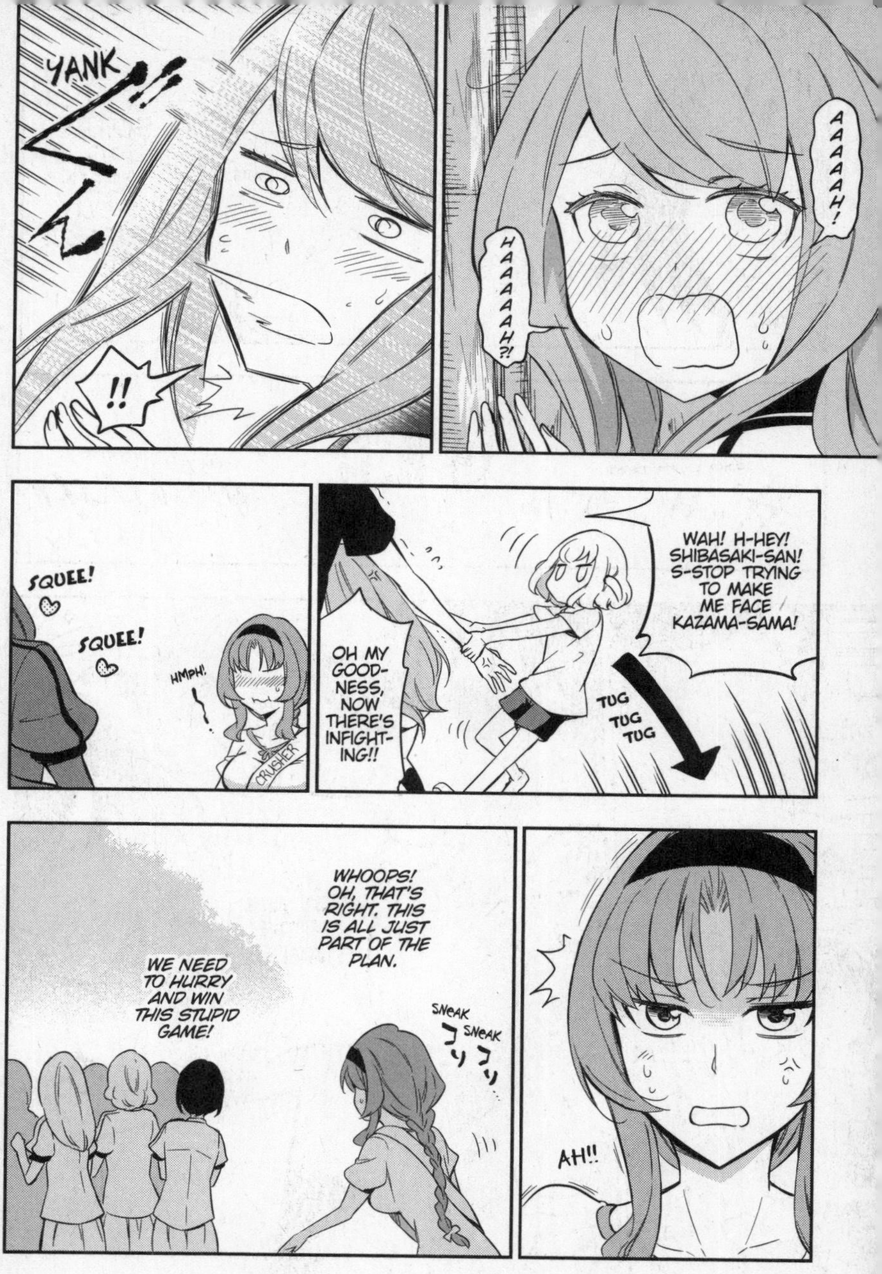
AAAAAH!
HAAAAAAH?!
YANK
!!
WAH! H-HEY! SHIBASAKI-SAN! S-STOP TRYING TO MAKE ME FACE KAZAMA-SAMA!
TUG TUG TUG
OH MY GOODNESS, NOW THERE'S INFIGHTING!!
SQUEE!
SQUEE!
HMPH!
CRUSHER
AH!!
WHOOPS! OH, THAT'S RIGHT. THIS IS ALL JUST PART OF THE PLAN.
SNEAK SNEAK
WE NEED TO HURRY AND WIN THIS STUPID GAME!

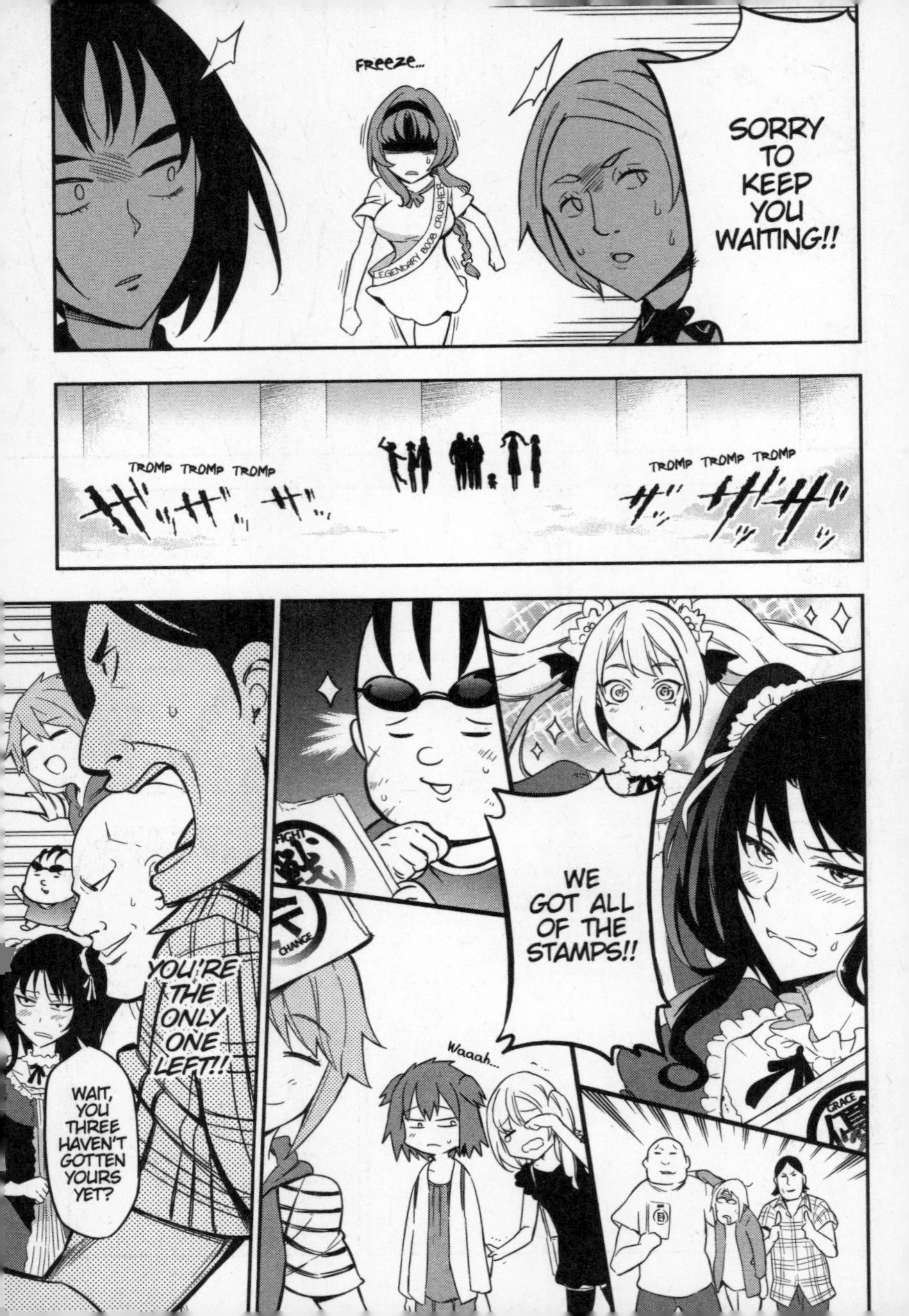
SORRY TO KEEP YOU WAITING!!
Freeze...
LEGENDARY BOOB CRUSHER
TROMP TROMP TROMP
TROMP TROMP TROMP
FIGHT
CHANGE
WE GOT ALL OF THE STAMPS!!
GRACE
Waaah...
YOU'RE THE ONLY ONE LEFT!!
WAIT, YOU THREE HAVEN'T GOTTEN YOURS YET?

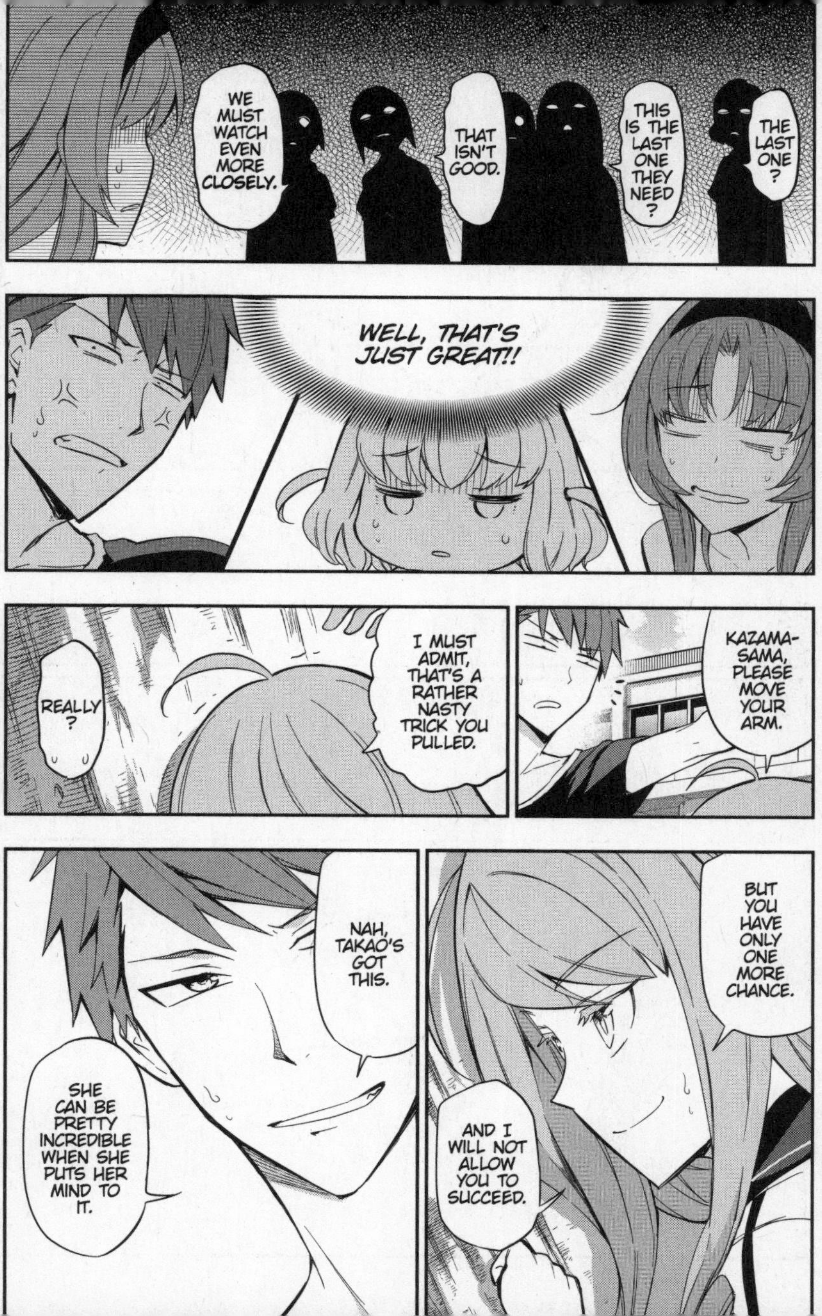
THE LAST ONE?
THIS IS THE LAST ONE THEY NEED?
THAT ISN'T GOOD.
WE MUST WATCH EVEN MORE CLOSELY.
WELL, THAT'S JUST GREAT!!
KAZAMA-SAMA, PLEASE MOVE YOUR ARM.
I MUST ADMIT, THAT'S A RATHER NASTY TRICK YOU PULLED.
REALLY?
BUT YOU HAVE ONLY ONE MORE CHANCE.
AND I WILL NOT ALLOW YOU TO SUCCEED.
NAH, TAKAO'S GOT THIS.
SHE CAN BE PRETTY INCREDIBLE WHEN SHE PUTS HER MIND TO IT.

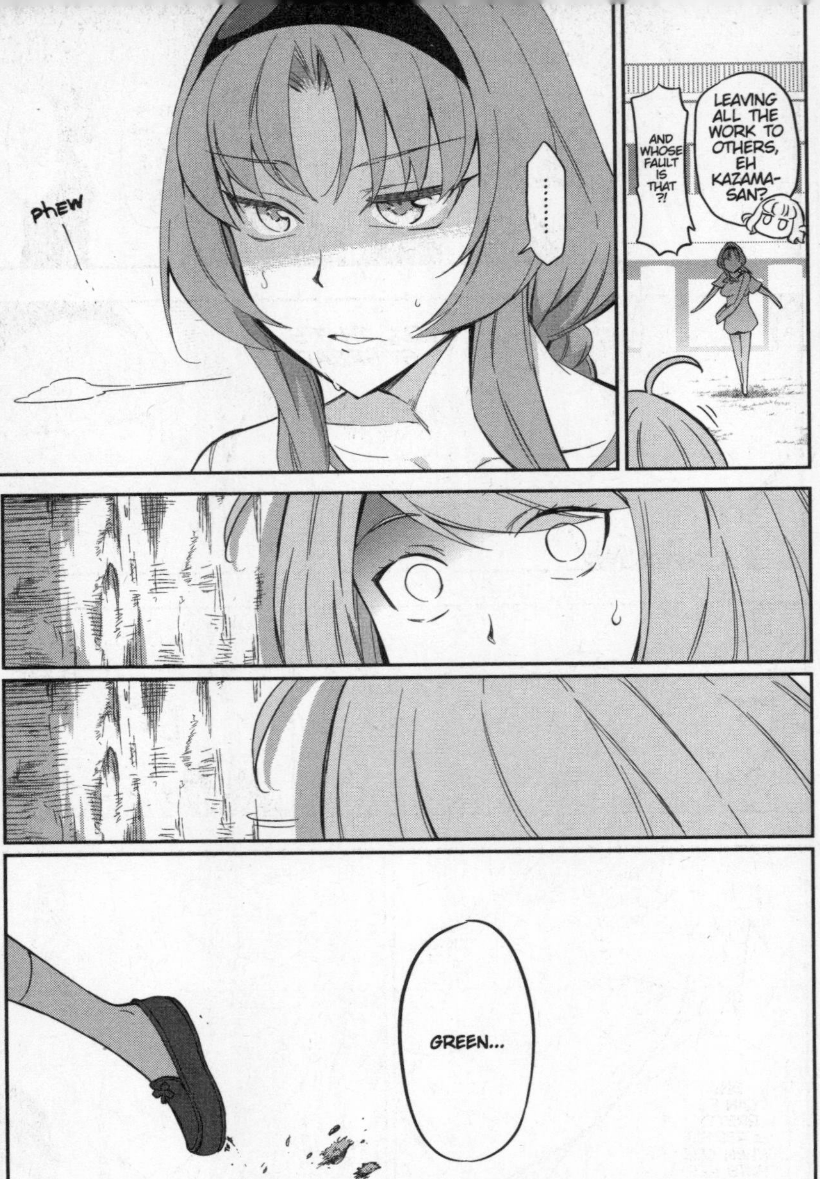
LEAVING ALL THE WORK TO OTHERS, EH KAZAMA-SAN?
AND WHOSE FAULT IS THAT?!
......
phew
GREEN...

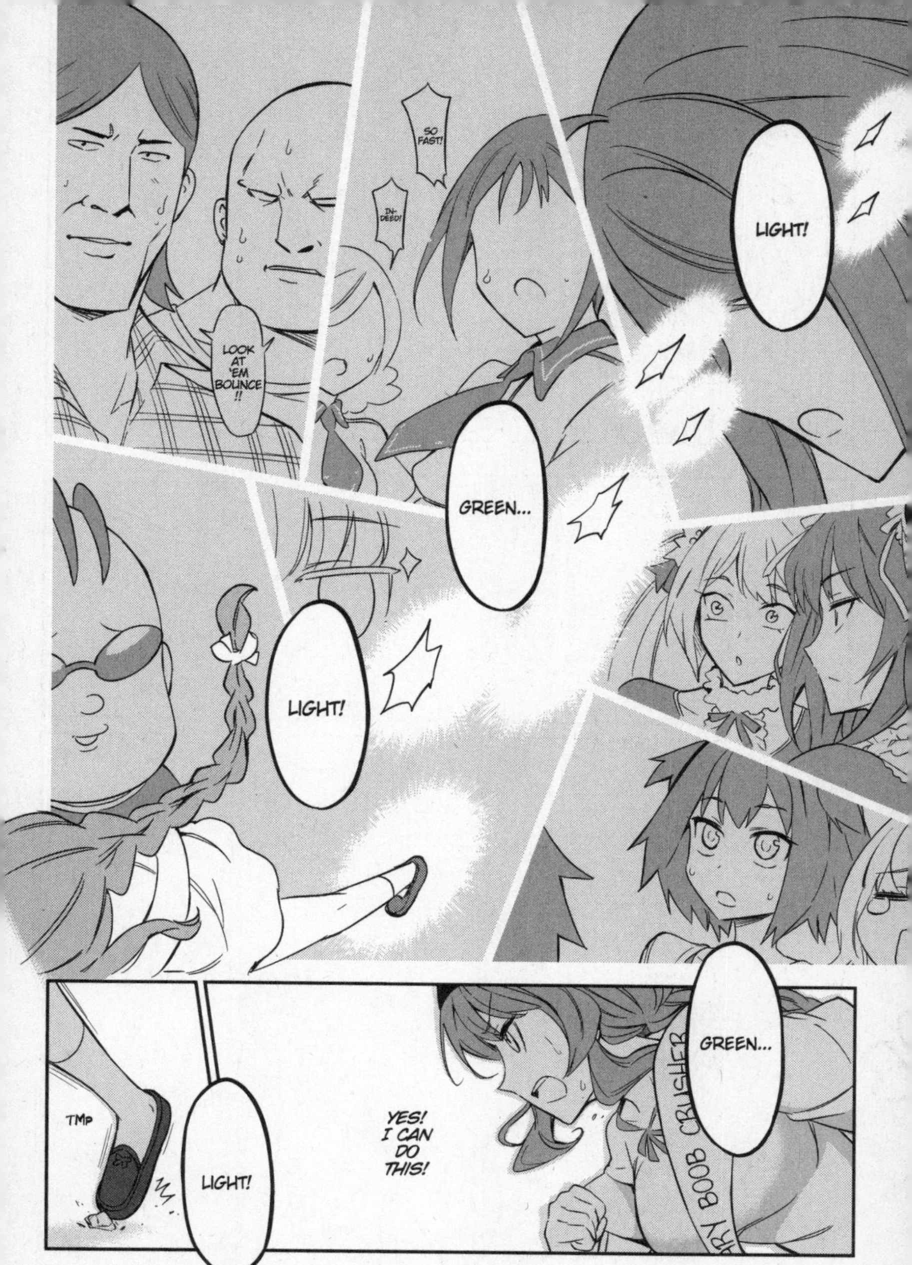
LIGHT!
SO FAST!
IN-DEED!
LOOK AT 'EM BOUNCE!!
GREEN...
LIGHT!
GREEN...
BOOB CRUSHER
YES! I CAN DO THIS!
LIGHT!
TMP

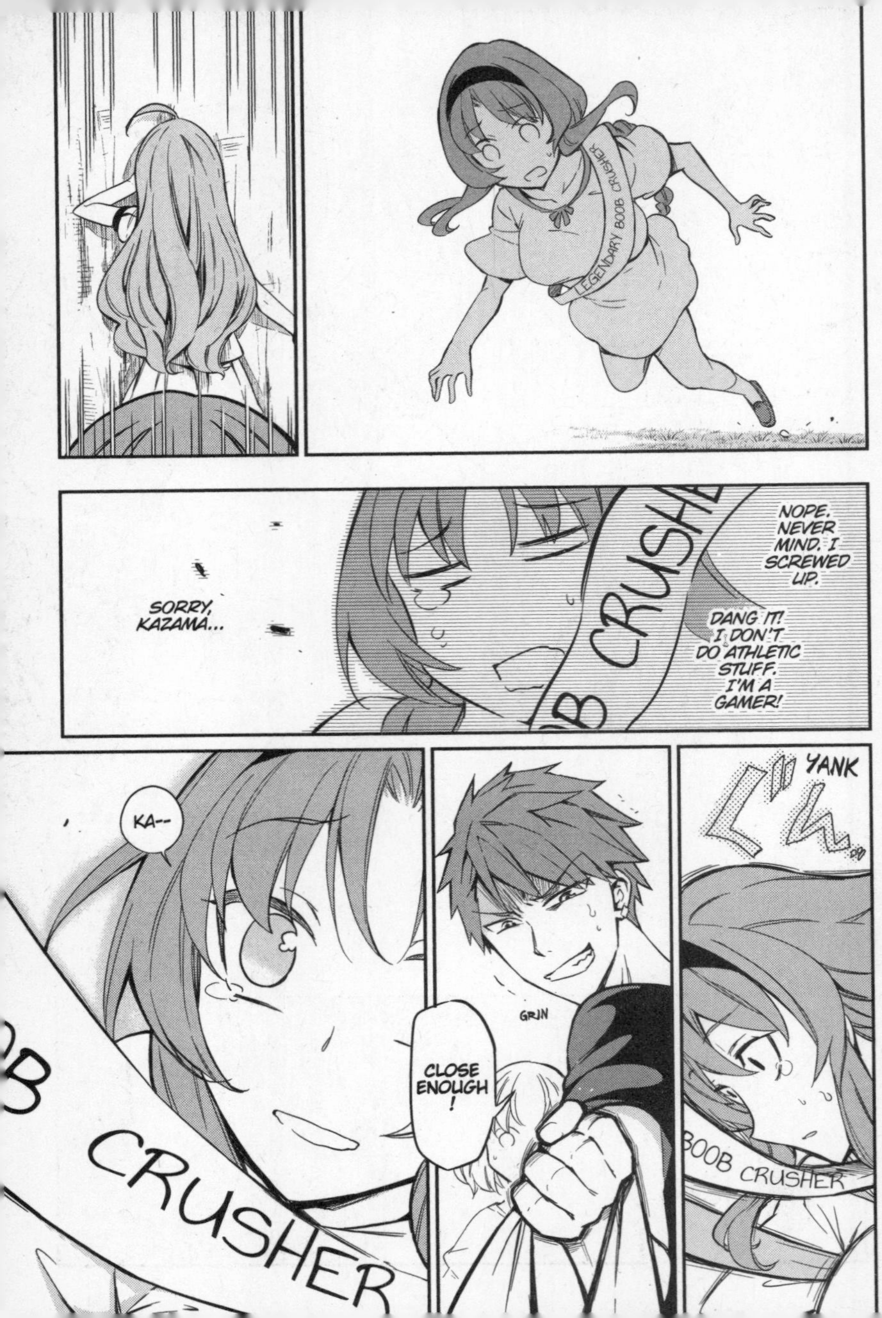

LEGENDARY BOOB CRUSHER
NOPE. NEVER MIND. I SCREWED UP.
DANG IT! I DON'T DO ATHLETIC STUFF. I'M A GAMER!
SORRY, KAZAMA...
YANK
BOOB CRUSHER
GRIN
CLOSE ENOUGH!
KA--

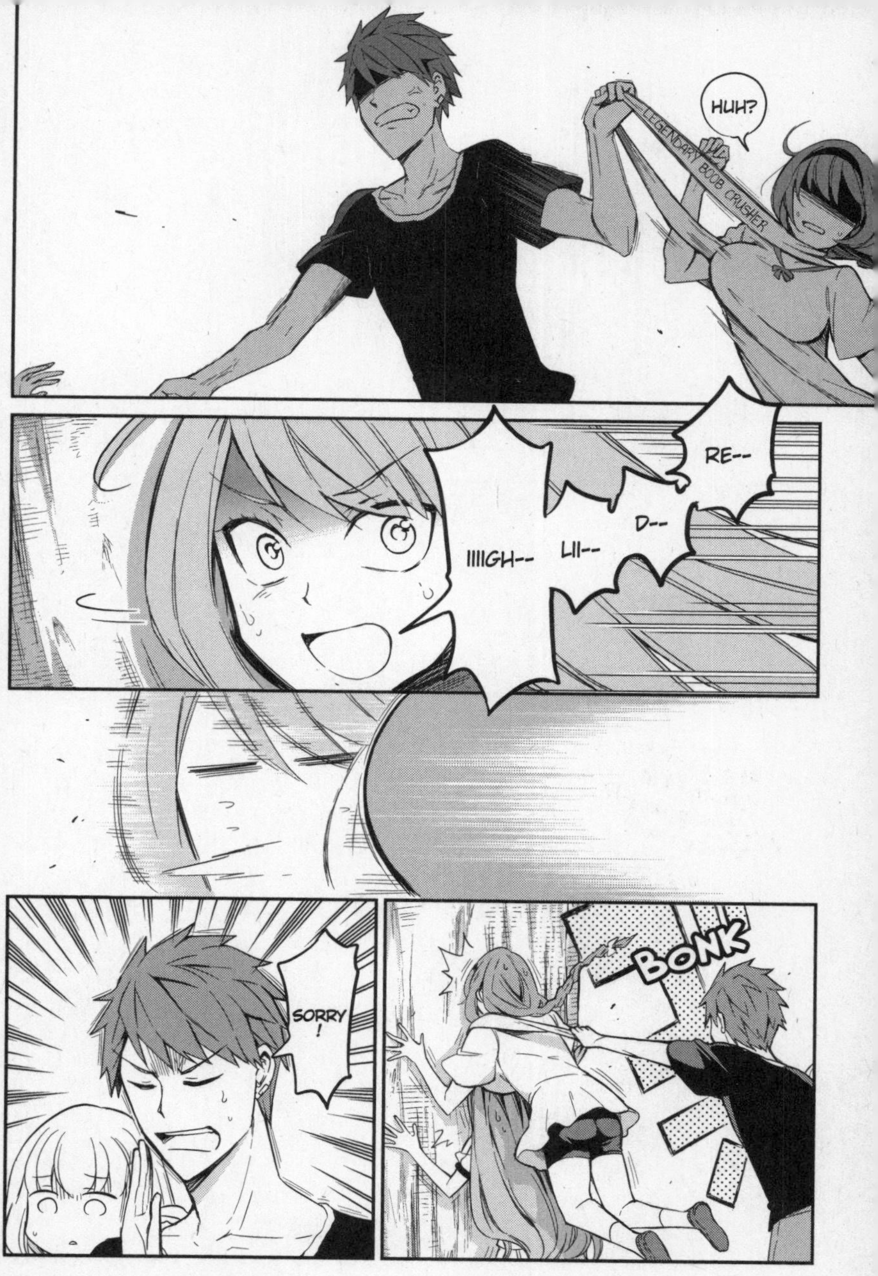
HUH?
LEGENDARY BOOB CRUSHER
RE--
D--
LII--
IIIIGH--
BONK
SORRY!

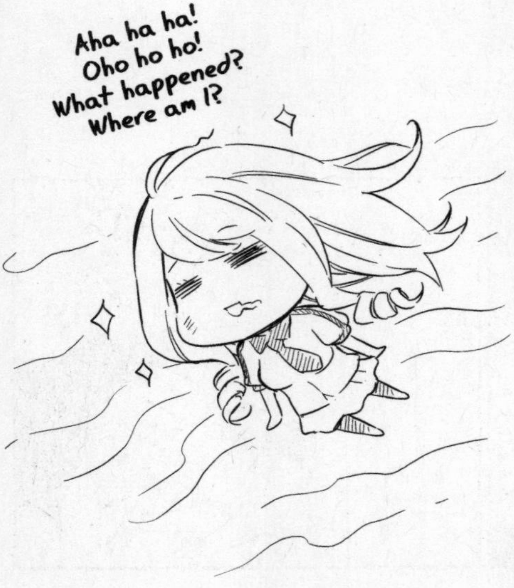
Aha ha ha!
Oho ho ho!
What happened?
Where am I?

D-FRAGMENTS

ディーふらぐ!

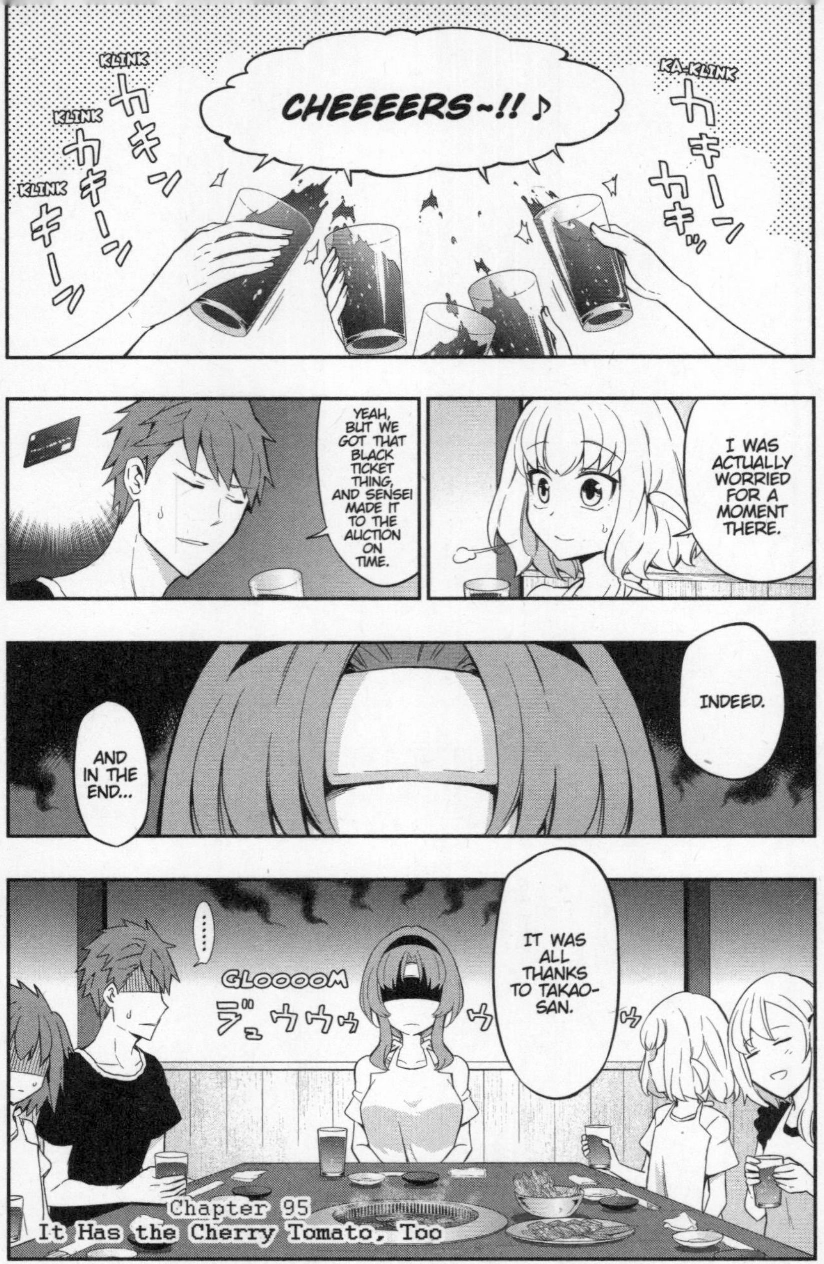
KA-KLINK
KLINK
KLINK
KLINK
CHEEEERS~!! ♪
I WAS ACTUALLY WORRIED FOR A MOMENT THERE.
YEAH, BUT WE GOT THAT BLACK TICKET THING, AND SENSEI MADE IT TO THE AUCTION ON TIME.
INDEED.
AND IN THE END...
IT WAS ALL THANKS TO TAKAO-SAN.
GLOOOOM
......

Chapter 95
It Has the Cherry Tomato, Too

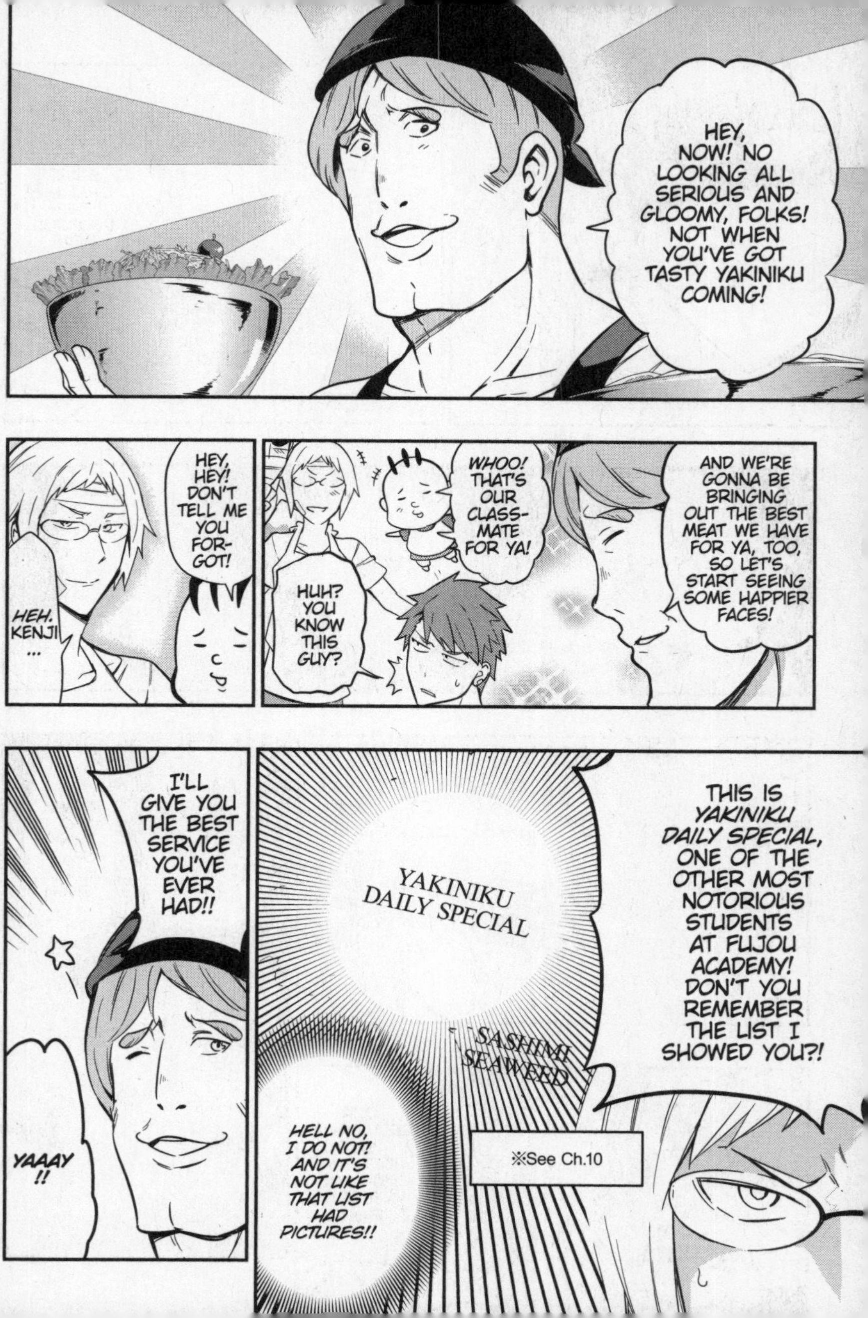
HEY, NOW! NO LOOKING ALL SERIOUS AND GLOOMY, FOLKS! NOT WHEN YOU'VE GOT TASTY YAKINIKU COMING!
AND WE'RE GONNA BE BRINGING OUT THE BEST MEAT WE HAVE FOR YA, TOO, SO LET'S START SEEING SOME HAPPIER FACES!
WHOO! THAT'S OUR CLASS-MATE FOR YA!
HUH? YOU KNOW THIS GUY?
HEY, HEY! DON'T TELL ME YOU FOR-GOT!
HEH. KENJI ...
THIS IS YAKINIKU DAILY SPECIAL, ONE OF THE OTHER MOST NOTORIOUS STUDENTS AT FUJOU ACADEMY! DON'T YOU REMEMBER THE LIST I SHOWED YOU?!
YAKINIKU DAILY SPECIAL
SASHIMI SEAWEED
※See Ch.10
HELL NO, I DO NOT! AND IT'S NOT LIKE THAT LIST HAD PICTURES!!
I'LL GIVE YOU THE BEST SERVICE YOU'VE EVER HAD!!
YAAAY !!

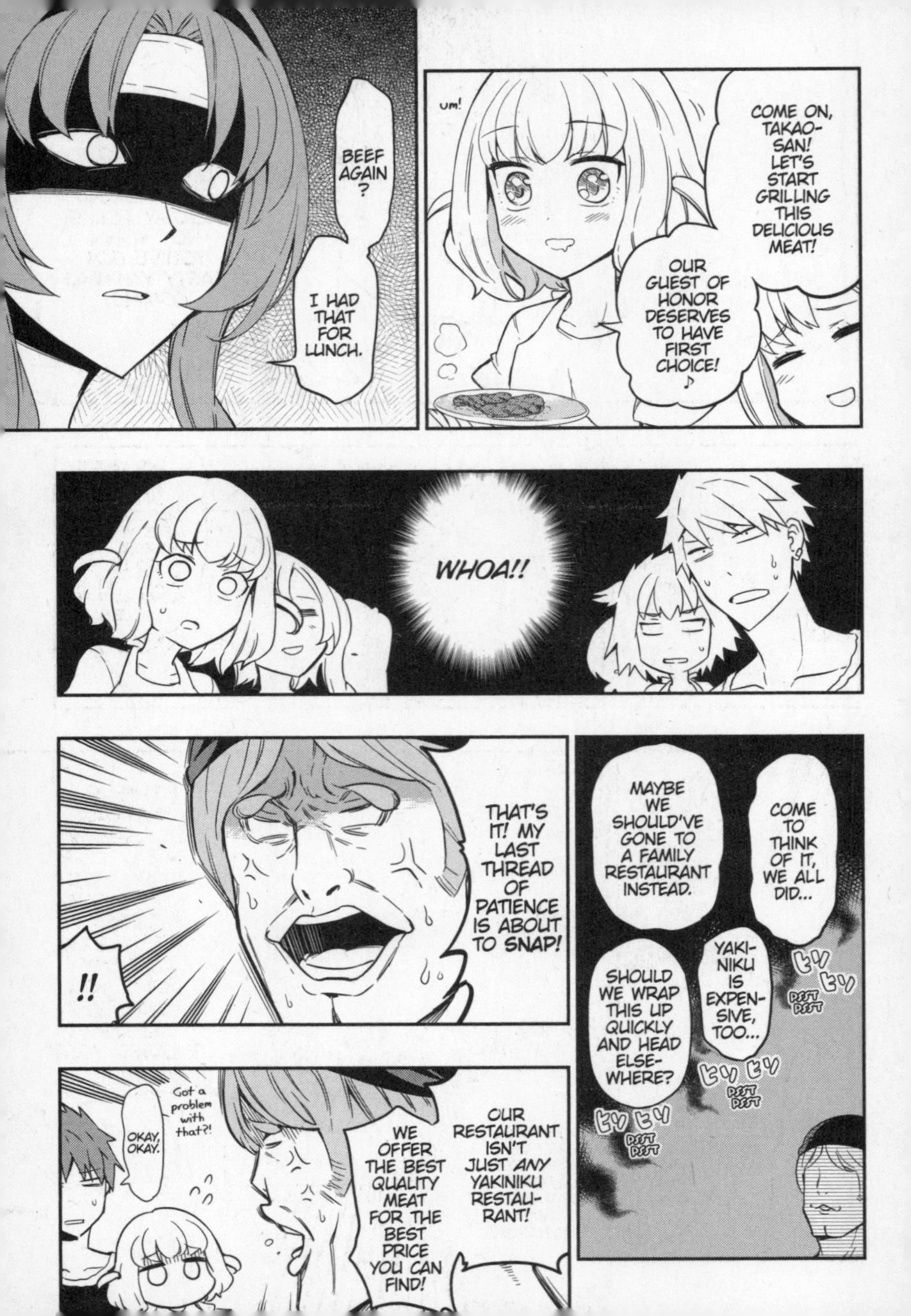
COME ON, TAKAO-SAN! LET'S START GRILLING THIS DELICIOUS MEAT!
UM!
OUR GUEST OF HONOR DESERVES TO HAVE FIRST CHOICE! ♪
BEEF AGAIN?
I HAD THAT FOR LUNCH.
WHOA!!
MAYBE WE SHOULD'VE GONE TO A FAMILY RESTAURANT INSTEAD.
COME TO THINK OF IT, WE ALL DID...
YAKI-NIKU IS EXPEN-SIVE, TOO...
ヒソ ヒソ
PSST PSST
SHOULD WE WRAP THIS UP QUICKLY AND HEAD ELSE-WHERE?
ヒソ ヒソ
PSST PSST
ヒソ ヒソ
PSST PSST
THAT'S IT! MY LAST THREAD OF PATIENCE IS ABOUT TO SNAP!
!!
OUR RESTAURANT ISN'T JUST ANY YAKINIKU RESTAU-RANT!
WE OFFER THE BEST QUALITY MEAT FOR THE BEST PRICE YOU CAN FIND!
Got a problem with that?!
OKAY, OKAY.

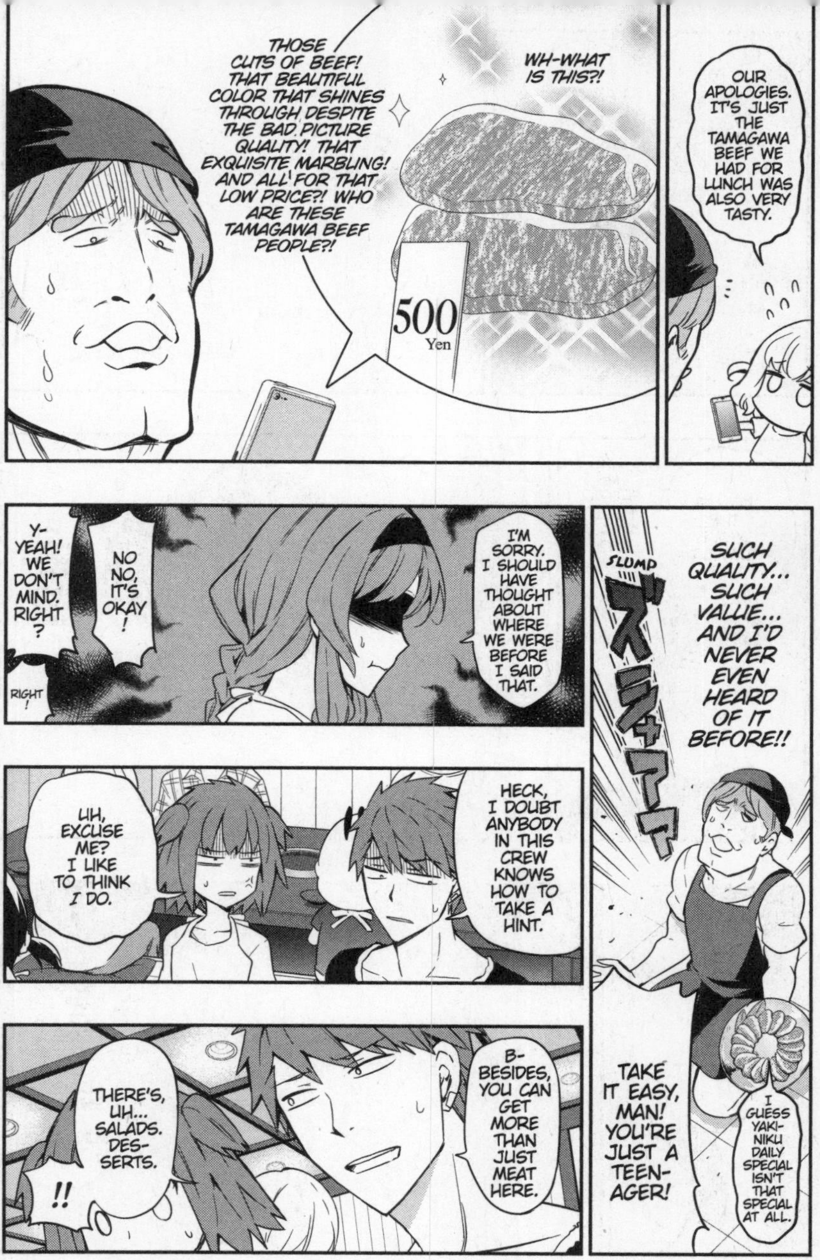
OUR APOLOGIES. IT'S JUST THE TAMAGAWA BEEF WE HAD FOR LUNCH WAS ALSO VERY TASTY.
WH-WHAT IS THIS?!
THOSE CUTS OF BEEF! THAT BEAUTIFUL COLOR THAT SHINES THROUGH DESPITE THE BAD PICTURE QUALITY! THAT EXQUISITE MARBLING! AND ALL FOR THAT LOW PRICE?! WHO ARE THESE TAMAGAWA BEEF PEOPLE?!
500 Yen
SLUMP
SUCH QUALITY... SUCH VALUE... AND I'D NEVER EVEN HEARD OF IT BEFORE!!
TAKE IT EASY, MAN! YOU'RE JUST A TEEN-AGER!
I GUESS YAKI-NIKU DAILY SPECIAL ISN'T THAT SPECIAL AT ALL.
I'M SORRY. I SHOULD HAVE THOUGHT ABOUT WHERE WE WERE BEFORE I SAID THAT.
NO NO, IT'S OKAY!
Y-YEAH! WE DON'T MIND. RIGHT?
RIGHT!
HECK, I DOUBT ANYBODY IN THIS CREW KNOWS HOW TO TAKE A HINT.
UH, EXCUSE ME? I LIKE TO THINK *I* DO.
B-BESIDES, YOU CAN GET MORE THAN JUST MEAT HERE.
THERE'S, UH... SALADS. DES-SERTS.
!!

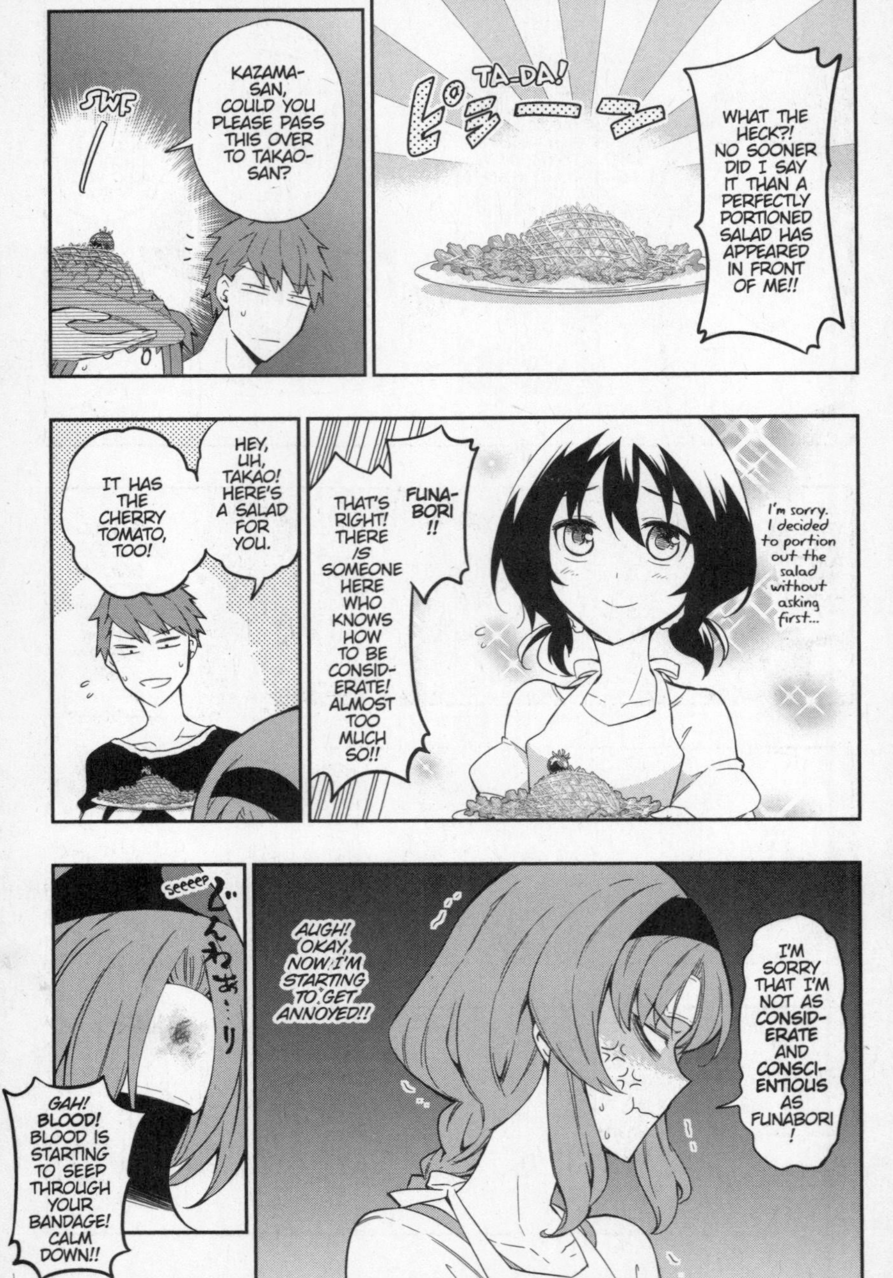
TA-DA!
WHAT THE HECK?! NO SOONER DID I SAY IT THAN A PERFECTLY PORTIONED SALAD HAS APPEARED IN FRONT OF ME!!
SWF
KAZAMA-SAN, COULD YOU PLEASE PASS THIS OVER TO TAKAO-SAN?
I'm sorry. I decided to portion out the salad without asking first...
FUNABORI!!
THAT'S RIGHT! THERE IS SOMEONE HERE WHO KNOWS HOW TO BE CONSIDERATE! ALMOST TOO MUCH SO!!
HEY, UH, TAKAO! HERE'S A SALAD FOR YOU.
IT HAS THE CHERRY TOMATO, TOO!
I'M SORRY THAT I'M NOT AS CONSIDERATE AND CONSCIENTIOUS AS FUNABORI!
AUGH! OKAY, NOW I'M STARTING TO GET ANNOYED!!
seeeep
じんわぁ…り
GAH! BLOOD! BLOOD IS STARTING TO SEEP THROUGH YOUR BANDAGE! CALM DOWN!!

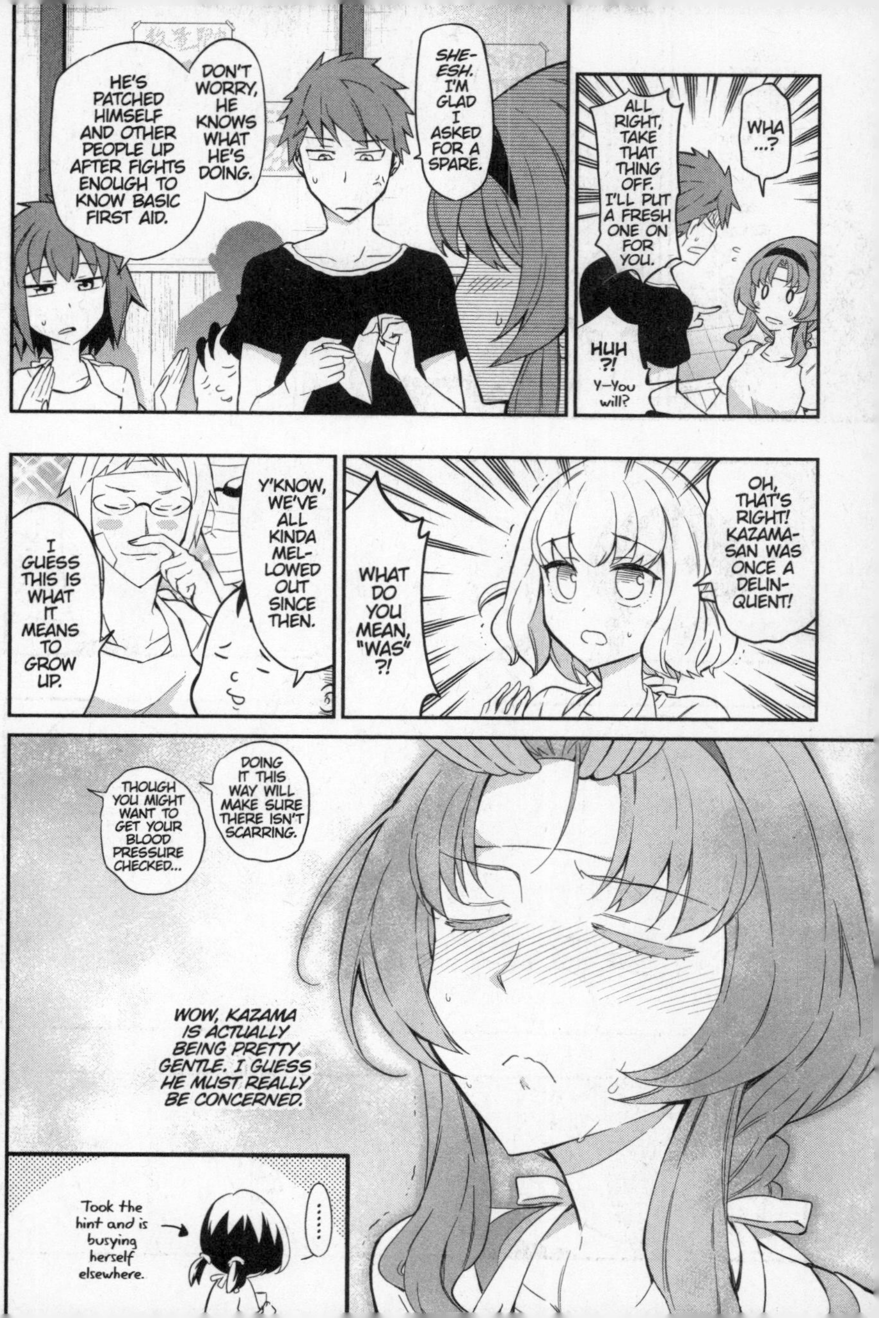
WHA ...?
ALL RIGHT, TAKE THAT THING OFF. I'LL PUT A FRESH ONE ON FOR YOU.
HUH ?! Y-You will?
SHE-ESH. I'M GLAD I ASKED FOR A SPARE.
DON'T WORRY, HE KNOWS WHAT HE'S DOING.
HE'S PATCHED HIMSELF AND OTHER PEOPLE UP AFTER FIGHTS ENOUGH TO KNOW BASIC FIRST AID.
OH, THAT'S RIGHT! KAZAMA-SAN WAS ONCE A DELIN-QUENT!
WHAT DO YOU MEAN, "WAS"?!
Y'KNOW, WE'VE ALL KINDA MEL-LOWED OUT SINCE THEN.
I GUESS THIS IS WHAT IT MEANS TO GROW UP.
DOING IT THIS WAY WILL MAKE SURE THERE ISN'T SCARRING.
THOUGH YOU MIGHT WANT TO GET YOUR BLOOD PRESSURE CHECKED...
WOW, KAZAMA IS ACTUALLY BEING PRETTY GENTLE. I GUESS HE MUST REALLY BE CONCERNED.
......
Took the hint and is busying herself elsewhere.

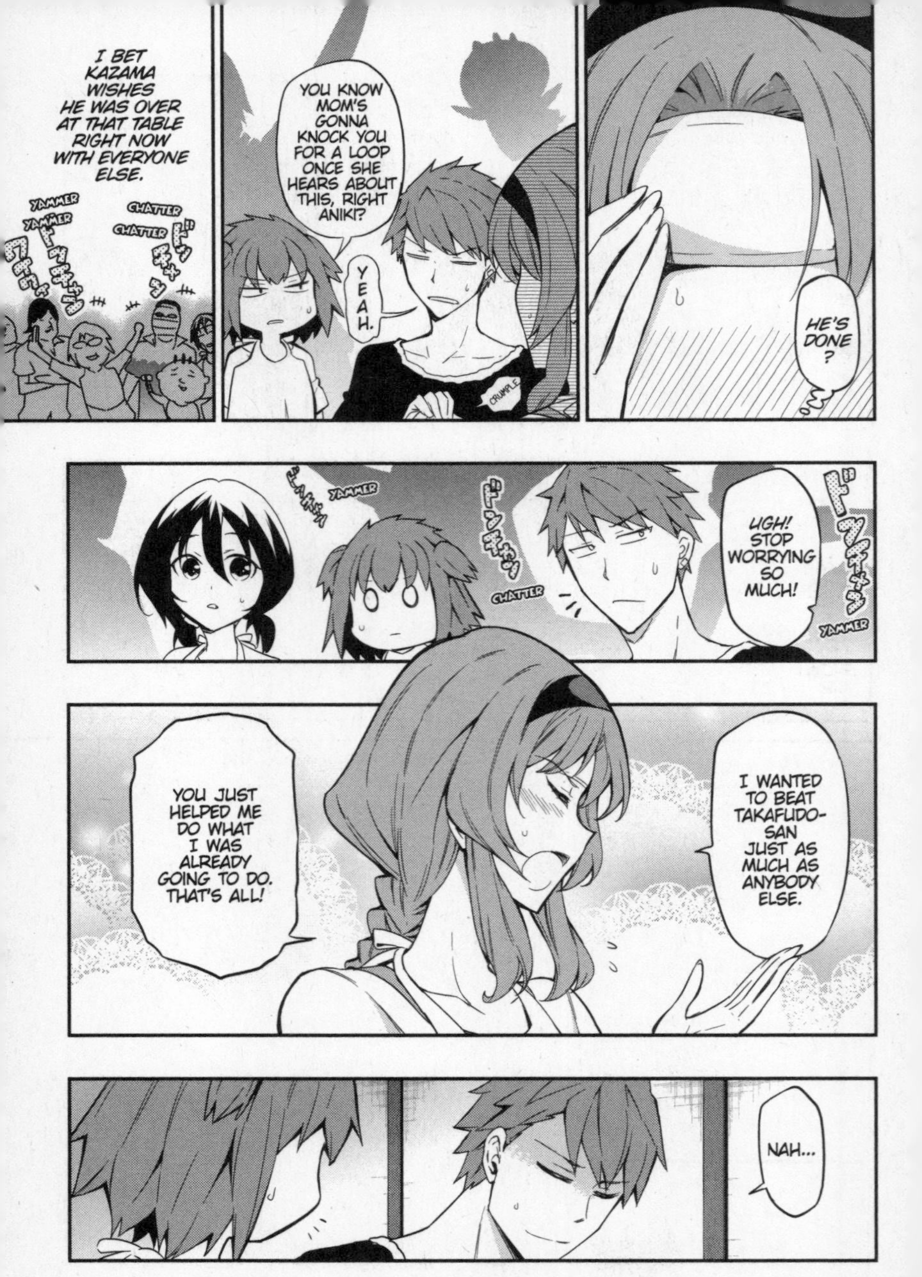
HE'S DONE?
YOU KNOW MOM'S GONNA KNOCK YOU FOR A LOOP ONCE SHE HEARS ABOUT THIS, RIGHT ANIKI!?
YEAH.
CRUMPLE
I BET KAZAMA WISHES HE WAS OVER AT THAT TABLE RIGHT NOW WITH EVERYONE ELSE.
CHATTER
CHATTER
YAMMER
YAMMER
UGH! STOP WORRYING SO MUCH!
YAMMER
CHATTER
YAMMER
I WANTED TO BEAT TAKAFUDO-SAN JUST AS MUCH AS ANYBODY ELSE.
YOU JUST HELPED ME DO WHAT I WAS ALREADY GOING TO DO. THAT'S ALL!
NAH...

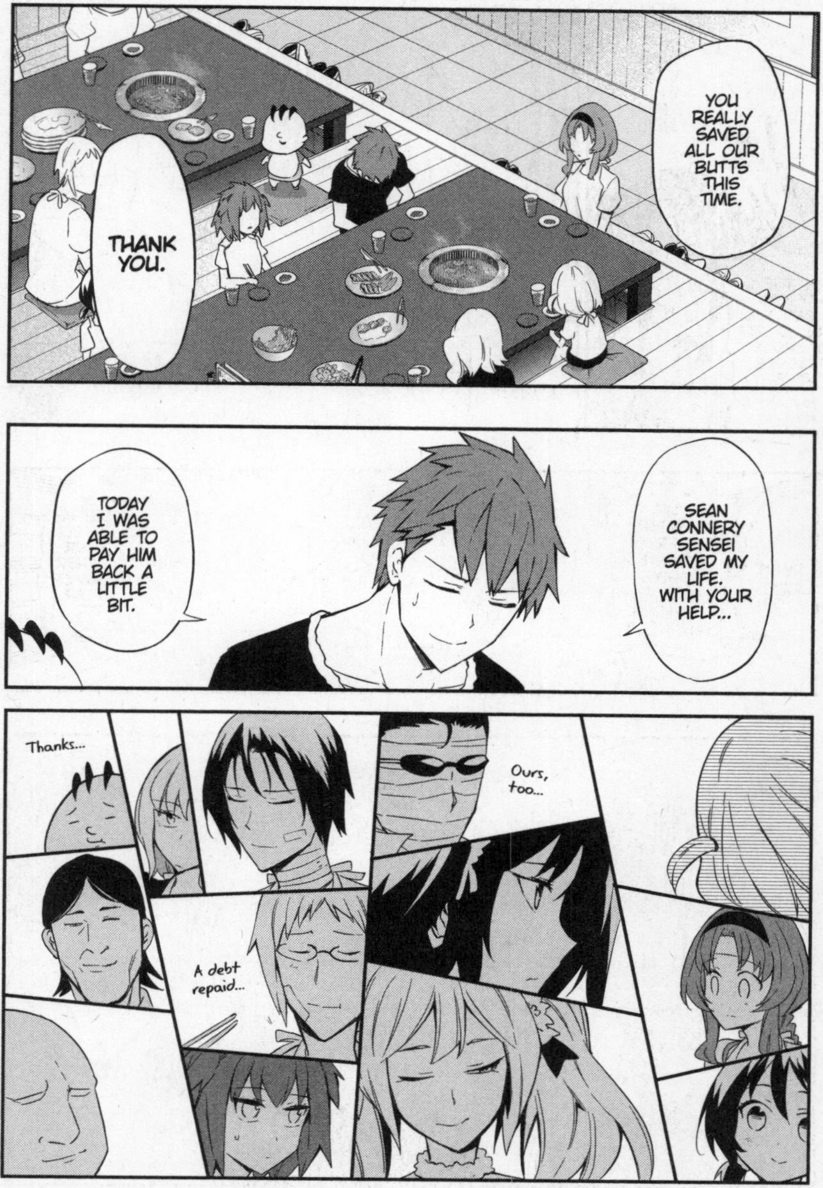
YOU REALLY SAVED ALL OUR BUTTS THIS TIME.
THANK YOU.
SEAN CONNERY SENSEI SAVED MY LIFE. WITH YOUR HELP...
TODAY I WAS ABLE TO PAY HIM BACK A LITTLE BIT.
Ours, too...
Thanks...
A debt repaid...

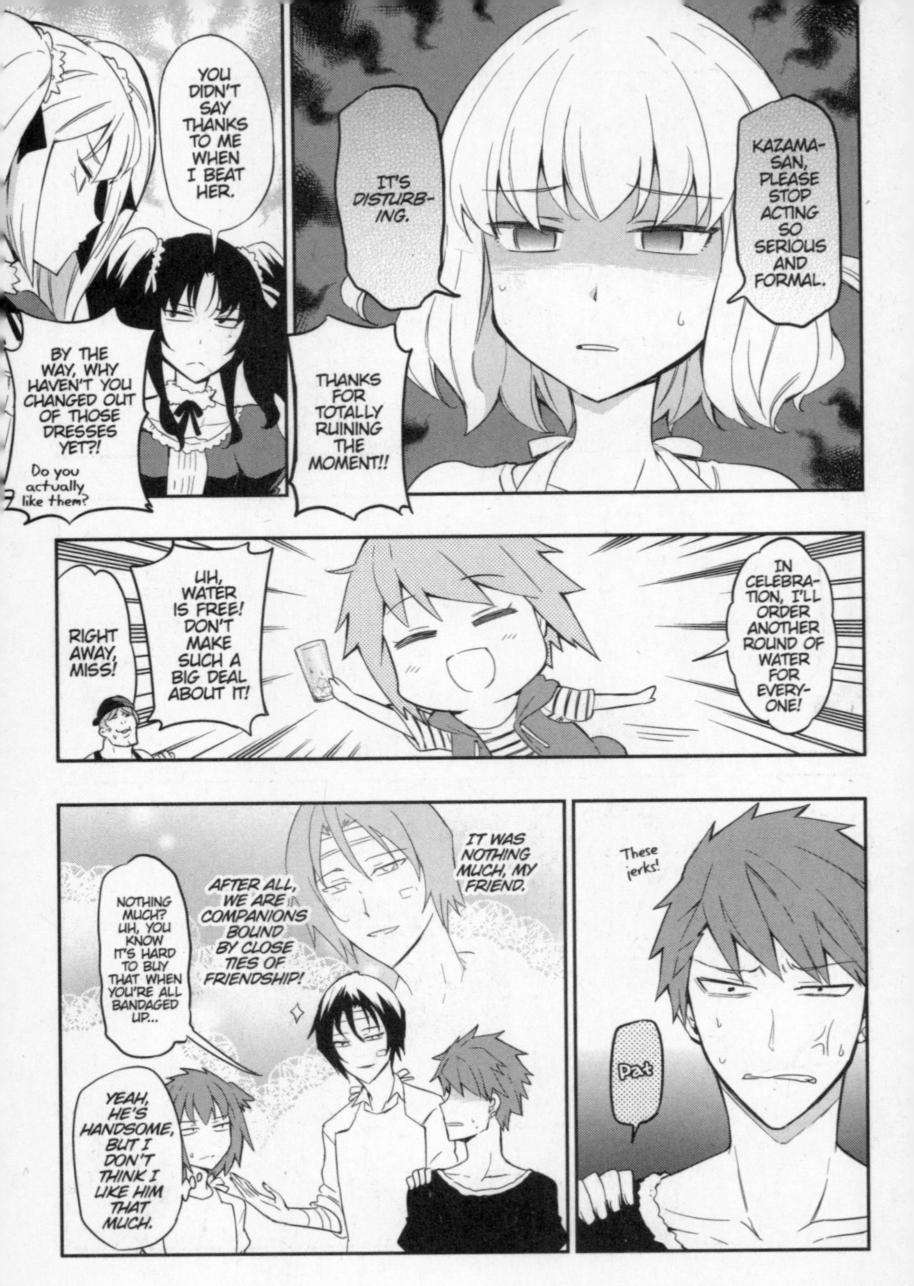

KAZAMA-SAN, PLEASE STOP ACTING SO SERIOUS AND FORMAL.
IT'S DISTURBING.
YOU DIDN'T SAY THANKS TO ME WHEN I BEAT HER.
THANKS FOR TOTALLY RUINING THE MOMENT!!
BY THE WAY, WHY HAVEN'T YOU CHANGED OUT OF THOSE DRESSES YET?!
Do you actually like them?
IN CELEBRATION, I'LL ORDER ANOTHER ROUND OF WATER FOR EVERYONE!
UH, WATER IS FREE! DON'T MAKE SUCH A BIG DEAL ABOUT IT!
RIGHT AWAY, MISS!
These jerks!
Pat
IT WAS NOTHING MUCH, MY FRIEND.
AFTER ALL, WE ARE COMPANIONS BOUND BY CLOSE TIES OF FRIENDSHIP!
NOTHING MUCH? UH, YOU KNOW IT'S HARD TO BUY THAT WHEN YOU'RE ALL BANDAGED UP...
YEAH, HE'S HANDSOME, BUT I DON'T THINK I LIKE HIM THAT MUCH.

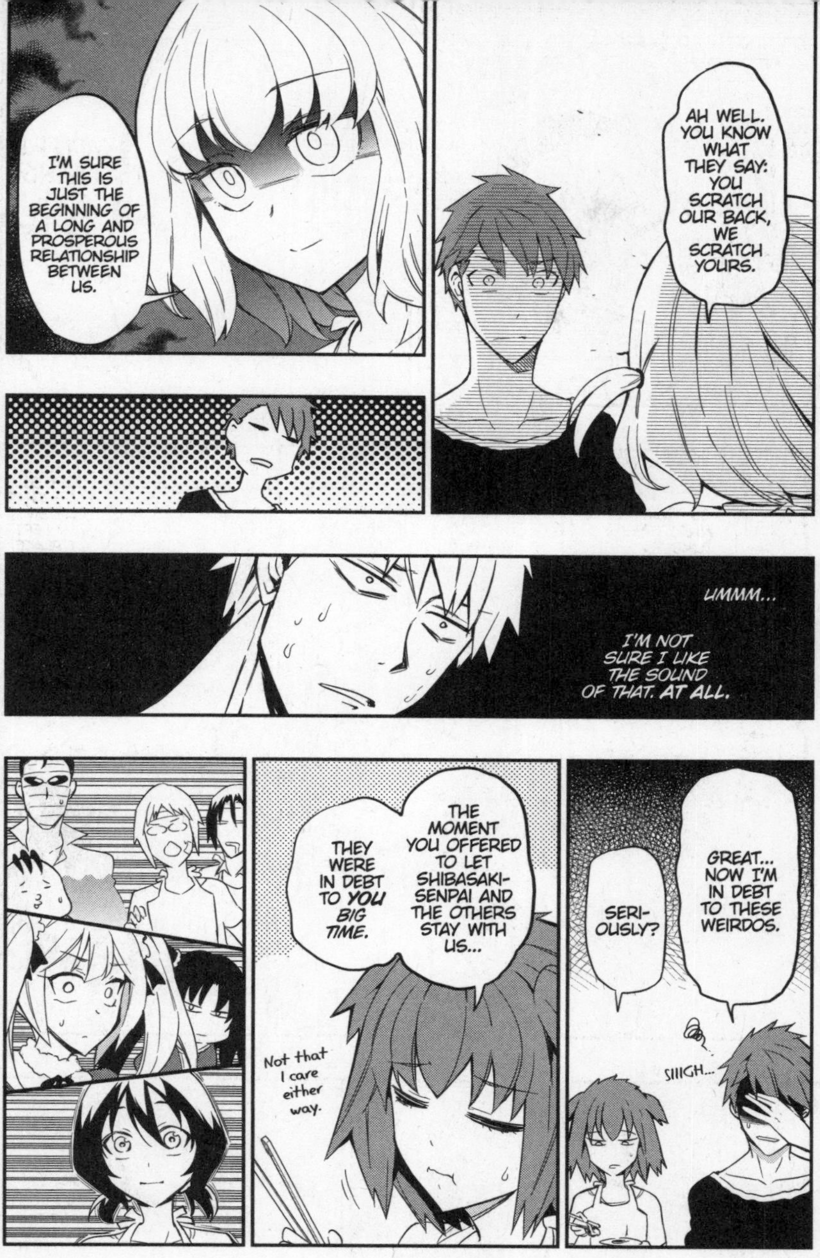
AH WELL. YOU KNOW WHAT THEY SAY: YOU SCRATCH OUR BACK, WE SCRATCH YOURS.
I'M SURE THIS IS JUST THE BEGINNING OF A LONG AND PROSPEROUS RELATIONSHIP BETWEEN US.
UMMM...
I'M NOT SURE I LIKE THE SOUND OF THAT. **AT ALL.**
GREAT... NOW I'M IN DEBT TO THESE WEIRDOS.
SERI-OUSLY?
SIIIGH...
THE MOMENT YOU OFFERED TO LET SHIBASAKI-SENPAI AND THE OTHERS STAY WITH US...
THEY WERE IN DEBT TO *YOU* *BIG TIME.*
Not that I care either way.

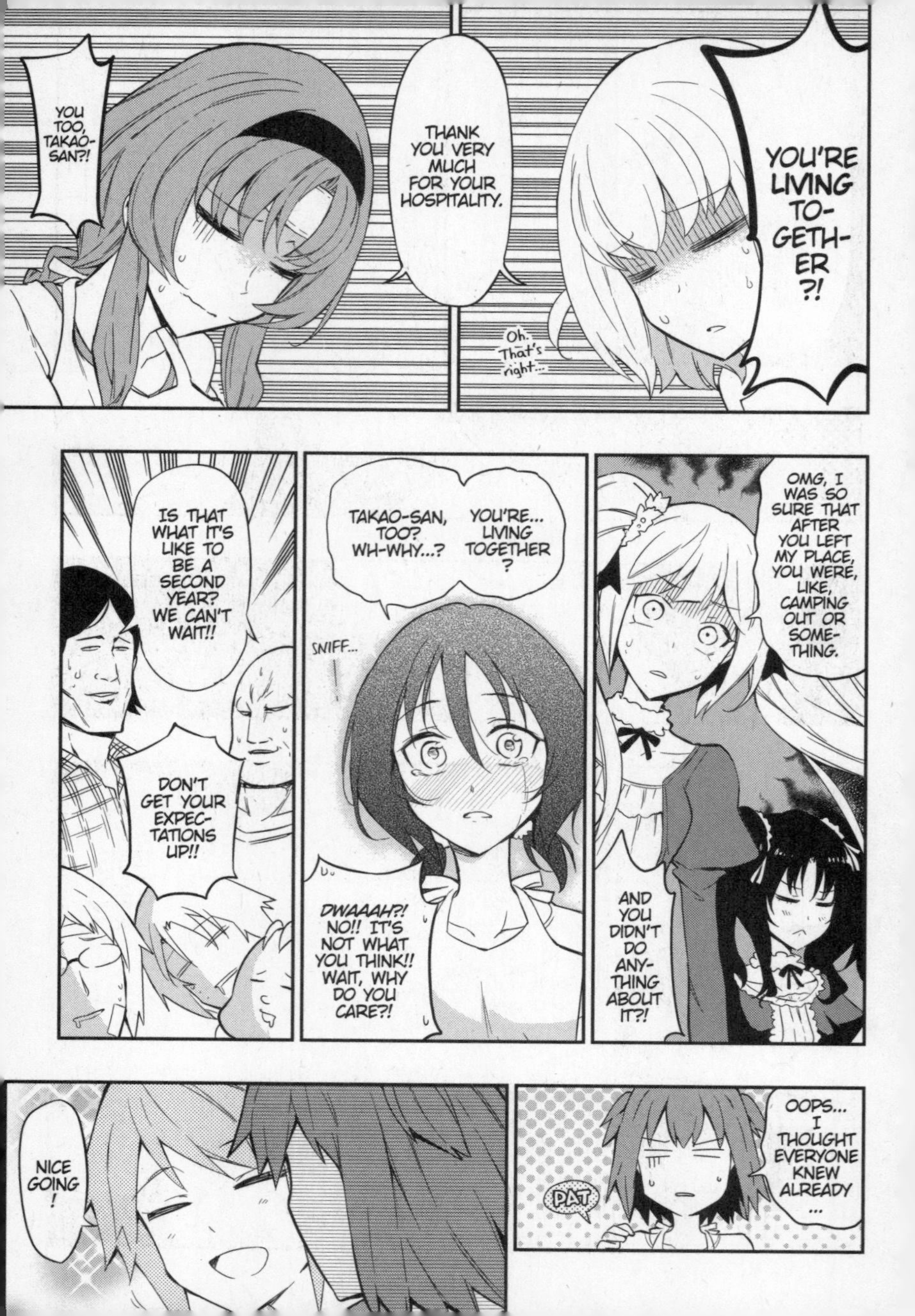
YOU'RE LIVING TO-GETH-ER?!
Oh. That's right...
THANK YOU VERY MUCH FOR YOUR HOSPITALITY.
YOU TOO, TAKAO-SAN?!
OMG, I WAS SO SURE THAT AFTER YOU LEFT MY PLACE, YOU WERE, LIKE, CAMPING OUT OR SOME-THING.
AND YOU DIDN'T DO ANY-THING ABOUT IT?!
YOU'RE... LIVING TOGETHER?
TAKAO-SAN, TOO? WH-WHY...?
SNIFF...
DWAAAH?! NO!! IT'S NOT WHAT YOU THINK!! WAIT, WHY DO YOU CARE?!
IS THAT WHAT IT'S LIKE TO BE A SECOND YEAR? WE CAN'T WAIT!!
DON'T GET YOUR EXPEC-TATIONS UP!!
OOPS... I THOUGHT EVERYONE KNEW ALREADY...
PAT
NICE GOING!

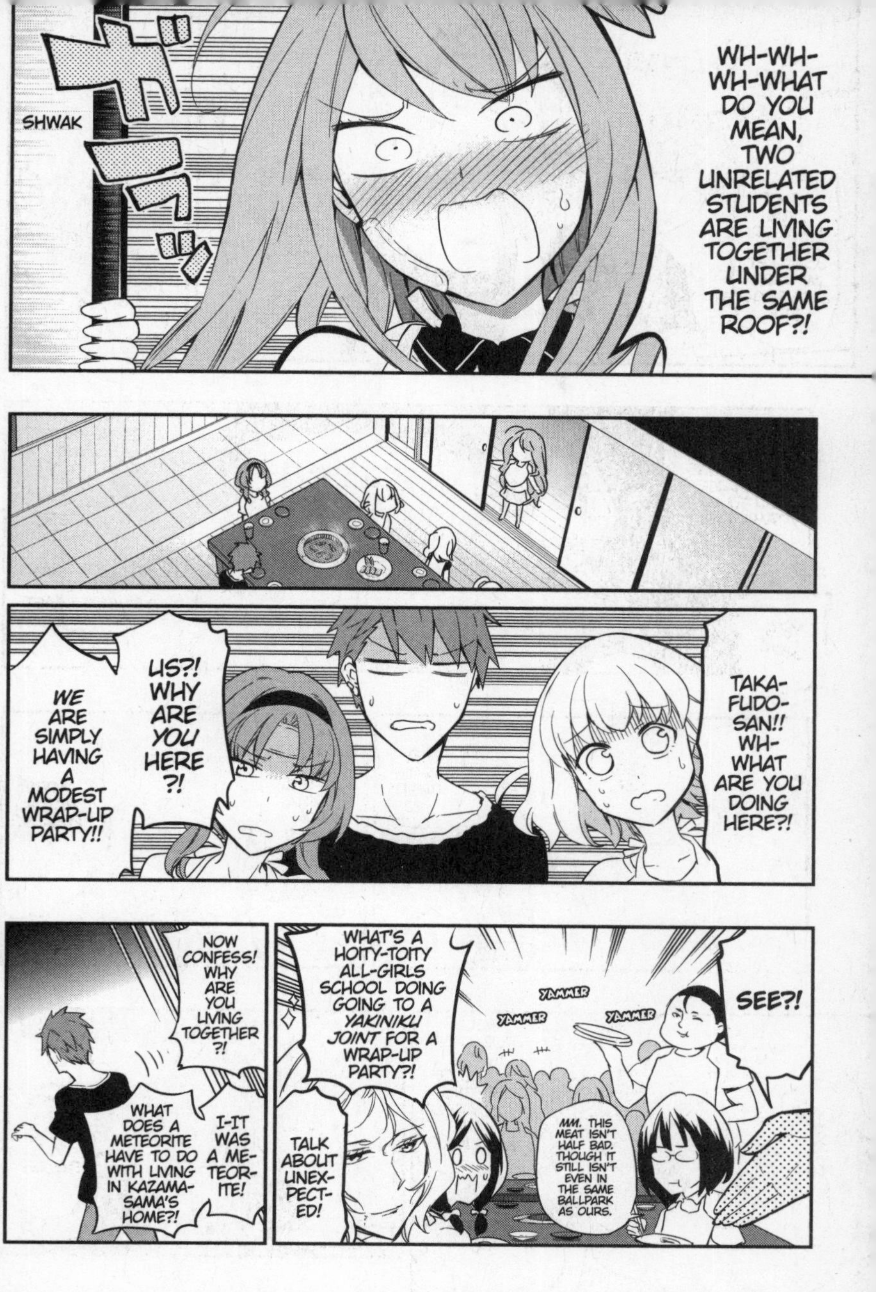
WH-WH-WH-WHAT DO YOU MEAN, TWO UNRELATED STUDENTS ARE LIVING TOGETHER UNDER THE SAME ROOF?!
SHWAK
TAKA-FUDO-SAN!! WH-WHAT ARE YOU DOING HERE?!
US?! WHY ARE *YOU* HERE?!
WE ARE SIMPLY HAVING A MODEST WRAP-UP PARTY!!
WHAT'S A HOITY-TOITY ALL-GIRLS SCHOOL DOING GOING TO A *YAKINIKU JOINT* FOR A WRAP-UP PARTY?!
SEE?!
YAMMER
YAMMER
YAMMER
MM. THIS MEAT ISN'T HALF BAD. THOUGH IT STILL ISN'T EVEN IN THE SAME BALLPARK AS OURS.
TALK ABOUT UNEXPECTED!
NOW CONFESS! WHY ARE YOU LIVING TOGETHER?!
I-IT WAS A METEORITE!
WHAT DOES A METEORITE HAVE TO DO WITH LIVING IN KAZAMA-SAMA'S HOME?!

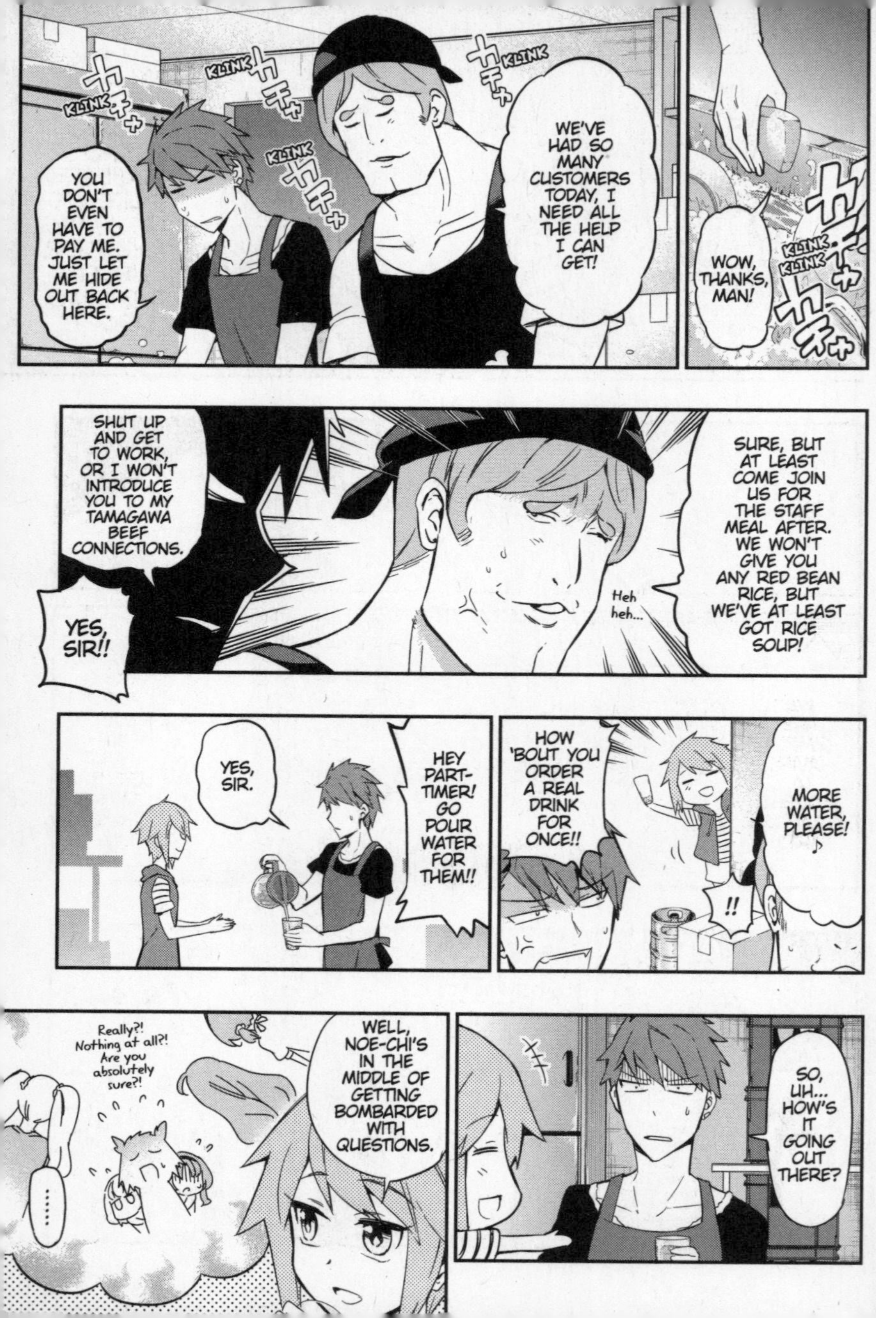
KLINK KLINK
WOW, THANKS, MAN!
KLINK
KLINK
WE'VE HAD SO MANY CUSTOMERS TODAY, I NEED ALL THE HELP I CAN GET!
KLINK
KLINK
YOU DON'T EVEN HAVE TO PAY ME. JUST LET ME HIDE OUT BACK HERE.
SURE, BUT AT LEAST COME JOIN US FOR THE STAFF MEAL AFTER. WE WON'T GIVE YOU ANY RED BEAN RICE, BUT WE'VE AT LEAST GOT RICE SOUP!
Heh heh...
SHUT UP AND GET TO WORK, OR I WON'T INTRODUCE YOU TO MY TAMAGAWA BEEF CONNECTIONS.
YES, SIR!!
MORE WATER, PLEASE! ♪
!!
HOW 'BOUT YOU ORDER A REAL DRINK FOR ONCE!!
HEY PART-TIMER! GO POUR WATER FOR THEM!!
YES, SIR.
SO, UH... HOW'S IT GOING OUT THERE?
WELL, NOE-CHI'S IN THE MIDDLE OF GETTING BOMBARDED WITH QUESTIONS.
Really?! Nothing at all?! Are you absolutely sure?!
......

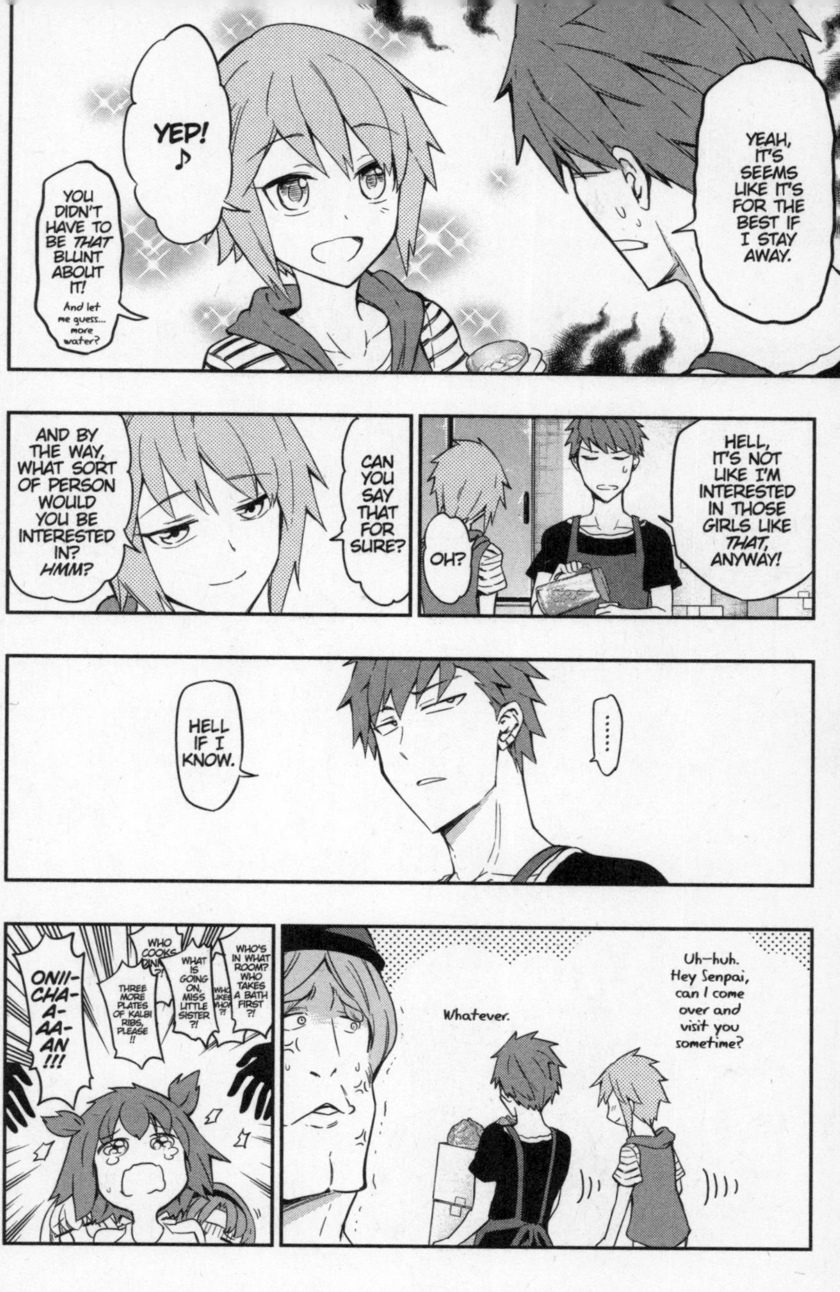
YEAH, IT'S SEEMS LIKE IT'S FOR THE BEST IF I STAY AWAY.
YEP! ♪
YOU DIDN'T HAVE TO BE *THAT* BLUNT ABOUT IT!
And let me guess... more water?
HELL, IT'S NOT LIKE I'M INTERESTED IN THOSE GIRLS LIKE *THAT*, ANYWAY!
OH?
CAN YOU SAY THAT FOR SURE?
AND BY THE WAY, WHAT SORT OF PERSON WOULD YOU BE INTERESTED IN? *HMM?*
......
HELL IF I KNOW.
Uh-huh. Hey Senpai, can I come over and visit you sometime?
Whatever.
WHO'S IN WHAT ROOM? WHO TAKES A BATH FIRST?!
WHAT IS GOING ON, MISS LITTLE SISTER?!
THREE MORE PLATES OF KALBI RIBS, PLEASE!!
ONII-CHA-A-AA-AN!!!

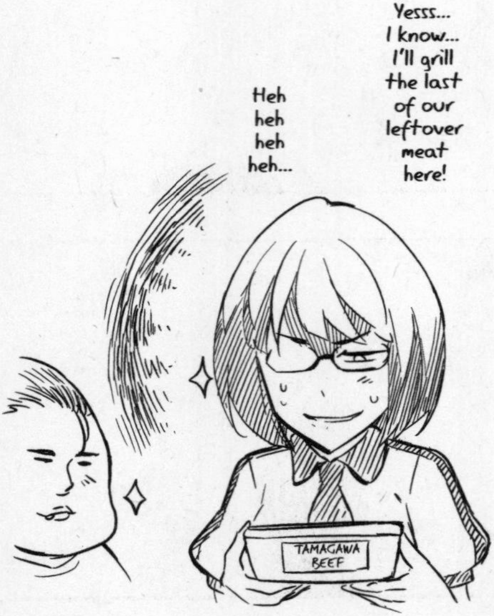
Yesss... I know... I'll grill the last of our leftover meat here!
Heh heh heh heh...
TAMAGAWA BEEF

D-FRAGMENTS ディーふらぐ！

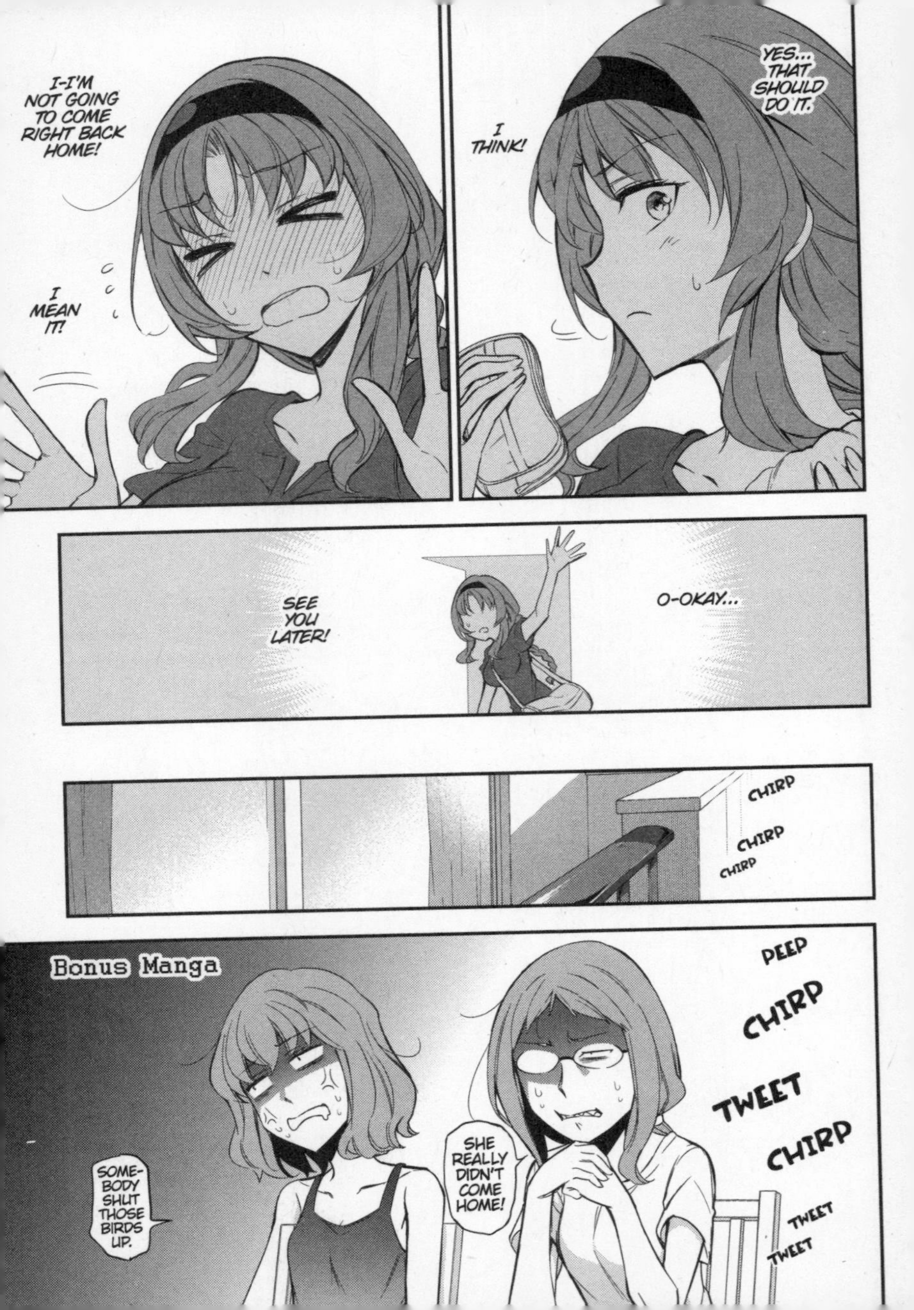
YES... THAT SHOULD DO IT.
I THINK!
I-I'M NOT GOING TO COME RIGHT BACK HOME!
I MEAN IT!
O-OKAY...
SEE YOU LATER!
CHIRP
CHIRP
CHIRP
Bonus Manga
PEEP
CHIRP
TWEET
CHIRP
TWEET
TWEET
SHE REALLY DIDN'T COME HOME!
SOME-BODY SHUT THOSE BIRDS UP.

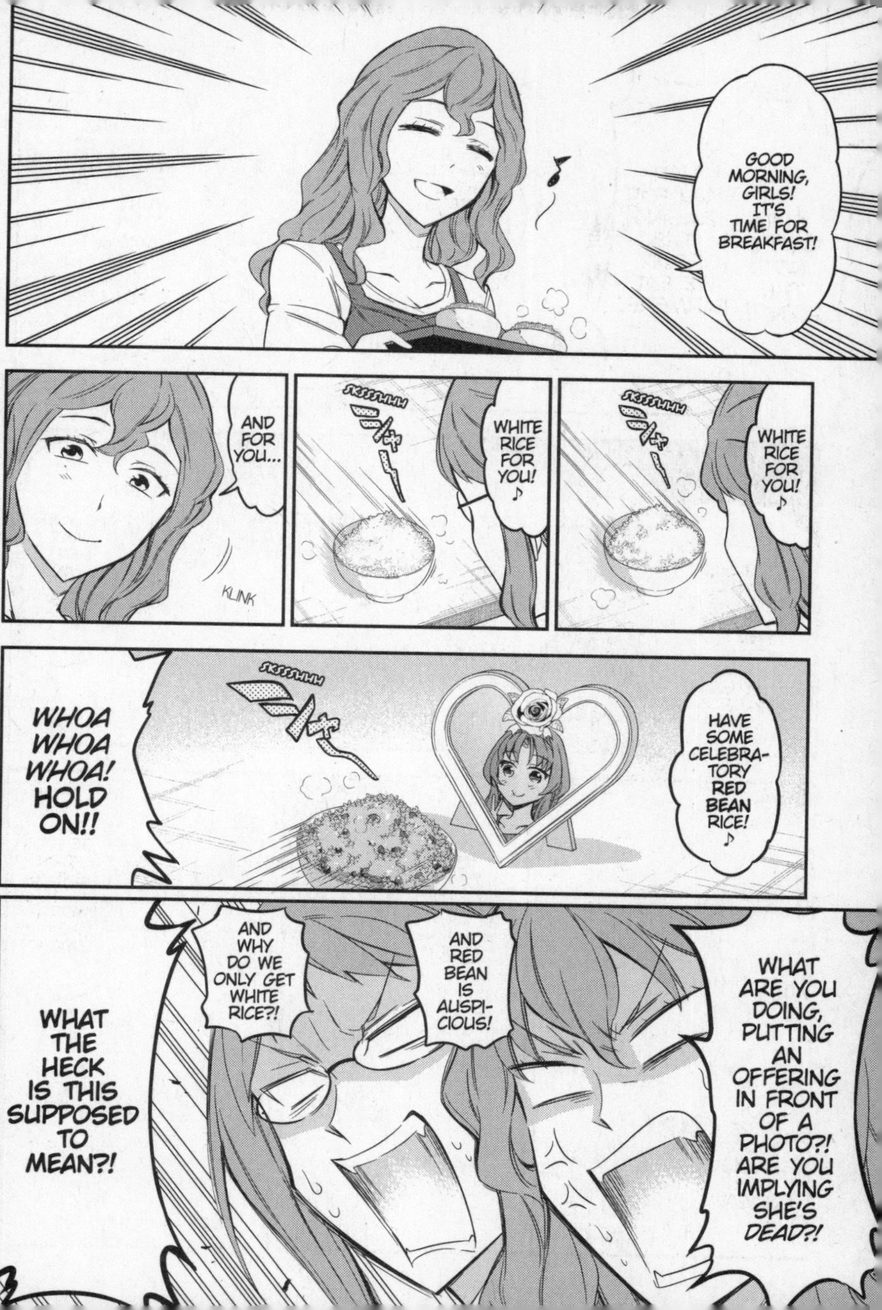
GOOD MORNING, GIRLS! IT'S TIME FOR BREAKFAST!
SKSSSHHH
WHITE RICE FOR YOU! ♪
SKSSSHHH
WHITE RICE FOR YOU! ♪
AND FOR YOU...
KLINK
HAVE SOME CELEBRATORY RED BEAN RICE! ♪
SKSSSHHH
WHOA WHOA WHOA! HOLD ON!!
WHAT ARE YOU DOING, PUTTING AN OFFERING IN FRONT OF A PHOTO?! ARE YOU IMPLYING SHE'S DEAD?!
AND RED BEAN IS AUSPICIOUS!
AND WHY DO WE ONLY GET WHITE RICE?!
WHAT THE HECK IS THIS SUPPOSED TO MEAN?!

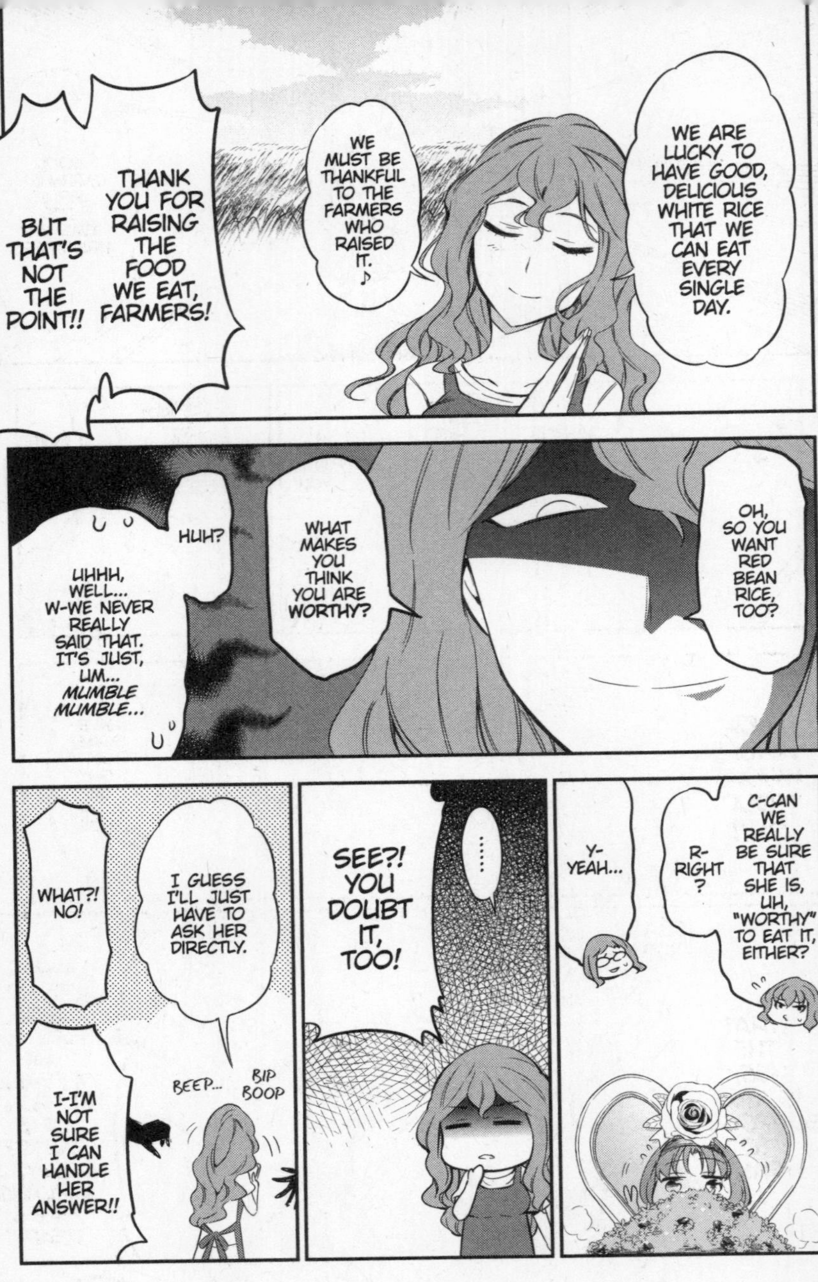
WE ARE LUCKY TO HAVE GOOD, DELICIOUS WHITE RICE THAT WE CAN EAT EVERY SINGLE DAY.
WE MUST BE THANKFUL TO THE FARMERS WHO RAISED IT. ♪
THANK YOU FOR RAISING THE FOOD WE EAT, FARMERS!
BUT THAT'S NOT THE POINT!!
OH, SO YOU WANT RED BEAN RICE, TOO?
WHAT MAKES YOU THINK YOU ARE WORTHY?
HUH?
UHHH, WELL... W-WE NEVER REALLY SAID THAT. IT'S JUST, UM... *MUMBLE MUMBLE...*
C-CAN WE REALLY BE SURE THAT SHE IS, UH, "WORTHY" TO EAT IT, EITHER?
R-RIGHT?
Y-YEAH...
......
SEE?! YOU DOUBT IT, TOO!
I GUESS I'LL JUST HAVE TO ASK HER DIRECTLY.
WHAT?! NO!
BEEP...
BIP BOOP
I-I'M NOT SURE I CAN HANDLE HER ANSWER!!

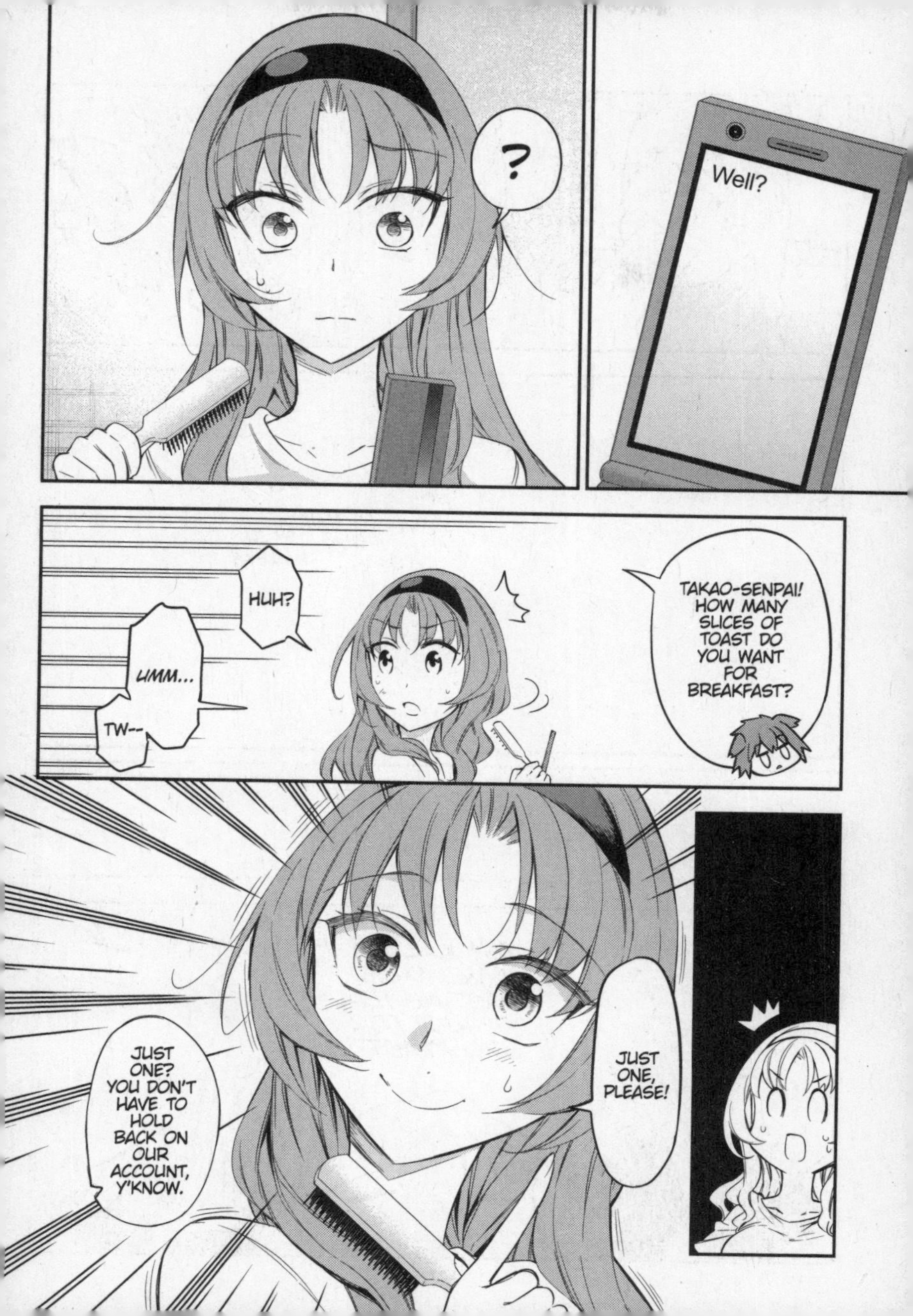
Well?
?
TAKAO-SENPAI! HOW MANY SLICES OF TOAST DO YOU WANT FOR BREAKFAST?
HUH?
UMM...
TW--
JUST ONE, PLEASE!
JUST ONE? YOU DON'T HAVE TO HOLD BACK ON OUR ACCOUNT, Y'KNOW.

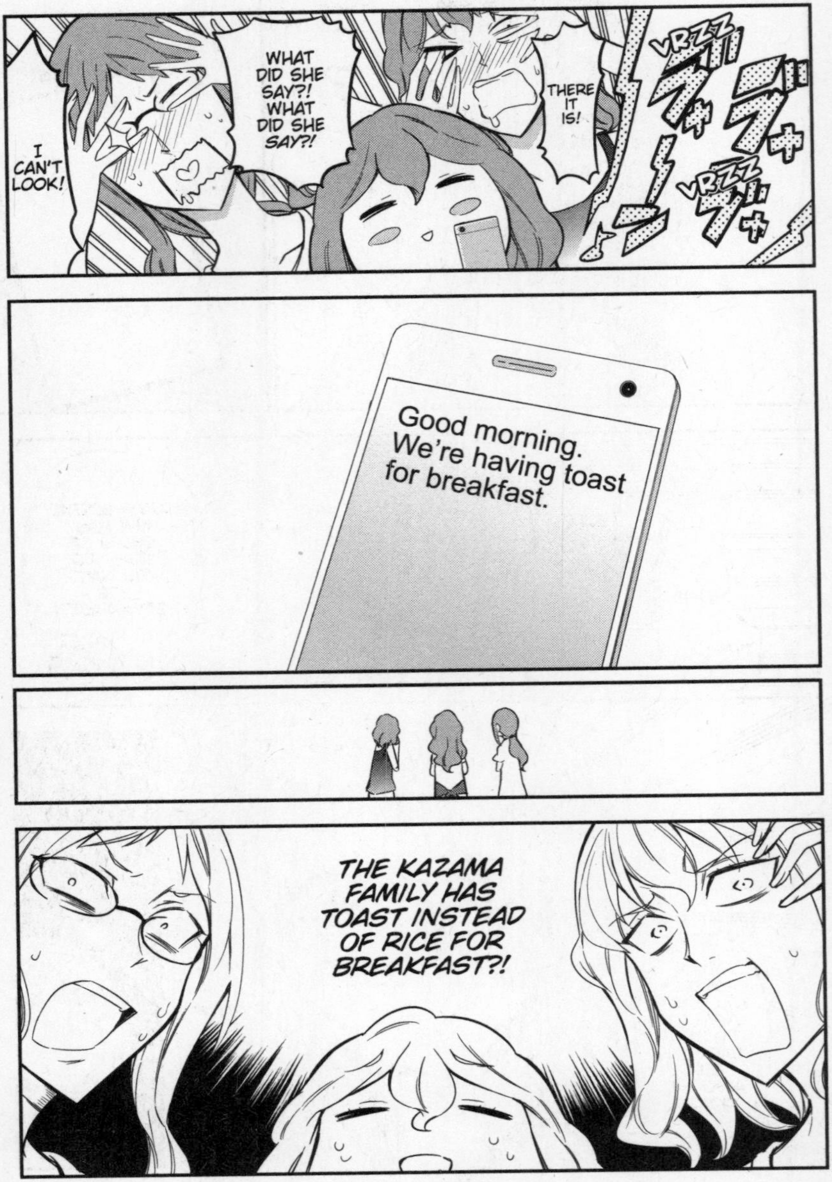
VRZZ
VRZZ
THERE IT IS!
WHAT DID SHE SAY?! WHAT DID SHE SAY?!
I CAN'T LOOK!
Good morning. We're having toast for breakfast.
THE KAZAMA FAMILY HAS TOAST INSTEAD OF RICE FOR BREAKFAST?!

END

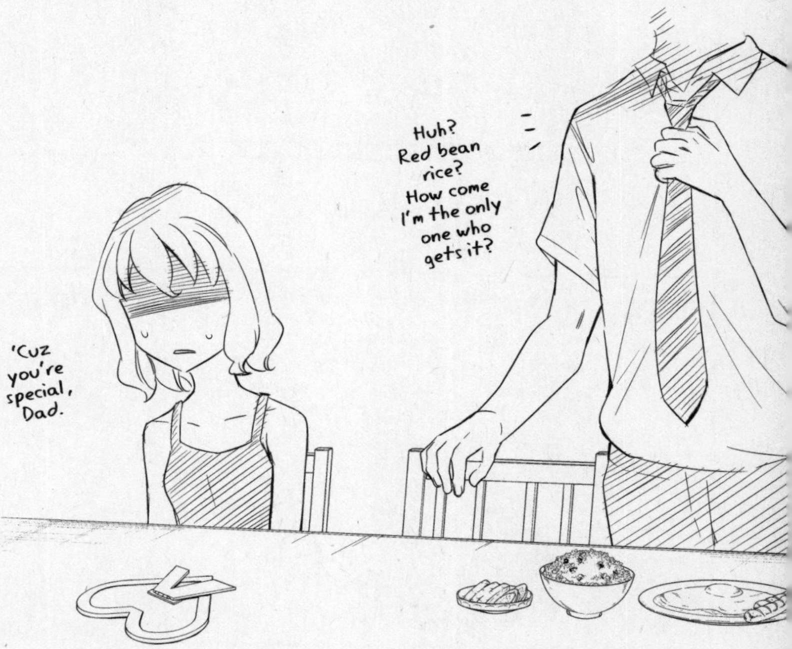
Huh? Red bean rice? How come I'm the only one who gets it?
'Cuz you're special, Dad.

D-FRAGMENTS ディーふらぐめんつ!

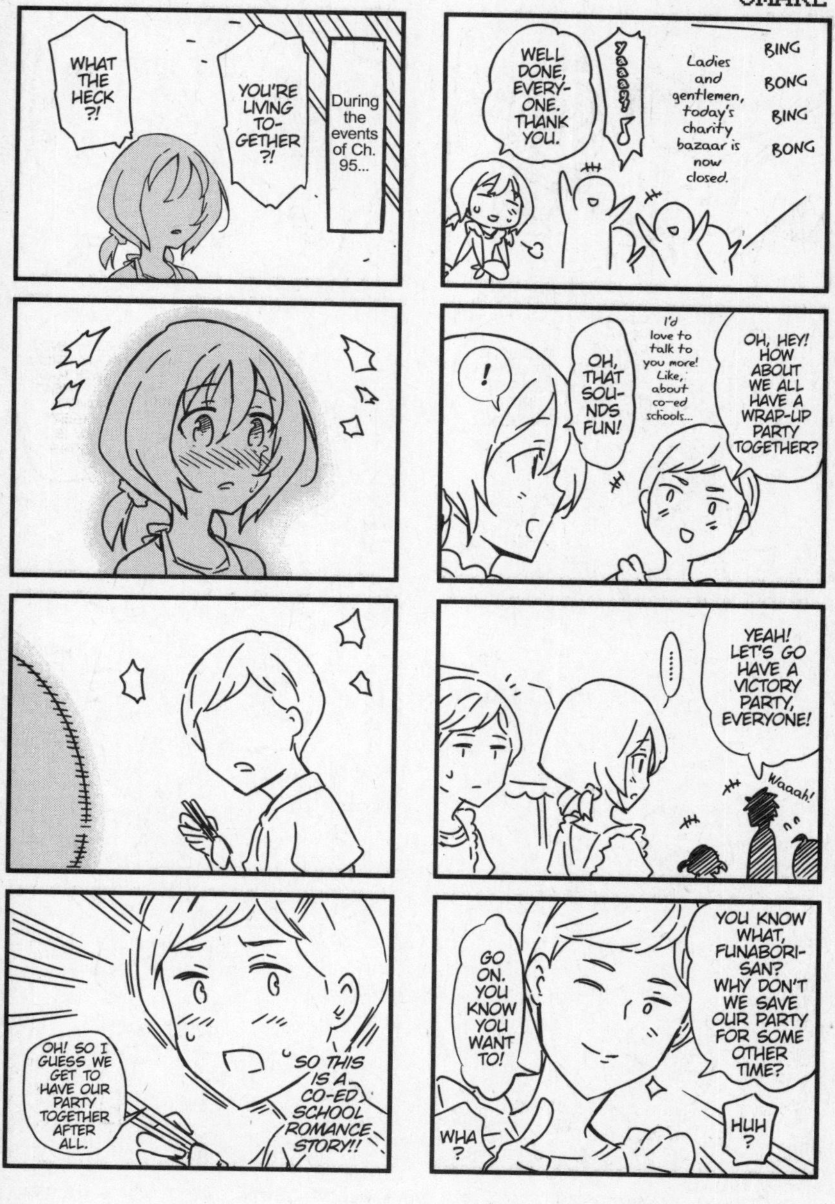
BING
BONG
BING
BONG
Ladies and gentlemen, today's charity bazaar is now closed.
Yaaay! ♪
WELL DONE, EVERY-ONE. THANK YOU.
OH, HEY! HOW ABOUT WE ALL HAVE A WRAP-UP PARTY TOGETHER?
I'd love to talk to you more! Like, about co-ed schools...
OH, THAT SOU-NDS FUN!
!
YEAH! LET'S GO HAVE A VICTORY PARTY, EVERYONE!
Waaah!
......
YOU KNOW WHAT, FUNABORI-SAN? WHY DON'T WE SAVE OUR PARTY FOR SOME OTHER TIME?
GO ON. YOU KNOW YOU WANT TO!
HUH?
WHA?
During the events of Ch. 95...
YOU'RE LIVING TO-GETHER?!
WHAT THE HECK?!
SO THIS IS A CO-ED SCHOOL ROMANCE STORY!!
OH! SO I GUESS WE GET TO HAVE OUR PARTY TOGETHER AFTER ALL.

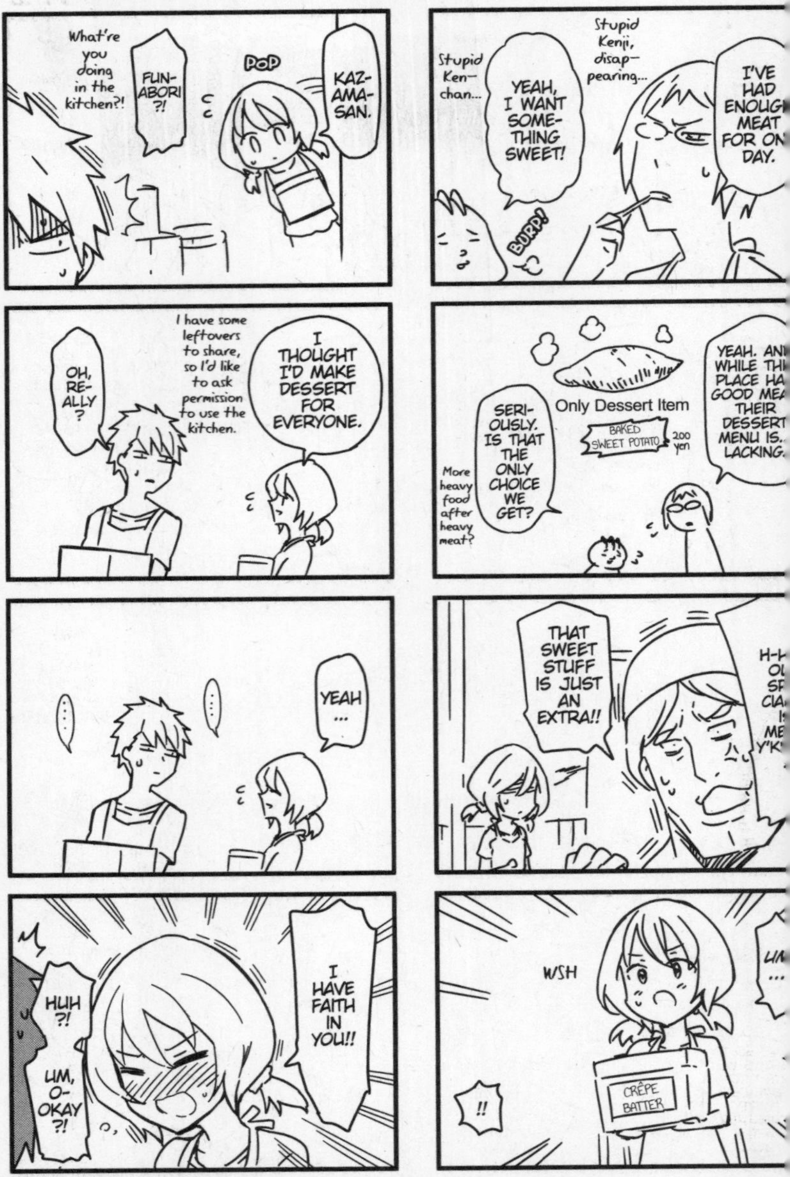
I'VE HAD ENOUG MEAT FOR ON DAY.
Stupid Kenji, disap-pearing...
YEAH, I WANT SOME-THING SWEET!
Stupid Ken-chan...
BURP!
YEAH. AN WHILE TH PLACE HA GOOD ME THEIR DESSERT MENU IS... LACKING.
Only Dessert Item
BAKED SWEET POTATO
200 yen
SERI-OUSLY. IS THAT THE ONLY CHOICE WE GET?
More heavy food after heavy meat?
THAT SWEET STUFF IS JUST AN EXTRA!!
UM ...
WSH
CRÊPE BATTER
!!
KAZ-AMA-SAN.
POP
FUN-ABORI?!
What're you doing in the kitchen?!
I THOUGHT I'D MAKE DESSERT FOR EVERYONE.
I have some leftovers to share, so I'd like to ask permission to use the kitchen.
OH, RE-ALLY?
YEAH ...
...
...
I HAVE FAITH IN YOU!!
HUH?!
UM, O-OKAY?!

SPECIAL THANKS!!
YUKINOJOU-SAN, KAWAMOTO-SAN (EDITOR), TOMIYAMA-SAN (COVER DESIGN), AND MY WONDERFUL R
ERS!!

SEVEN SEAS ENTERTAINMENT

S0-ARY-684

D-FRAG!

story and art by **TOMOYA HARUNO**

VOLUME 12

TRANSLATION
Adrienne Beck

ADAPTATION
Claudie Summers

LETTERING AND RETOUCH
William Ringrose
M. Victoria Robado

LOGO DESIGN
Courtney Williams

COVER DESIGN
KC Fabellon

PROOFREADING
Danielle King
B. Lana Guggenheim

EDITOR
Shannon Fay

PRODUCTION MANAGER
Lissa Pattillo

EDITOR-IN-CHIEF
Adam Arnold

PUBLISHER
Jason DeAngelis

FOLLOW US ONLINE: *www.sevenseasentertainment.com*

READING DIRECTIONS

This book reads from *right to left*, Japanese style.
If this is your first time reading manga, you start
reading from the top right panel on each page and
take it from there. If you get lost, just follow the
numbered diagram here. It may seem backwards at
first, but you'll get the hang of it! Have fun!!

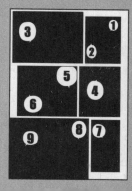